How French Moderns Think

HAU
Books

Hau Books are published by the
Society for Ethnographic Theory (SET)

www.haubooks.org

How French Moderns Think

The Lévy-Bruhl Family, from "Primitive Mentality" to Contemporary Pandemics

Frédéric Keck

With a foreword by Michael M. J. Fischer

Hau Books
Chicago

An earlier version was published as *Préparer l'imprévisible. Lévy-Bruhl et les sciences de la vigilance*
© 2023 Presses Universitaires de France, French edition

© 2023 Hau Books

Cover image: Photograph of Dyak child, 1912
Private collection

Cover design: Daniele Meucci
Layout design: Deepak Sharma, Prepress Plus Technologies
Typesetting: Prepress Plus Technologies (https://prepressplustechnologies.com)

ISBN: 978-1-914363-02-3 [paperback]
ISBN: 978-1-914363-03-0 [PDF]
LCCN: 2023945315

Hau Books
Chicago Distribution Center
11030 S. Langley Ave.
Chicago, Il 60628
www.haubooks.org

Hau Books publications are marketed and distributed by The University of Chicago Press.
www.press.uchicago.edu

Printed in the United States of America on acid-free paper.

In memory of Paul Rabinow (1944–2021)
teacher, mentor, friend

Contents

Contents

Foreword

Michael M. J. Fischer

Frédéric Keck's book on the Lévy-Bruhl family tells a story of the French sociological tradition through four generations: Lucien, his son Henri, a Roman law scholar, his grandson Raymond, a social statistician, and his great-grandson Daniel, a vaccine specialist, and great-granddaughter Viviane, a specialist in environmental law. These four generations have shifted—in French political terms—from the Dreyfus Affair in the middle of the Third Republic to the Audin Affair during the Algerian War of Independence. They witnessed the repetition of state or army lies and trials in which the accused were scapegoated or, indeed, in Alfred Dreyfus's case, made to undergo a ritual of sacrifice, being stripped of rank and personhood, to cover up the honor of the army. Keck brilliantly casts these trials as ones, in Lévy-Bruhl's terms, about the shift from "primitive mentality" to more complex understandings of how things go wrong in complex societies. "Primitive" in much, if not all of, Keck's reading has to do with the rise of irrational movements—Nazism in the 1930s and the preceding anti-Semitism in Dreyfus's case of the 1890s to 1909—in societies that, he suggests, have no better way of dealing with threat and looming catastrophe than to whip up irrational passions around external causes. Indeed, one might think here of the Trump and Bolsonaro politics of today's world.

As Keck writes, "when social anthropology in France emerged in the late nineteenth century in the context of the Dreyfus Affair, it offered several ways of integrating the irrational within rationality." He continues:

At first, Dreyfus, Lévy-Bruhl, and Jaurès opposed the "civilized mentality" of the French Enlightenment to the "primitive mentality" of the Catholic army. But as the warning signs multiplied of what the Dreyfus Affair prefigured—*the rise of colonial violence* in the world *and anti-Semitism in Europe*—"primitive mentality" and its forms of mystical participation appeared as the only intellectual resources available to prepare society for these threats. (emphasis added)

Frédéric Keck situates Lucien Lévy-Bruhl as a major figure of the French intelligentsia and political elite amid other contending figures—allies and critics—including Henri Bergson, Émile Durkheim, and Marcel Mauss in the founding of social theory but also Franz Boas and John Dewey in the United States (US), and, in the later generation, Claude Lévi-Strauss, Emmanuel Levinas, and many others. By following out the next three generations of the Lévy-Bruhl family as they, in turn, became well-known players, Keck shifts the stakes in social theory along with the rise of changing techniques of social statistics (still crude at the time of Durkheim and Lévy-Bruhl), microbiology (Lévy-Bruhl's first son), the sociology of crime and penal theory (Lévy-Bruhl's second son), epidemiology and public health (Lévy-Bruhl's third son, who met his wife at the Pasteur Institute and became an expert in gas accidents), phenomenology, structuralism, cybernetics, and vaccine development.

At issue are four key foci of attention:

The first of these foci is the rise of statistics and epidemiology and of other new sciences of the twentieth century (cybernetics and structuralism) for modeling chance occurrences. The Lévy-Bruhl family members play leading roles in each step along the way. Keck builds upon his earlier book on avian influenza where he contrasts two logics dealing with such unexpected disasters, or catastrophes, or new epidemics: *prevention* (in the nineteenth century) and *preparedness* (in the twentieth and twenty-first centuries). The transition is one from actuarial tables as they were used in the insurance industry in the nineteenth century for dealing with industrial accidents (what Charles Perrow calls "natural accidents" that occur with such statistical regularity that the calculation of premiums can be based on them) to contemporary techniques of disaster management. The key term here is the role of chance as being external or internal to explanation, a point I further elaborate on in the three other foci of attention.

The second is the way in which the unexplained is dealt with in statistical or structural terms rather than as a relationship between the individual and the social. One might think here of the shift in organizational theory in the United States from blaming individuals who caused things to go wrong to focusing on failures of the system that allowed an individual failure to cause harm to the larger system. Here Keck points out that, after the Second World War, two powerful intellectual currents threatened to sideline Lucien and his son Henri's sociological work. These were German phenomenology and American structuralism, the latter of which Lévi-Strauss, following Roman Jakobson, would champion. But a third path, which Henri pioneered, was the transformation of statistical procedures for governance. Henri is an important transitional figure who works in restructuring the administrative statistical services and then returns to Roman law, which he uses to try to fit into his father's work in a more Durkheimian tradition, as a transition between finding the truth in criminal cases through procedures of proof versus the Christian tradition of forcing a confession. Structurally, these are two different modes of apprehending the truth, which can be read as two different mentalities or two different deep structures or unconscious patterns (again think of the organizational behavior theories above). Henri Lévy-Bruhl traces how accusations of criminality in Roman law are transformed by codification of trust through letters of credit in evolving commercial law. This a brilliant reading and, in a way, this argument regarding the penal system fits with the analyses of penal systems that Michel Foucault took from Georg Rusche and Otto Kirchheimer's *Punishment and Social Structure*, both authors members of the Frankfurt School (Rusche and Kirchheimer 1939). Pragmatically, what forced these changes, Keck argues, is the rise of white-collar crime (the "smart crime") of fraud, breaches of trust, and swindling, which Henri had to deal with and which were understood as new categories of crime after the Second World War.

Third, even though Lévi-Strauss plays a minor role in this book, his work plays an important role in Keck's attempt to solve the problem of explanations that cannot be reduced to how individuals think but rather seem to be matters of structure, deep patterns that are unconscious and that operate like language—the example par excellence is when individual speakers cannot explain the rules but can tell when a sentence is or is not grammatical. Each generation of the Lévy-Bruhl family, Keck argues, is trying to solve these problems and the way in which its members solve them from generation to generation throws light both on the changes in the sciences of the day (new explanatory modes) and on the political issues that intersected with these conceptual problems. Levinas is another important figure who plays a minor role in the book but is an important transgenerational figure who wants to use phenomenology against the rise of fascism. Even though one of his teachers, Martin Heidegger, was a facilitator of fascism, Levinas also studied with Edmund Husserl and attended the famous debate at Davos between Ernst Cassirer and Heidegger: so it is not just Levinas as an individual but also Levinas as a transgenerational figure who is trying to defang the fascist uses of phenomenology.

Fourth, Lévy-Bruhl himself is brought to life in quite a different way than his usual dismissal as an evolutionist who thought tribal peoples were "prelogical" and mystical participants in non-rational ideas and who needed to be civilized to become modern. Keck does not hide the elements in Lévy-Bruhl's writing that make him appear this way, but he points out that, repeatedly toward the end of his life, Lévy-Bruhl denies that "prelogical" was the right vocabulary. And in moves quite similar to those Lévi-Strauss made later, he insists that both primitive and civilized mentalities can coexist and, indeed, as Freud pointed out, that the savage/primitive/prelogical/a-logical is always there beneath the surface of the civilized. "Mentality" is another archaic term for today's reader, but, as Keck fittingly observes, for Lévy-Bruhl it provides a third position—in contrast to race, geography, or cultural determinism—from which to offer external explanations for why different groups of people think differently. Lévy-Bruhl and Boas (who certainly engaged in forceful debates with each other) came to see themselves as allies. Keck points out that Marcel Proust argues that the term "mentality" was introduced at the time of the Dreyfus Affair and that Émile Zola used it to describe the judge's reasoning. For this Keck cites Paul Rabinow from his book *French Modern* (1989: 167): "Lévy-Bruhl warned that although social sentiments were the hardest ones to change, giving scientific forms to moral representations was the only path to the rational construction of norms for modern society." Perhaps even more important is the notion of solidarity (which Keck says Lévy-Bruhl, with Durkheim, was among the first to use) that come from a variety of "moral environments"; and crucial, perhaps, is the observation that Lévy-Bruhl criticized evolutionism in moral matters by agreeing with Fustel de Coulanges that there could be no primitive humanity prior to the formation of the idea of responsibility and that ideas of responsibility are formed through *moeurs* (mores), institutions, and rituals. "Participation" is another term that needs to be rethought as the way that collective representations are experienced by individuals. Indeed, the prominent American psychological anthropologist Anthony Wallace would famously argue that culture is not something shared but something participated in, understanding cultures as being like languages.

The book falls roughly into two periods: the first two parts (1857–1914 and 1914–1939) bring to life the socialist politics of the defenders of Dreyfus, the politics around Jaurès and Léon Blum, and the struggles over how to think about the colonial world; the third part (1939–2020, that is from the death of Lucien Lévy-Bruhl to the present) is a rich account of the succeeding generations, tracing complexity and not linearity. Raymond (Lucien's grandson) is sent to the United States on a Rockefeller grant to learn the techniques of random sampling developed under the New Deal and Keck reads these new statistical techniques as approaches to what he would today call disaster preparedness as opposed to risk prevention. Here I would have liked more on the training of colonial statisticians by Raymond, showing how the importation of this knowledge was not just for France but also its colonies. Raymond is also at the center of controversy over the use of the price index and Valéry Giscard d'Estaing's use of it to lower wages, without presumably affecting other forms of benefit. The final chapter in this part is on Daniel and Viviane Lévy-Bruhl and the need to develop new forms of epidemiology and environmental monitoring: a move from those used earlier by the Pasteur Institute, which had relied on risk by studying social classes, to one relying on sentinel networks of physicians and naturalists able to better pick up the first signs of potential epidemics.

This all is a tour de force, full of details, including some informed suppositions where proof is lacking, for example regarding the files that Lévy-Bruhl had accumulated on the Dreyfus Affair and that were destroyed by the Nazis. The book offers rich material to reevaluate the theoretical developments over the course of the troubled twentieth century when policy, politics, war, and epidemics intersect and create new forms of the unexpected. In a very Durkheimian turn of phrase, Keck observes "events anticipated have changed form," that is, anticipation, prevention, and preparedness are all collective representations with different forms at different historical conjunctures, depending on different kinds of data collection, different forms of analysis, and different conceptions of how the social operates. This book is a major accomplishment that changes how we think about the social sciences in France and elsewhere. It will be a provocative text for many scholars to work from, not just in the history of anthropology and the history of science but also in the history of policy-making and its statistical and other techniques, the history of Jews in the French secular state, and the politics of the left from the early twentieth century to the present.

Michael M. J. Fischer

Acknowledgments

The idea for this book emerged about ten years ago around an article I planned to write with Frédéric Audren and Emmanuel Didier on the members of the Lévy-Bruhl family that each of us had studied: Lucien, Henri, and Raymond. While I continued this project on my own, Frédéric and Emmanuel's initial impulse has never ceased to stimulate me.

Through my encounter with Daniel Lévy-Bruhl at the Pasteur Institute in 2011 during a seminar on the questions of proof and decision in public health, I was able to meet some of Lucien Lévy-Bruhl's descendants: Viviane, Milo, Sacha, Ulysse, and Pierre Lévy-Bruhl, as well as Michel Léon. I warmly thank them for giving me access to the oral history and the written archives of the family, and for following with benevolence the realization of this book.

I presented the findings from my work at the Institute for Contemporary Publishing Archives (Institut mémoires de l'édition contemporaine, IMEC) at Christophe Prochasson's seminar at the École des hautes études en sciences sociales in 2012. His remarks, as well as those of Gilles Candar and Frédéric Worms, allowed me to improve my article and publish it under the title "Lévy-Bruhl, Jaurès et la guerre" in the *Cahiers Jaurès*.

The colloquium organized by Emmanuelle Chevreau, Frédéric Audren, and Raymond Verdier around Henri Lévy-Bruhl at the Université Panthéon-Sorbonne in 2015 was for me the first opportunity to present my hypotheses to several members of the Lévy-Bruhl family and to measure the delicacy of this work of restitution.

I was able to consult the Lucien Lévy-Bruhl collection of the Musée du quai Branly–Jacques Chirac in 2018 thanks to Carine Peltier (who aided access to the photographs) and Stéphanie Leclerc-Caffarel (who helped with the objects) in the company of members of the Lévy-Bruhl family—another restitution experience.

Gaëtan Thomas's thesis, defended in 2018, on French vaccination policies helped me push the time frame of this book to the contemporary era. I thank him for giving me access to his interviews with Daniel Lévy-Bruhl.

I wish Alain Desrosières had read this book, as he was one of the first to encourage me in its writing. My encounter with Béatrice Touchelay allowed me to extend the work she and Alain Desrosières had done with Raymond Lévy-Bruhl.

I thank Daniel Demellier and Muriel Hilaire-Soule for giving me access to the archives of the Pasteur Institute, where I found the traces of Marcel Lévy-Bruhl, as well as Michaël Davy and Sandra Legout for their help in publishing his photograph.

I presented this book in progress at conferences at the Graduate Institute of International Studies in Geneva at the invitation of Grégoire Mallard; the University of Southern California in Los Angeles at the invitation of Andrew Lakoff; Fudan University in Shanghai at the invitation of Huang Bei; and the University of Berkeley at the invitation of Stefania Pandolfo.

I have shared my enthusiasm for the history of the Lévy-Bruhl family in friendly and scholarly discussions with Ivan Ascher, Alain Bernard, Romain Bertrand, Luc Boltanski, Frédéric Brahami, Julien Clément, Jessica De Largy Healy, Philippe Descola, Souleymane Bachir Diagne, Sarah Frioux-Salgas, Marie Gaille, Carlo Ginzburg, Ghassan Hage, Xie Jin, Isabelle Kalinowski, Mathieu Kleyebe Abonnenc, Rémi Labrusse, Monique Lévi-Strauss, Emmanuelle Loyer, Pierre Macherey, Patrice Maniglier. I thank them for their listening and their encouragement.

I am grateful to the Canadian Institute of Advanced Research for support of the editing and illustrations for this book. For editing and production, I want to thank Theo Busto, Deborah Durham, Kriti Kapila, Molly Mullin and Jane Sabherwal.

My mother, Bernadette, my father, Gérard, my aunt Geneviève, and my uncle Francis have accompanied me with their affection in writing the story of this family that is not theirs but that has a "family resemblance."

Thanks to Joëlle for being my Alice, my Lucie, my Odette, my Fanchette, my Lisette...

Except where otherwise marked, all translations from French to English are by the author.

Abbreviations

IDEA	Institute for the Development of Applied Epidemiology (Institut pour le développement de l'épidémiologie appliquée)
IMEC	Institute for Contemporary Publishing Archives (Institut mémoires de l'édition contemporaine)
INSEE	National Institute of Statistics and Economic Studies (Institut national de la statistique et des études économiques)
INVS	Institute of Health Vigilance (Institut national de veille sanitaire)
SFIO	Socialist Party (Section française de l'Internationale ouvrière)
SNS	National Statistics Service (Service national des statistiques)
UK	United Kingdom
UNESCO	United Nations Educational, Scientific and Cultural Organization
US	United States of America
WHO	World Health Organization

Introduction

Lucien Lévy-Bruhl became (in)famous for a series of books he published on "primitive mentality" between 1910 and 1939 (Goldman 1994; Merlié 1989; Keck 2008). These books were widely read by colonial officers and by the educated public. With logical clarity, they presented a variety of observations made by missionaries and travelers about non-European societies. They aimed to attenuate the violence of the colonial system by understanding "how natives think," as the English translation of his 1910 book had it, and to ignite curiosity about forms of life other than those of the "white, adult civilized man," a bold statement with which he opened this book. With his books and articles on "primitive mentality," Lucien Lévy-Bruhl played a major role in vulgarizing ethnology, a science aimed at studying and comparing human societies; yet he also supported the field's scientific development when, in 1925, he together with Marcel Mauss and Paul Rivet founded the Institute of Ethnology at the University of Paris, which organized scientific expeditions in Africa, Amazonia, and New Caledonia. Lévy-Bruhl is associated with the ambiguous mixture of empathy and paternalism that, in France, is considered characteristic of the scholars of the Third Republic, betrayed by the clumsy term "prelogical" that he used to describe "primitive mentality." Lévy-Bruhl is often caricatured as an "armchair anthropologist" who divided "primitive societies" from those he called "civilized" and who argued that the former were incapable of logical thought.

Despite the colonial heritage that makes him suspicious in a post-colonial world, this book seeks to revitalize the political thinking of Lucien Lévy-Bruhl by exploring the similarities between his time and ours. The COVID-19 pandemic has led us to question the capacity of the state to be prepared for unpredictable threats, including the emergence of a new virus. This is a question that Lucien Lévy-Bruhl addressed when he reflected on the novel aspects of the First World War: its worldwide expansion, which upset previous power configurations, and the use of industrial weapons and toxic gases, which led to changes in the atmosphere. When he described "primitive mentality" as a "participation in forces imperceptible to the senses and yet real" (Lévy-Bruhl 1910: 22), Lévy-Bruhl attempted to think, through the detour of ethnology, about the power of the invisible forces that surrounded him. He wrote in a personal note entitled "Unpredictability": "Expect the unexpected and prepare everything to channel and direct it" (Lévy-Bruhl 1917a). When he justified the creation of the Institute of Ethnology in 1925, he again used the word "prepare" to describe the shock that colonization produced:

> [At the institute,] the future administrators of our colonies will be able to prepare themselves to understand the societies so different from ours where they will have to live, with the formidable mission of finding a transition between the institutions of those societies and ours that does not predetermine a crisis, fatal for the natives and disastrous for us. If the catastrophe can be avoided, it will be by dint of intelligent and persevering sympathy. (Lévy-Bruhl 1929b: 85)

The role of ethnology, in his view, was to mitigate the shock that led colonial officers and local societies to disastrous conflict.

This reformist insistence on understanding as a way to mitigate future disaster first took shape when sociologists reflected on the French Revolution. If this event divided different mentalities within the same society, it was also possible to mentally bridge the gap between the "primitive" and the "civilized" and thus produce a unified humanity by an effort of reflexivity. In the French philosophical debate between positivism and spiritualism that took place in the nineteenth century, the "civilized mentality" transforms the "primitive mentality" from spontaneous rules of action to reflexive laws of development. By opposing "primitive mentality" and "civilized mentality" as two modes of collective organization, a community of feelings and a rational legislation—which are also two ways to anticipate future events—the French sociological school attempted to resolve the revolutionary crisis and avoid its catastrophic consequences (Karsenti 2006).

Borrowing Auguste Comte's motto "Knowledge leads to foresight, foresight leads to action," the French republican state relied on scientists to calculate the risk of industrial accidents (Ewald 2020). But the insurance techniques of the welfare state left on the margins other means of anticipating the future, which Comte had qualified with the paradoxical expression "logic of sentiments" and which Lévy-Bruhl explored in his works on "primitive mentality." The First World War led Lévy-Bruhl and his contemporaries to revalorize these colonial margins not only as economic and military resources but also as mental resources. When he compared the trust of modern individuals in the regularity of the laws of nature and the attention of "primitive societies" to the mystical phenomena that disrupt ordinary events, Lévy-Bruhl did not argue that one was superior to the other, as evolutionary anthropology did, but accentuated the contrast between two modes of thought that are available to any human mind anticipating future events.

> We have such a well-established continuous feeling of intellectual security that we do not see how it could be shaken; for, supposing even the sudden appearance of a completely mysterious phenomenon, the causes of which would at first entirely escape us, we would nevertheless be convinced that our ignorance is only provisional, that these causes exist, and that sooner or later they can be determined. Thus, the nature in which we live is, so to speak, intellectualized in advance. It is order and reason, like the spirit that thinks and moves in it. Our daily activity, down to its humblest details, implies a quiet and perfect confidence in the invariability of natural laws. The primitive's attitude of mind is quite different. The nature in which he lives presents itself to him under a completely different aspect. All objects and beings are involved in a network of mystical participations and exclusions: they are the context and the order of these objects. (Lévy-Bruhl 1922: 17)

Lévy-Bruhl was, thus, one of the first to argue that human societies perceive dangerous events differently and that the calculation of risk is only one among them (Douglas and Wildavsky 1982). We can understand Lévy-Bruhl's thinking about participation in relation to a debate between two of his fellow alumni from the Normal Superior School (École normale supérieure) in Paris, Émile Durkheim and Henri Bergson, about how human action manages uncertainty. Lévy-Bruhl's *La mentalité primitive*, published in 1922, should be read in discussion with the books they published, one ten years earlier and the other ten years later: Durkheim's *Les formes élémentaires de la vie religieuse* (Durkheim 1912) and Bergson's *Les deux sources de la morale et de la religion* (Bergson 1932).

Durkheim describes the forms that emerge in sacrifice, conceived as a ritual operation through which society protects itself against external forces by reaffirming its categories, in a way that can be compared to the work of experts when they assess risks and recommend governments to take precautionary measures. Bergson shows how prophets and mystical heroes manage to recapture "the intention of nature" in situations of crisis by inventing new norms (Bergson 1932 [1935: 105]), which is very similar to the contemporary work of whistleblowers who raise alarm in the public space and help experts create new categories of risk. While Durkheim thinks of the unpredictable as a threat to collective organization and Bergson thinks of it as a resource for collective creation, Lévy-Bruhl describes how societies prepare for the unpredictable by means of "mystical participation."

One contemporary technique of preparedness allows us to capture what Lévy-Bruhl had in mind. Sentinels are living beings situated at the limits of the social space where they perceive early warnings of future threats. They blur the opposition between humans and nonhumans by sending signs of the presence of a danger or an enemy that make sense across the species border. When he asks how the moral sentiments of "primitive societies" tolerate contradictions that are refused by modern logic, Lévy-Bruhl asks for an anthropology of sentinels: how does one take the perspective of the sentinel on environmental threats without reducing it to the more organized forms of public alert? The sentinel, in this sense, introduces forms of normativity below the level where whistleblowers act: not in a public debate on justice but in the relations between humans and nonhumans as a resource of signs for collectives (Chateauraynaud and Torny 1999; Keck 2020).

In historical accounts of anthropology, Lucien Lévy-Bruhl is often inscribed in the progressive formation of the notion of the symbolic as a universal foundation for a reconstruction of modern societies, from Comte to Claude Lévi-Strauss via Durkheim. The symbolic integrates the feeling that results from contradictions and transgressions to produce a stable representation of the social, thus extending foresight to the constitutive events of society, experienced in the mode of crisis (Karsenti 1997). This book, by contrast, proposes to inscribe Lévy-Bruhl into another intellectual genealogy, that of the sentinel raising warning signals of impending catastrophes.

This is also a family history, since I show that Lévy-Bruhl's vigilant attention to sentinels was transmitted to his descendants over four generations. I started thinking about this family genealogy in 2003 when I met Lucien Lévy-Bruhl's grandson Raymond Lévy-Bruhl, who was one of the first members of the National Institute of Statistics and Economic Studies (Institut national de la statistique et des études économiques). In 2010, I began discussions with his great-grandson Daniel Lévy-Bruhl, who was working as an epidemiologist at the National Institute of Health Vigilance (Institut national de veille sanitaire), renamed the French Agency for Public Health (Santé publique France), and with his great-granddaughter Viviane Lévy-Bruhl, who was a specialist of environmental law working at the French Institute (Institut de France). Lucien Lévy-Bruhl had three sons: Marcel, a microbiologist who worked at the Pasteur Institute, Henri, a jurist who founded the Institute of Roman Law (Institut de droit romain), and Jean, a chemist who studied the effect of gases during the First World War and who was the father of Raymond and the grandfather of Daniel. These filiations invited me to question the links between the ethnology of "primitive mentality" and the science of norms governing the relations between humans and invisible beings in their environment. How did these four generations of civil servants work for the French state through different institutions of knowledge to anticipate the future with the help of ethnology, microbiology, law, chemistry, statistics, and epidemiology?

My discussions with Daniel Lévy-Bruhl and other descendants of Lucien Lévy-Bruhl gave me access to the correspondence between Lucien Lévy-Bruhl and his wife Alice during the Dreyfus Affair and during his travels after the First World War. Lucien Lévy-Bruhl was a cousin-in-law to Alfred Dreyfus and active behind the scenes throughout the affair, particularly by supporting the actions of his friend Jean Jaurès. During his travels in the interwar period, he attempted to propagate norms of justice that resulted from the Dreyfus Affair in a world preparing both for a new war and for the end of colonial empires. When Dreyfus returned from prison in 1898, the linguist Jean Psichari wrote him a letter in which he declared: "Every Frenchman must be grateful to you. You have been there like a soldier at his post. As an advanced sentinel, you have seen the day of justice finally shine" (Duclert 2006: 571). The sentinel here designates a position at the limits of social space that allows for the emergence of a new modality of justice beyond its organized forms. It must be recalled here that the French colonial and military officers who sent Dreyfus to the penal colony of Cayenne were unable to demonstrate his guilt and that the success of those who defended him led to the formulation of new norms of justice that transformed the French military organization and labor politics, leading to the first participation of socialist leaders in the government. The hypothesis presented in this book is the following: Lucien Lévy-Bruhl saw in Alfred Dreyfus a sentinel of justice, but it would take the experience of the war for him to observe other figures of resistance to the colonial state and build what can be called an anthropology of sentinels. When I started to understand how Lucien Lévy-Bruhl's political thought was marked by the Dreyfus Affair, I encountered an obstacle: a box carrying the label "Dreyfus Affair" that Lucien had given to his son Jean in 1939 to pass onto his grandson Raymond, then nineteen years old, disappeared when the German army occupied Jean's apartment in Paris during the Second World War. It is not possible to reconstitute the letters and articles in this box, but I will use two letters that survived, sent by Dreyfus to Lévy-Bruhl in 1894 and 1917 respectively, to suggest a hypothesis about their content.

In order to fill this gap in the archive and reestablish the link between Lévy-Bruhl's anthropological work and his political commitment, this book follows the transformations of the social sciences in France through colonial troubles and global wars, which are perceived and anticipated by the Lévy-Bruhl family through the memory of the Dreyfus Affair. Such a hypothesis leads me to link, in this intellectual biography, three forms of historical writing often kept separate. First, I offer an intellectual history of philosophy and the social sciences in France, studying the alliances and divergences between actors in scientific institutions, particularly in relation to questions concerning responsibility and chance. Second, I address an environmental and global history connecting theoretical debates in France to transformations in relationships between humans and their environment that took place with a greater intensity in the colonies, such as vaccination campaigns in the Philippines or deforestation in Brazil. Finally, this is a history of French Judaism that questions the effect of the *émancipation* of the Jewish community on republican thought. These three combined efforts allow me to outline a French genealogy of what is now called "preparedness."

For Jewish intellectuals, the trial of Alfred Dreyfus was a harbinger of the wave of anti-Semitism that would ravage Europe in the following years and threaten the republican values they had endorsed. As a Jewish member of the French army, Dreyfus was accused of a crime of treason he had not committed and sent to prison for several years where he almost died before receiving a retrial and a presidential pardon. In a seminal book, American historian Michael Marrus noted that "the French Jewish community was less prepared than it might have been for an impending tragedy" (Marrus 1980: 7). He thus projected retrospectively a form of disaster preparedness dating from after the Second World War onto forms of anticipation that were available for the Jewish community at the turn of the century. At the forefront of these forces was socialism, embodied at the time by Jaurès who inscribed events within a horizon of justice. Marrus with irony thus quoted a declaration made by Léon Blum:

> The Jew has the religion of Justice as the Positivists have the religion of Fact or Renan the religion of Science. The idea of inevitable Justice alone has sustained and united the Jews in their long tribulations. Their Messiah is nothing other than the symbol of eternal Justice, which may leave the world for centuries, but which cannot fail to reign one day. Is this not the spirit of socialism? (Marrus 1980: 135)

This book questions how "socialism"—a term that may be as dated as "primitive mentality"—provided Lévy-Bruhl and his descendants with an ideal of justice and truth that prepared them for future disasters. Paul Rabinow has called these thinkers "French moderns": reformers, engineers, and architects who equipped the French Republic with norms and forms through new styles of thought and institutions producing a knowledge of the social. "Lévy-Bruhl," Rabinow wrote, "warned that although social sentiments were the hardest ones to change, giving scientific forms to moral representations was the only path to the rational construction of norms for modern society" (Rabinow 1989: 167). Rabinow also noted that the French state required the Jewish community to renounce private interests and attachments and enter a space of collective representations. What the Jews found in Paris, he says, "was an attenuation of marked social boundaries as well as the moral ties that thrive when these boundaries and their associated persecutions are strong" (Rabinow 1999: 22). Rabinow proposes the term "purgatory" to describe the space in which private interests and moral attachments are represented in France under the secularization of the sacred, transforming techniques of prevention and insurance into a precautionary principle. Following Rabinow, Stephen Collier and Andrew Lakoff have described how techniques of preparedness emerged in the US before the Second World War and were articulated at the beginning of the Cold War, such as simulations of disasters in critical infrastructures (Collier, Lakoff, and Rabinow 2004; Collier and Lakoff 2022). In this genealogy of experts concerned with the maintenance of democratic rule during states of emergency, sentinels were implemented to perceive early warning signals for events whose probability could not be calculated but whose consequences were perceived as catastrophic. These techniques of preparedness were then extended to generic threats when the specter of a nuclear attack faded away.

This book argues that French moderns thought about techniques to anticipate future disasters through the detour of "primitive mentality." While they relied on the French state to organize prevention by the laws of statistics, they asked how "premodern" societies or "stateless societies" prepare for future disasters without relying on "laws of nature." Marshall Sahlins, who passed away one day before Paul Rabinow after following a very different intellectual track at the University of Chicago, wrote in his book *How "Natives" Think*, the title of which is an ironical reference to Lévy-Bruhl: "One cannot do good history, not even contemporary history, without regard for ideas, actions and ontologies that are not and never were our own" (Sahlins 1995: 14). This book asks how Lévy-Bruhl anticipated the future in a modern fashion by taking a nonmodern perspective, that of the sentinel of injustice in the French colonial state.

The ideal of truth and justice inherited from the French Revolution and realized in social norms by a socialist politics informed how the Lévy-Bruhl family related to statistics as a scientific knowledge about collectives and as a mode of intervention in society. By contrast with other families of statisticians, such as the Bernoullis in the eighteenth century or the Bertillons in the nineteenth century, they did not use statistics to reinforce the state; rather, they continually updated statistics to serve a failing state, since the French state used "statistics" to discriminate against Jews during the Dreyfus Affair and the Vichy regime. On the other hand, the Lévy-Bruhl family could be described statistically as sharing common properties with Jewish families of their time. Raymond Lévy-Bruhl, who was one of the great actors in the history of statistics in France, humorously said in 1954: "My personality is only the point of intersection of a certain number of statistical facts" (*Informations* 1955). This book explores the space between biographies of singular personalities and the history of statistics in France. It follows how a family of French moderns multiplied knowledges of surveillance to anticipate global threats on the French territory, in its complicated relations between the metropole and the colonies, reinventing the nonmodern as a source of renewal.

PART I: RESPONSIBILITY (1857–1914)

CHAPTER I

The *émancipation* by the University

Lucien Lévy-Bruhl and Claude Lévi-Strauss can be considered the two founders of French ethnology. Their names are both Jewish and double-barreled. As Lévi-Strauss once noticed, this duality may indicate an unstable origin that led to their ethnological vocation.[1] Their names link the most ancient Jewish name associated with divination in the kingdom of Israel—Levi—with names attached to the culture of the German Empire—Bruhl and Strauss—while their first names are borrowed from Roman antiquity, as if they should attenuate the contradictions of the family name by a classical filiation. The father of Claude Lévi-Strauss, Raymond, had added to the name of his paternal grandfather, Lévi, that of his maternal grandfather, Isaac Strauss, in memory of the splendor of the court of Napoleon III where the latter was conductor at the Opera Ball of the Second Empire (Fabre 2012). Similarly, Lucien Lévy-Bruhl composed his name from that of his father and that of his wife to show the success of his republican marriage and to begin a new genealogy. In this book, I refer to him as Lucien Lévy-Bruhl throughout his life, even

---

1. In July 1981, Lévi-Strauss replied the following to a question from a journalist at the *Nouvel Observateur* about Sartre's assertion that "the Jew is spontaneously an ethnologist": "I admit that in sociology and ethnology there is a remarkable proportion of Jews. Perhaps we should not attach more importance to this than to the remarkable proportion of double names among ethnologists, which has also been noticed." On Lévi-Strauss's analysis of proper names, see Derrida (1976).

though he was authorized to bear this name only in 1902. These double-barreled family names and classical first names indicate a common trajectory of Jews in France since the French Revolution, captured by the French term *émancipation*.

Science of Judaism and "Mental Alienation"

Lucien Lévy-Bruhl was born in Paris on April 10, 1857, to Sylvain Lévy, a chemical salesman born in Metz, and Arlestine Bernard. His father was often traveling because of his work and Lucien spent much of his time with his mother and his two sisters, who shared his taste for literary studies. On April 12, 1882, he married Alice Bruhl, daughter of David Bruhl and Clothilde Hadamard, in Paris, having met her through her sister, also named Alice—both Alices went to the same school in central Paris. The Hadamard family sold jewelry and drapery in Metz. Lucien's paternal grandfather, Léon Lévy, had worked for Alice's great-uncle Obry-Ephraïm Hadamard in a printing shop in Metz until 1830, when he moved to Paris.[2] Within the framework of the republican meritocracy, the marriage with Alice Bruhl thus completed in Paris an alliance begun half a century earlier in Metz in the presses of a printing house. On the other side, the Bruhl family, which had come from Worms in Germany, were involved in the diamond trade in Paris; they gave Alice as dowry a trousseau of 25,000 francs and a portfolio of stock market shares (Levi 2007). The double-barreled name "Lévy-Bruhl" marked an alliance between the "court Jews," who supported the commercial enterprises of the Empire through financial networks, and the "Jews of knowledge," who climbed up the ladder of the republic through academic merit (Arendt 1968; Milner 2006). The knowledge he acquired on the benches of the republican school he attended gave Lévy-Bruhl access to a family fortune that assured his personal comfort and the means to support his friends and colleagues.

---

2. Obry-Ephraïm Hadamard (1787–1854) was a printer in Metz from December 21, 1812, to April 30, 1830, when he moved to Paris. He was the father of the Arabist David Hadamard (1821–1849) and the painter Auguste Hadamard (1823–1886) and the grandfather of the actress Zélie Hadamard (1849–1902) and of the mathematician Jacques Hadamard (1865–1963). Viviane Lévy-Bruhl preserves in her personal collection a document signed by August Hadamard to terminate a two-year work contract by Léon Lévy, Metz, April 21, 1830.

In the recollections of those who knew him, Lucien Lévy-Bruhl was described as being exceptionally bright and clever. These qualities enabled him to pass the exam of the Normal Superior School in 1876, where he met a range of bright young scholars who would play a central role in his career. He was second to Salomon Reinach, who came from a family of wealthy bankers and brilliant polymaths. The graduation photograph shows Lévy-Bruhl as a young man with a rebellious look under a proud beret. In spite of his good academic results, Lucien Lévy-Bruhl was the target of insults from his classmates, either because of his Jewish name or because of his modest background. He was one of the only scholarship holders at the Normal Superior School and had to work as a tutor in the summer to finance his studies, which prompted a stay in Switzerland in the summer of 1876 and one in Sussex, England, in 1878. A letter that he received while in Sussex suggests that he was not at ease in the monastic atmosphere of the Normal Superior School: the letter's author, his classmate Camille Jullian, urged him to take advantage of the happy English climate "far from the gossip of the Normal Superior School."[3] After passing the *agrégation* in philosophy in 1879, a competitive examination to qualify those who would become teachers in public schools, Lucien Lévy-Bruhl taught at the high school in Poitiers. In a letter to Reinach, he expressed boredom and lamented his difficulty in getting down to work. Having given up on a thesis in metaphysics, he thought of starting a thesis on responsibility because he was fascinated by madness. "This is a study of passions and of mental alienation that interests me greatly."[4]

---

3. IMEC letter from Camille Jullian to Lucien Lévy, September 3, 1878.
4. Maison de l'Orient et de la Méditerranée Jean Pouilloux in Lyon, Salomon Reinach Archives, letter no 10108976/9, letter from Lucien Lévy to Salomon Reinach, June 5, 1881. This letter is published in Nisio (2019). The term "aliénation mentale" was coined by Philippe Pinel in his *Traité medico-philosophique sur l'aliénation mentale, ou la manie* in 1798 (Pinel 1798). It was used by his student Jean-Étienne Esquirol in his doctoral thesis in 1805, "Des passions considérées comme causes, symptômes et moyens curatifs de la maladie mentale" (Esquirol 1805), and to translate William Ellis's *A Treatise on the Nature, Symptoms, Causes, and Treatment of Insanity* (Ellis 1838) into *Traité de l'aliénation mentale, ou De la nature, des causes, des symptômes et du traitement de la folie* (Ellis 1840) (see Foucault 2009).

Lucien Lévy-Bruhl's relationship with Judaism can be described as distanced, since he was not brought up reading the sacred texts or respecting religious rituals, and he did not count a rabbi among his direct ancestors. In the letters his mother sent him while he was in Sussex, she had to remind him to write to his grandmother for religious holidays and not to travel during Yom Kippur. His early letters exchange good wishes with his parents and sisters for Rosh Hashanah. When he received Reinach's *Handbook of classical philology* (Reinach 1880), he wrote to his fellow student at the Normal Superior School: "If I were in the least competent, my dear friend, I would have used this entire letter to tell you about your book and to praise it, which it undoubtedly deserves—but this is Hebrew to me."[5] Lucien Lévy-Bruhl thus established a complicity with the specialist in ancient Greek by considering Hebrew a dead language. Indeed, Salomon Reinach, and even more so his brother Joseph, a lawyer and politician, embody, in the eyes of contemporary historians, "an assimilating Franco-Judaism that implies, in the end, the complete negation, in the public arena, of Jewish particularism, its pure and simple dissolution within a universally apprehended Frenchness" (Birnbaum 1992: 27).

Distancing oneself from the Jewish tradition was indeed the principle of an emancipated Jewish community within the French Republic. On September 1, 1879, Lucien Lévy-Bruhl received a letter of congratulations for his success in the *agrégation* in philosophy from Zadoc Kahn, who had just founded the Society for Jewish Studies (Société d'études juives) on the model of the German Wissenschaft des Judentums (Studies of Judaism) (Simon-Nahum 2018). Zadoc Kahn studied and taught at the rabbinical seminary of Metz between 1856 and 1867, before being appointed chief rabbi of the consistory of Paris and then chief rabbi of the consistory of France, where he consistently defended the integration of the Jews of France into the republic (Chaumont and Kuperminc 2007). Lucien Lévy-Bruhl's marriage to Alice in 1882 established family ties with Zadoc Kahn, whose daughter Berthe married Alice's brother Henri.

Around the same time that Lucien Lévy-Bruhl was becoming ensconced in the Jewish community, his distanced relationship to Judaism was challenged when his first publication project was rejected in 1880 by the *Revue d'études juives*. It was an article on the theory of passions in Spinoza, which Théodore Reinach, a brilliant young Hellenist and

---

5.   Salomon Reinach Archives, letter no 10108976/9, Letter from Lucien Lévy to Salomon Reinach, June 5, 1881.

member of the committee of the journal, also the brother of Salomon and Joseph Reinach, criticized for not speaking sufficiently of the influence of the Jewish tradition on Spinoza. Lévy-Bruhl, who throughout his life claimed his fidelity to Spinoza's doctrine while mixing it with Hume's skepticism,[6] read the philosopher of the substantial union of soul and body as an important author for the science of the human mind but not for the "scientific study of Judaism." Théodore Reinach's letter deserves to be quoted to measure the gaps between these two human sciences in search of institutional credit:

> It seemed to us that, from the historical point of view, Spinoza's philosophy fits perfectly into the framework of our journal, whereas from the dogmatic point of view, it can only be admitted by way of exception and with the greatest precaution. ... We are just born, we are weak, we are credited with good looks, but in order to survive, we need the sympathy and active support of scholars from all countries who are concerned with Judaism; and we will only succeed in inspiring their confidence by clearly affirming from the beginning, by the choice of our articles, both the special character of our studies and the truly scientific spirit that animates us.[7]

Reinach's refusal was certainly difficult for Lévy-Bruhl, but it did not discourage him from launching his research in moral philosophy rather than in the science of Judaism.

Naturalistic Approach to Moral Emotions

Lucien Lévy-Bruhl's first successful publication was also silent on Judaism, even though it concerned a Jewish author, Heinrich (Henri) Heine. This article, published by the *Nouvelle revue* in 1881, emphasized that

6. In a letter to the British anthropologist Edward Evans-Pritchard in 1934, Lévy-Bruhl distinguished himself from the founders of ethnology by claiming to be a descendant of Spinoza and Hume: "I had the ambition to add something to the scientific knowledge of human nature by using the essential data of ethnology. My training was philosophical, not anthropological. I proceed from Spinoza and Hume rather than from Bastian and Tylor" (Lévy-Bruhl 1957: 413).

7. IMEC, Letter from Théodore Reinach to Lucien Lévy, November 6, 1880.

Heine's perspective on the relationship between France and Germany was particularly valuable, since he lived in both countries and spoke both their languages. According to the young philosopher and contrary to the portrait given by Germaine de Staël, Heine showed that Germany was not only a country of metaphysical schools but also a country of military barracks, where the feeling of hatred toward France was especially strong because of its ideological foundation. If he perceived in Germany the signs of the war to come in 1870, Heine discovered in France that "the great task of his time is *émancipation*" (Lévy-Bruhl 1881: 342), a term that in French means both progress through knowledge and liberation from serfdom. This term not only designated for Heine a task for the Jews, who should free themselves from their minority condition according to the Napoleonic precept, but a task for all citizens who had to appropriate the movement of ideas resulting from the French Revolution:

> Not very suited for a politics of action, Heine was more adept at foreseeing a future towards which his preoccupations constantly carried him. The relations between France and Germany worried him, and, looking further ahead, he questioned the future destiny of democracy in Europe and noted the first symptoms of a great social revolution. (Lévy-Bruhl 1881: 355)

If Heine seemed in his eyes to be divided between "the generous democratism of his heart" and "the aristocracy of his mind," Lucien Lévy-Bruhl noted that this separation between the heart and the mind was attenuated by the development of a "popular or democratic or naturalist art" which put scientific truth within reach of the multitude. Lucien Lévy-Bruhl's first article thus concluded optimistically on the possibility of scientifically enlightening human behavior, which expressed with a touching naivety the ideal of *émancipation* of this young man, then aged twenty-four. "Mankind has so far suffered its history; it is time that it finally takes control, like a child who, becoming a man, begins to know what he wants and to want what he does" (Lévy-Bruhl 1881: 383).

This first publication by Lévy-Bruhl thus sketched an ethnological approach within Europe. If the border between Germany and France was the place where the signs of future conflict could be perceived, at the point where two apparently incompatible national characters met, it was possible to produce a scientific knowledge based on the literary forms that were circulating between these territories and that accompanied social transformation. Lévy-Bruhl noticed that German romanticism, which mourned the loss of a communal ideal and found it only in nostalgia, is replaced in France by a naturalist literature that, through the novels of Flaubert and Zola, spread the spirit of observation throughout the society. While Heine was still divided between the heart and the mind when he asked himself whether the revolution would be one of democratic *émancipation* or one of class struggle, Lévy-Bruhl saw in the diffusion of knowledge promised by the public university system a means of holding onto these two aspects of humanity, because he considered popular literature a form of knowledge where Heine still searched for the unity of language (Karsenti 2017: 117–18).

Lévy-Bruhl's confidence in knowledge may have come from his time in England as a tutor where he acquired a facility in reading English authors, even if he did not attend the Universities of Oxford or Cambridge. Although he was to establish himself as one of the specialists in the relations between France and Germany without ever crossing the Rhine during his studies—unlike his fellow students who left to do internships in German laboratories (Digeon 1959)—Lévy-Bruhl did not seem torn between these two nations and did not express any nostalgia for the Alsace-Lorraine of his parents. In the manner of an English naturalist, he considered the border between Germany and France a place where he could observe the democratic transformations that affected industrial societies by influencing moral passions. His second publication, entitled "Darwin on morality," emphasized the need for a "naturalistic" approach to moral emotions, based on scientific observations and not philosophical systems (Lévy-Bruhl 1883). Lévy-Bruhl's conception of the border between France and Germany can be formulated as follows: it is the place where sentinels can perceive signs of an impending conflict following the experimental method of natural history, because the effects of ideas on bodies are more visible there than elsewhere.[8]

A History of Political Ideas

Lucien Lévy-Bruhl shared this experimental approach to moral phenomena with Émile Boutmy, founder of the Free School of Political

---

8.   Heine wrote in his late poem "Lost Child," originally published in 1851 in *Romancero*: "As a sentinel post in the war for freedom/I have stayed without complaint for thirty years/I fought without a hope of victory/I knew I would not return unharmed" (Heine [1851] 1997: 145).

Sciences (École libre des sciences politiques). He gave courses there be-tween 1885 and 1895, while he was a professor of philosophy at the Lycée Louis-le-Grand (the main high school in Paris) and awaiting a position at the University of Paris-Sorbonne. Émile Boutmy created this school in the aftermath of France's defeat of 1870 in its war with Prussia. He gave it two goals: to compensate for the lack of knowledge in ad-ministration among the French elite and to instill an empirical approach to political facts that did not limit itself to the formal procedures of the state. Boutmy himself applied this method to English and American societies by observing, below the level of state history, the moral and political life of a society that gives a people a sense of unity. His method was inspired by the "psychology of peoples" (*Völkerpsychologie*) that lin-guists were then developing in Germany, but it was less dependent on the system of language and more attentive to the multiplicity of causes that make up collective life. Lévy-Bruhl summarized Boutmy's method as follows:

> According to him, political philosophy consists essentially in discov-ering how causes subordinate each other, how they intersect, how they intertwine, sometimes concurring and sometimes opposing in their effects. But on the other hand, the network of causes is so complicated … that it is practically impossible to arrive at rigorous knowledge of the causes solely by observing the effects. This is where what Mr. Boutmy calls "the divinatory sense of the psychologist" in-tervenes. This sense seizes, in the complex physiognomy of a people, the essential feature that makes its character and that orders the oth-ers. (Lévy-Bruhl 1906: 801–802)

For Lévy-Bruhl, assigning a character to a people runs the risk of sub-stantializing a set of historical facts in a formula; but it shows how the unity of a society emerges from below, by deciphering the idea toward which social affects converge, rather than from above, by describing the legal apparatus of the state. Lévy-Bruhl retained from Boutmy the as-sumption that *émancipation* does not occur through assimilation by the state but through participation in the state, defined as a place where a plurality of forms of life is expressed through an affective anticipation of the future rather than in a scientific observation of the present. For Lévy-Bruhl, political science was not a science of the state, which is the original meaning of "statistics," but rather an observation of the condi-tions of social life that make the state possible.

In the courses he gave at the Free School of Political Sciences, Lévy-Bruhl applied this method to Germany. From these courses, he developed a series of articles and then a book entitled *Germany since Leibniz: Essay on the development of national consciousness in Germany 1700–1848* (Lévy-Bruhl 1890d). It is worth noting that he chose not to begin the history of Germany with Martin Luther, who translated the Bible into German in the sixteenth century, but with Gottfried Leibniz, who strove a century later to bring Germany into a European system of peace despite the diversity of its political forms. In this book, Lévy-Bruhl attempted to understand how this pacific idea of Germany produced a national sentiment during the nineteenth century that was used by the Prussian state in an aggressive way. The method that Lévy-Bruhl adopted was, therefore, experimental and not systematic: it did not postulate the unity of a people but it observed how the idea of this unity spread by overcoming social resistance, with periods of incubation and periods of rapid growth comparable to the movements of a living organism. At the end of this history, the Bismarckian state did not appear as a necessary development—contrary to what some readers of Georg Hegel suggested at the time (Bourgeois 1989)—but as one form among others of national consciousness. It was, therefore, necessary to be vigilant to this emerging form while keeping alternatives in view.

During his teaching at the Free School of Political Sciences, Lucien Lévy-Bruhl met the jurist Moisei Ostrogorski, who had fled the pogroms in Russia and with whom he built a lasting friendship. In 1885, Ostrogorski defended a thesis on the origin of universal suffrage and developed a reflection on political parties that would have a great influence on political science, notably through the sociology of Max Weber (Ostrogorski 1993). He showed that parties in the United Kingdom (UK) and the United States (US) are real political enterprises that require total commitment from their members and that these parties modify the game of political decisions by internal rules that can go against the general interest. Ostrogorski's study of the diversity of political parties can be compared to Lévy-Bruhl's analysis of the diversity of national forms in Germany. Both show that collective entities participate in a general idea that they concur to realize, one through partisan programs and the other through forms of literary expression. After his thesis, Ostrogorski traveled to the UK and the US and was elected to the Russian Duma in 1906. The abundant correspondence he maintained with Lévy-Bruhl informed the latter of the political situation in Europe at large and of the threats to Jews in the various countries of the continent. Ostrogorski left political life after the Russian Revolution of 1917 and died in 1921.

Strikingly, Lévy-Bruhl's last publication on Germany was in 1895, just as the Dreyfus Affair began. Lévy-Bruhl then took up his position as lecturer in modern philosophy at the Sorbonne where he gave a series of lectures on French philosophy (Lévy-Bruhl 1899b). But this very publication, entitled "The crisis of metaphysics in Germany," seemed to amount to a statement of failure. After having published a work on one of the founders of German Romanticism, the philosopher Friedrich Jacobi (Lévy-Bruhl 1894), Lévy-Bruhl now noted that metaphysics had disappeared in Germany with the rise of a positive spirit shared by conservative and socialist thinkers. The militarization of the Prussian state coincided, according to him, with the German socialists' adoption of the principle of class struggle. Lévy-Bruhl predicted the appearance of a new metaphysician who would think about the conditions of life in Germany and, in particular, the industrial activities that were developing on the margins of the Prussian state. The socialist debate on Karl Marx's writings lacked, in his eyes, a metaphysics that would fill the gap between the current description of the world and the coming revolution. Here again, Lévy-Bruhl called for a science of sentiments closer to English naturalism than to German positivism: "The theorists of German socialism claim to proceed in an exclusively scientific way and profess to despise sentiment. That may be so, but sentiment serves them and they do not disdain to be served. What will happen if the prediction of the triumph of German socialism does not come true? It will be a decisive crisis" (Lévy-Bruhl 1892c: 557).

For lack of a sufficiently solid metaphysics, the German socialists, according to Lévy-Bruhl, "compose with the sentiment that dominates the nation" and rely on Bismarckian militarism in case of war (Lévy-Bruhl 1895a: 362). In the transition from a metaphysics of the ideal to a positive psychology, the possibility of a knowledge produced by a sentiment, that is by the perception of signs of emergence at the margins of national constructions, was lost in Germany. Similarly, Lévy-Bruhl observed that German literature had not been able to deal with new social problems in an original way but contented itself with reproducing literary models that originated in France and England. For him, the only contemporary innovation in Germany was in music: Lévy-Bruhl, a great fan of Richard Wagner, whom he played on the piano in his family circle, took up Arthur Schopenhauer's definition of music as "a metaphysics that has become sensitive" (Lévy-Bruhl 1892a: 373).

This "knowledge by sentiment," which Lévy-Bruhl elaborated in his thesis, would soon be put to the test in the Dreyfus Affair. In his eyes, knowledge by sentiment was much better able to perceive signs of the future and organize their distribution than positive law; in that sense it was a better driver of *émancipation* than science itself. Lévy-Bruhl's first articles were thus a contribution to the debate on socialism that was taking place in France in this period. As Lévy-Bruhl rejected the Marxist principle of class struggle, he proposed in his thesis on responsibility a singular mode of knowledge and action based on the sentiment of justice. This proposal brought him close to his two schoolmates at the Normal Superior School, Émile Durkheim and Jean Jaurès, as we will see in the next two chapters.

CHAPTER 2

The Critique of Criminology

Lucien Lévy-Bruhl depicted his thesis on "the idea of responsibility," defended in 1883, as a contribution to public debate. While his first articles were situated in the intellectual space of literary journals located between France, Germany, and England, in which Lévy-Bruhl addressed the heritage of the French Revolution and the coming of the First World War, his first book, published in 1884, addressed those interested in problems of social life: "I lived in Paris and went to Amiens for my classes. I had a subscription to the railway. The manager of the Gare du Nord, who knew me, said to me one day: 'Have you written a book on responsibility? Give it to me! I'm interested in responsibility'" (Lévy-Bruhl 1929b: 76).

A philosophy thesis for a stationmaster: this is the context in which Lévy-Bruhl, within the framework of the Third Republic, reformulated the conception of responsibility elaborated by Emmanuel Kant in the late eighteenth century. This context was organized around two new facts: on the one hand, the acceleration of the movement of people and goods, which made it necessary to think about insurance against the accidents of industrial life, in competition with the state system of insurance set up in Germany; on the other hand, the trauma of the Commune of 1871 and anarchist attacks against political figures, which led to measures of security contradicting the republican attachment to liberties. This double context justified the statement with which Lévy-Bruhl opened his thesis: "The question of whether or not a man is responsible for a certain action arises much more often today than in the past" (Lévy-Bruhl 1884a: 12).

Positivist Criminology in Italy and Germany

By the late nineteenth century, a new science had emerged that appeared to dissolve the moral notion of responsibility: criminology. Using the observation of the regularities of social life, it defined crime as an exception to these rules. From the perspective of social defense, it was not necessary to consider the criminal a responsible subject: it sufficed to show that criminal acts were outside the rules of social life and could be anticipated according to the laws of criminology (Blanckaert 1994; Foucault 1994). In *The criminal man*, published in Italy in 1876, Cesare Lombroso relied on observations in asylums, barracks, and prisons to assert that crime manifested biological malformations and a regression to an earlier stage of development of the human species (Lombroso 1876). Delinquency could thus be explained by degeneration and crime by primitive savagery. One of his disciples, Raffaele Garofalo, used statistics to collate these observations and to make the criminal appear as an enemy who had unconsciously declared war on society. Such theses were received well in France after the repression of the Commune because the link between criminals, enemies, and savages justified sending Communards to the prisons of New Caledonia.

Although criminology was based on shaky biological foundations that could easily be refuted, it highlighted the role of statistics in the regulation of social life. Statistics replaced criminal law, which exposes the subject to a sanction, with social defense, which identifies dangerous individuals by their deviation from the norm. Crime then appeared as a risk that modern individuals had to accept because of the complexities of social life. This was the path that German civil law explored in the late nineteenth century and that French jurists and physicians took up. Indeed, Germany had developed a legal system that made it possible to establish no-fault liability by transferring the burden of workers' accidents to the companies that employed them, notably through the 1838 law on railroads that, in 1871, was extended to all industry. The psychology of Gustav Fechner and Wilhelm Wundt echoed this legal development, explaining the actions of individuals not by free will but by a set of excitations. The French doctor Charles Feré relied on their work to explain, in opposition to the Italian theory of the heredity of crime, that security was a public service demanding the contribution of every citizen; this reframed criminality in the language of insurance.

History and Philosophy of Responsibility

Faced with these Italian and German scientific currents that dissolved the notion of subjective responsibility in criminology and psychology, Lévy-Bruhl endeavored to defend it. In his thesis, he combined the two teachings he had received at the Normal Superior School: that of Émile Boutroux on Kantian criticism and that of Numa Fustel de Coulanges on ancient history.

Lévy-Bruhl described the enthusiasm with which his generation received Boutroux's teaching several times. "He gave us a lecture on Kant's philosophy that so overwhelmed us that all we could talk about was the *Critique of Pure Reason*" (Lévy-Bruhl 1929b: 76). Indeed, Boutroux aimed at bringing together the philosophy of knowledge and practical philosophy through an analysis of moral emotions. Beyond discovering the Kantian text in its technicality, the philosophers of Lévy-Bruhl's generation were inspired by the very idea of critique as the possibility of placing themselves at the transcendental level of conditions of possibility. Lévy-Bruhl wrote in a tribute published in the journal *Critique philosophique*, edited by Charles Renouvier, that

> more and more, the criticist doctrine is spreading: the proofs of its influence are becoming greater every day and for those who know a little about our students, there is no doubt that a good part of the philosophical youth is fed by it. (Lévy-Bruhl 1892b: 72)

Kant's criticism allowed Lévy-Bruhl's generation of philosophers to distance themselves from Hegel's philosophy, which had constituted the basis of academic teaching during the Second Empire through its translation by Victor Cousin, and to think differently about consciousness. Where Hegel had described the development of a substance that gradually becomes aware of itself, Kant posited a set of relations that are concentrated in centers of belief. In a series of articles on "the psychology of the primitive man," Renouvier criticized German philosophy and English anthropology (Renouvier 1874, 1879). Both made the mistake, in his eyes, of postulating a natural primitive germ from which humanity would develop, whereas historical observation showed rather a diversity of "moral environments" constituted by mutual reactions to historical accidents, in a modality of cohesion that Renouvier was one of the first to call "solidarity" (Blais 2000; Mucchielli 1998). The figure of the "primitive" thus arrived early in the

work of Lucien Lévy-Bruhl through Renouvier's critique of evolutionism in anthropology.

In his analysis of the idea of responsibility, Lévy-Bruhl rejected the
conception of a primitive humanity prior to the formation of the idea of
responsibility. The whole difficulty of the debate on responsibility, in his
view, came from the fact that responsibility was usually defined as understanding and accepting the law, whereas for Lévy-Bruhl the law only
codified preexisting beliefs constituted in social life. This was a strong
criticism of the idea of a "good savage" that Jean-Jacques Rousseau had
defended. "One can imagine an artificial and solitary man whose innocence would shame our social vices. In reality, man lives everywhere
in society, even in New Guinea, and it does not seem that the looser the
bonds of society, the closer man is to innocence" (Lévy-Bruhl 1884a: 59).

Here Lévy-Bruhl followed Fustel de Coulanges's demonstration on
the ancient city. Fustel showed that, before the law was formulated by
the institution, the rule manifested itself by its sacred character as a belief
shared through ritual practices (Héran 1987; Karsenti 2013). He spoke
of "old beliefs that, in the long run, disappeared from people's minds but
left long after them usages, rituals, and forms of language from which
even the unbeliever could not free himself" (Fustel de Coulanges 1984:
25). This field of beliefs preceding laws, which Lévy-Bruhl qualified by
the term "morals" (*moeurs*) and which German philosophy referred to
as *Sittlichkeit*, ignores the modern distinction between piety, morality,
and legality: it is a set of prescribed actions that gives rise to approval or
reprobation. According to Lévy-Bruhl, Christianity introduced the distinction between piety, morality, and legality through the idea of merit,
which interiorized sanction within consciousness. The postulation of
a God external to human laws led to a dissociation between objective
responsibility ruled by laws and subjective responsibility accessible to
consciousness. If the function of schools and tribunals in this process
was to strengthen the idea of merit by connecting objective and subjective responsibility, they should not encourage, according to Lévy-Bruhl,
a sacrifice of the individual to society. The notion of justice should, thus,
be separated from notions of legality and merit and should keep the
meaning it had in old piety.

What Lévy-Bruhl meant by justice was rather vague at this stage,
probably because his engagement with socialism was still shy. But he
claimed it strongly against "positivism." With the use of this term, he
targeted a mode of thinking that seeks natural laws to prescribe the
government of society, as can be found in the use of criminology to

reorganize society. The critical philosophy of Renouvier allowed Lévy-Bruhl to oppose positivism on the grounds that knowledge is relative to a subject and that the feeling of justice is the only way to reach an absolute object by organizing solidarity among humans, thus opening a separation between nature and society.

> Positivism says: "Be content with the given world!" ... This way of understanding the relativity of our knowledge offends what is highest and noblest in human nature, that inner voice that cries out, "Do not be content with the given world!" Positivism is a dogmatism of human nature. In our eyes, if man must resign himself to not knowing the absolute, it is on condition of having the thought of it constantly present. (Lévy-Bruhl 1884a: 184)

Claiming the right of individual consciousness against the laws observed by positivism, Lévy-Bruhl brought a solution to the philosophical question of responsibility close to that which Raymond Saleilles had proposed in legal debates. For Saleilles, the responsibility for work-related accidents should rely on an individualization of the penalty (Saleilles 1898). Prevention of accidents should not be a form of expiation because the Christian notion of justice differs from the old notion of vengeance. Individualizing a penalty meant assessing the degrees of freedom of the individuals involved in the accident, that is calculating the risks they have taken, in order to reduce these risks by delegating them to the social organization. By the way it punished crime, Saleilles said, modern social life thus produced individuals who tended to forget their social obligations.

Sociology of law at that time was an attempt to explain this paradoxical situation of modern societies, as it started not from the individual being punished but from the punishing society. Émile Durkheim recommended studying responsibility in primitive societies, while Gabriel Tarde described criminals in industrialized societies where they were aggregated like corporations. Durkheim defined punishment as a way to restore society to the situation prior to the crime that disturbed it. This led him to conceive of society as a consciousness endowed with its own representations and categories, and to distinguish forms of law according to forms of solidarity. In his view, the so-called primitive societies displayed a form of solidarity that could be qualified as "mechanical," in the sense that they present the punishment in an undifferentiated way for all individuals, by contrast with the "organic solidarity" of modern societies where penalty depends on the social situation of the criminal (Durkheim 1933). Tarde remarked that the degrees of freedom that Saleilles proposed the judge to analyze did not take into account all the forms of crime available in the statistics. It was better, for Tarde, to speak about a criminal character, or even an innate predisposition, to understand how certain individuals commit transgressive acts that will be imitated by others and that are qualified legally as criminal (Lévy-Bruhl 1890b).

If Lévy-Bruhl was critical of the positivism of criminology, he appraised Tarde and Durkheim's sociology of law as a renewal of the discipline founded by Auguste Comte and Herbert Spencer. In an article published in 1895 under the title "Sociological questions," he claimed that these two sociologists articulated in new ways moral and social issues (Lévy-Bruhl 1895b). They showed that more justice would improve life in society, but also that a more just social organization would increase moral ideas. If he supported Durkheim's views on the necessity of comparing forms of justice, Lévy-Bruhl asserted that travelers' observations in remote societies were not reliable (Lévy-Bruhl 1884a: 138) and he contented himself with the literary description of the working-class districts of London and Berlin where high rents forced families into dense and unsafe housing (Lévy-Bruhl 1895b: 781). The sentiment of injustice led him to ask for a reorganization of the rules of justice. Hence, Lévy-Bruhl's distinction in his thesis between two forms of responsibility was not a dualism between object and subject but corresponded to two modes of articulation between crime and sanction: one in which they adequately fit together and the other in which they do not. The Dreyfus Affair was, then, an opportunity for Lévy-Bruhl to question this connection between crime and sanction, as it immersed him in an actual case involving questions of justice and responsibility that he had considered speculatively in his thesis.

CHAPTER 3

The Dreyfus Affair: A Matrix for Ethnology

In December 1894, Lévy-Bruhl was summoned to the prison rue du Cherche-Midi, in the center of Paris, as a civil witness for artillery officer Alfred Dreyfus who had just been accused of the crime of high treason based on a scrap of a note found in a wastebasket in the German Embassy. The two men were tied by family, for Dreyfus had married Lucie Hadamard, Alice Bruhl's cousin, four years earlier (Burns 1991). At the first military trial of Dreyfus, which took place behind closed doors, Lévy-Bruhl declared that "no motive could explain [why] a thirty-five-year-old captain, a graduate of the Polytechnic School (École polytechnique) and the War School (École de guerre), to whom happiness, fortune, and life smiled, [would commit] a crime as monstrous and stupid as that which was imputed to him."[1] This testimony was based on Lévy-Bruhl's reflection on responsibility: in his view, the magnitude of the crime could not justify Dreyfus's punishment if the absence of a motive did not allow it to be attributed to a specific individual. The gap between society's reaction to the crime and the individual's sentiment of injustice questioned the foundations of French sociology and opened it to the ethnological study of the variations of justice.

---

1. These words were reported after Lucien Lévy-Bruhl's death in 1939 by the journalist Antoine Charpentier in the weekly journal *La griffe* (Charpentier 1939).

Lévy-Bruhl Facing Dreyfus in Jail

What could Lucien Lévy-Bruhl have thought of his relative Alfred
Dreyfus, who was reputedly cold and distant? One is tempted to apply
to Lévy-Bruhl what Léon Blum wrote: "The Jews of Dreyfus's age, who
belonged to the same social stratum, who, like him, had passed difficult competitions, ... were exasperated by the idea that hostile prejudice
would limit their impeccable careers" (Blum 1932 [1935: 26]). This sociological reasoning on the ambivalence of the Jewish elites of the Third
Republic toward Dreyfus probably does not account for the complex
sentiments Lévy-Bruhl must have felt toward his cousin-in-law, but the
parallels between the two men's social trajectories are striking. Alfred
Dreyfus was born in 1859 in Mulhouse to a family of textile merchants
and entered the Polytechnic School in 1878. In 1893, after graduating
from the War School, he did an internship at the army headquarters,
where his German language skills were appreciated, and he gained the
rank of captain. There he was accused, on October 15, 1894, of leaking
military secrets to the German army. As a professor of philosophy at
the Sorbonne, Lévy-Bruhl was in a good position to defend Dreyfus,
having experienced the same rapid rise in the meritocratic institutions
of the republic. It must be noticed that Dreyfus came from an Alsatian
Judaism more integrated into the rural economy, whereas Lévy-Bruhl
came from a poorer but more urban Lorraine Judaism. This might have
encouraged Lévy-Bruhl to be more modest and cautious in his public
appearance while Dreyfus was criticized for his perceived arrogance and
overt ambition. Yet the biographical comparison suggests that Dreyfus
offered Lévy-Bruhl a mirror to observe what would happen to him if an
accident of history interrupted a seemingly irreversible trajectory. This is
how the captain presented himself to the philosopher in a letter dated
December 27, 1894:

> I see today, to my expense, that it is sometimes more difficult to live
> than to die. What a beautiful drama one could make from my unfor-
> tunate history, my dear Lucien. There is enough to inspire a philoso-
> pher such as you. I was happy and proud, husband of an admirable
> woman, father of two charming babies, owner of a fortune largely
> sufficient for my modest tastes, surrounded by a family that loved me.
> ... I had everything at last! What a terrible collapse. And then, how
> much I understand this rage and this anger of a whole people, hear-
> ing that an officer is a traitor. There is no punishment great enough

to punish such a crime ... but the traitor is not me; and I am even convinced that it is not an officer. I would have preferred to be sentenced to death. At least there would be no more discussion possible. But now my nights are spent in continuous struggles between the desire to finish with this treacherous life and the hope, one day, to see my name rehabilitated by the discovery of the wretched author of the incriminated letter. ... Do you understand, my dear Lucien, all the tumultuous fights in my soul, all these ghosts haunting my brain? Is there a justice on earth? Unfortunately I do not have this deep faith that makes martyrs. Until now my conscience alone has given me all the courage I have shown; I hope that my conscience will allow me to fight to the end. (Duclert 2006: 291)

The "drama" that Dreyfus depicted so poignantly put on stage an officer accused of treason because of how the handwriting on a piece of paper—known in the affair as the *bordereau*—that revealed information about the maneuvers of the French army resembled his own handwriting. The officer's suffering was twofold: being accused and condemned for a crime he had not committed; and knowing that the honor of the army, to which he was viscerally attached, had been scorned by a criminal who remained free. The Ministry of War, led by General Mercier, wished to resolve the turmoil caused by the discovery of the *bordereau* by giving Dreyfus the possibility of committing suicide; but Dreyfus did not believe enough in the army to become a "martyr." He was left with his conscience in which two forces clashed with each other: his trust in the army and his conviction that he was innocent.

By enacting a series of "ghosts"—"honor," "homeland," "justice," "Judaism," "anti-Semitism"—this "drama" played out the speculative opposition that Lévy-Bruhl had constructed in his thesis ten years earlier in a singular way. The Statistical Section of the General Staff, headed by Lieutenant-Colonel Sandherr, a native of Mulhouse and known for his anti-Semitism, had indeed recovered the *bordereau* from a wastebasket at the German Embassy in Paris while monitoring the activities of the military attaché Maximilian von Schwartzkoppen. A graphology report written for the military trial by Alphonse Bertillon, who had set up a system for classifying anthropometric photographs at the Paris prefecture, attested that Dreyfus was indeed the author of the *bordereau*. To contradict this "objective" demonstration of his responsibility, Dreyfus could only offer the "subjective" sentiment of his innocence, taking as witness his cousin, who shared the same meritocratic trajectory in the republican education system. Because a military tribunal accused him of a crime he did not commit, Dreyfus's faith in the army and his faith in justice, which had coincided until then, dissociated. Individual conscience was, thus, not a sufficient criterion for justice because it was irreversibly split into two incompatible beliefs. If we want to take up the notions proposed by Lévy-Bruhl in his thesis, the first trial of Dreyfus opposed legality to piety as two contrasting views on morality. Henceforth, supporters of Dreyfus had to transform his sentiment of innocence into evidence, to place it in contrast with the evidence of the criminological experts.

The army suggested another solution for the troubles that affected Dreyfus's conscience. Faced with his refusal to commit suicide, his superiors organized a ceremony of degradation in the courtyard of Les Invalides (a hospital for wounded soldiers in the middle of Paris) on January 5, 1895, to mark his social death. The signs of his military identity were publicly destroyed, his saber was broken, and his decorations were removed from his chest, one after the other, under the gaze and cries of a hateful crowd. Since Dreyfus's individual conscience could not, by itself, put an end to the disturbance that affected him in spite of itself, what Durkheim will call "collective consciousness" had to reassert the order that has been disturbed.

Dreyfus, as a victim of the crowd's emotions, was sent to the penal colony of Cayenne (also called Devil's Island, off the coast of French Guiana), where an almost certain physical death awaited him. The strategy of the first Dreyfusards (his supporters)—Mathieu Dreyfus, Bernard Lazare, but also Lucien Lévy-Bruhl—was to enlist a growing number of actors in supporting the officer's innocence, so as to avoid the anti-Semitic accusation that they were defending him because of Jewish solidarity. They turned first to the lawyer René Waldeck-Rousseau, who defended Dreyfus at his first trial. After the degradation ceremony, they contacted Salomon Reinach, who informed his brothers Joseph and Théodore. Then they contacted Lucien Herr, in charge of the library of the Normal Superior School, where he had great influence on students such as Blum and Charles Péguy because of his knowledge of German socialism. They also contacted the historian Gabriel Monod, who mobilized his Protestant networks. In this way, Lévy-Bruhl's development of his scientific and political network can be "considered in many ways as the starting point of the involvement of scholars in the affair, even before it broke out in 1898" (Duclert 2006: 288).

Zola and Jaurès as Whistleblowers

A major turn in the Dreyfus Affair was when Major Georges Picquart discovered, at the Bureau of Statistics, that the real author of the *bordereau* had been Major Ferdinand Walsin Esterhazy and opposed his superiors who requested him to cover up these facts. Émile Zola revealed this on January 13, 1898, in his famous article "J'accuse," published in Georges Clemenceau's newspaper, *L'Aurore*. Zola's motivation, following his naturalist literary style and his anarchist political convictions, was to purge French society of the "virus" of anti-Semitism that had infected it since the "Panama scandal," when the bankruptcy of a Jewish businessman investing in the Panama Canal led to a wave of accusations against Jewish bankers. When he presented the facts that Picquart had discovered to the public, Zola took the position of "pastor of a whole people" by exposing himself to public vindication and taking upon himself the emotional burden that had fallen on Dreyfus through a process qualified by Zola as "human sacrifice" (Zola 2010: 98, 136). When the army accused him of defamation, Zola went into exile in London. But the trial against Zola led the Ministry of Justice to demand Dreyfus's return from Cayenne and the organization of a new trial to examine the evidence against him in Rennes in 1899.

Zola's position in the Dreyfus Affair can be described as a secular and naturalized version of Christian sacrifice. The famous writer took upon himself the burden of sacrifice because he considered Dreyfus as the embodiment of the ideal of justice, thus leaving aside Dreyfus's personal history and feelings. After his return from exile, Zola published a piece entitled "Justice" in *L'Aurore* in which he described an imagined meeting with the captain: "Ah! I confess that the idea of his return, the thought of seeing him free, of shaking his hands, overwhelms me with an extraordinary emotion that fills my eyes with happy tears" (Zola 2010: 136). In a letter he sent to Dreyfus a few days before the beginning of the Rennes trial, Zola identified the captain with an idealized France: "At this hour, our task is to bring you, along with justice, appeasement, to calm our poor and great country at last, by finally completing our work of reparation, by showing the man for whom we have fought, in whom we have embodied the triumph of human solidarity. When the innocent man rises, France will once again become the land of equity and goodness" (Zola 2010: 319).

Lévy-Bruhl's personal position in the Dreyfus Affair was quite different and much closer to the public position defended by Jean Jaurès.

In 1894, having just been reelected deputy for Carmaux, Jaurès declared that the deportation of Dreyfus, whom he described as a Jewish bourgeois officer, was less severe than the execution of miners on strike in his homeland of Tarn, thus taking up an anti-Semitic argument that circulated in socialist circles. In 1898, however, when he lost his mandate as a deputy and taught philosophy at the Faculty of Toulouse, Jaurès understood, perhaps with Lévy-Bruhl's help, that if he defended Dreyfus against the army and its experts, he was better placed to defend the miners and the workers against the capitalist mineowners. Jaurès's strategy was to show that the French state used the same lies against Dreyfus as against the miners, and to show it in such a way that the ideal of truth and justice would emerge from the legal case.

In preparation for the Rennes trial, Jaurès wrote *Les preuves* (*Proofs*), which Lévy-Bruhl described as "a masterpiece of exact analysis and eloquent logic" (Lévy-Bruhl 1916b: 34). His "dialectical ingenuity" (Blum 1932 [1935: 137]) deconstructed the accusations against Dreyfus by displaying their contradictions, using his philosophical training at the service of legal reasoning. His first target was Alphonse Bertillon, whom Jaurès described as an "anthropometrist," in contrast to his brother, "a knowledgeable statistician," who had joined the Dreyfusard side. To explain the dissimilarities between the handwriting of the *bordereau* and that of Dreyfus, Bertillon had invented a theory of "double writing" and "self-forgery": Dreyfus would have imitated the handwriting of his brother Mathieu and his wife to make it appear that the *bordereau* was not his. Instead of starting from the facts and working toward the verdict, Bertillon thus deduced the facts from the captain's presumed guilt, a form of reasoning Jaurès described in *Les preuves* as "incredible sophistry," "insane logic," and "supreme madness" (Jaurès 1998: 108). Bertillon appeared as a charlatan and a magician when he claimed he could read Mathieu Dreyfus's handwriting in the *bordereau*, as a "Macbeth's cauldron in which the imagination of Mr. Bertillon, an incomparable witch, mixes, crushes, and distorts the elements" (Jaurès 1998: 114). Following Jaurès, the criminologist reasoned wrongly, first, by asserting that the *bordereau* was both written and not written by Dreyfus and, second, by transforming his error into a system through mathematical formulas. While many observers had criticized Bertillon's system as the product of madness, Jaurès displayed its rationality to argue against it.

In his demonstration's second step, Jaurès tried to explain how the army introduced these lies into people's minds, which he described as characterized by "common sense, our national virtue" (Jaurès 1998: 153).

His accusations targeted Minister of War Godefroy Cavaignac, who had maintained the accusation against Dreyfus despite Picquart's revelations of Esterhazy's guilt. Jaurès reproached Cavaignac for surfing on the wave of anti-Semitism that arose after the financial scandals of the preceding decade and for leaping from a suspicious fact to a set of proofs by "contagion" (Jaurès 1998: 195). If the *bordereau* was the element around which the system of accusation was built, deconstructing the attribution of the *bordereau* to Dreyfus destroyed the entire accusation. But the contradiction that Jaurès noted seemed to escape his opponents because they reasoned according to another logic: "For them, the guilt of Dreyfus is like an immaterial and timeless essence that survives the moral ruin of all the witnesses and the failing of all the evidence" (Jaurès 1998: 268). Jaurès, thus, staged the Dreyfus Affair as an opposition between a rational way of thinking targeting the truth of facts and an irrational way of thinking driven by primitive emotions—or between "common sense" (*bon sens*, a term Jaurès borrowed from René Descartes's *Discourse on the Method* published in 1637) and "bad faith" (*mauvaise foi*, a term Jean-Paul Sartre [1946] expanded on in his analysis of anti-Semitism based on the works of Lévy-Bruhl). While Dreyfus was accused of being Jewish, as if it were a criminal character that determined him to betray France for Germany, Jaurès's reasoning showed that primitive solidarity was on the side of the prosecutors, who thought illogically or "wildly."

Jaurès thus provided a philosophical formulation to a feeling that gained ground in public opinion as the affair unfolded (Harris 2010). The "savage" was not the criminal who rebelled against society or the "Jewish syndicate" secretly organized to defend Dreyfus, but the military authorities who accused him without proof. The affair brought French society back to an earlier stage of justice where it arbitrarily designated victims to put an end to a disturbance and to restore society's honor. This idea can be found in the writings of the journalist Jules Cornély in *Le Figaro*:

> The investigation proved this truth recognized by the majority of the scientists: that man is refractory to any modification and that between the civilized and the savage there is hardly the thickness of the clothing. It has plunged us back into the Middle Ages, into the Inquisition, into arbitrary and harsh justice. (Duclert 2006: 626)
> For if we are not savages and if this man is a victim of our errors … what other name than remorse can be given to the feeling that his sight awakens? (Duclert 2006: 634)

While Zola defended an ideal of truth by sacrificing his career and his life, Jaurès gave dialectical expression to a conviction that animated the world of scholars and that would be constitutive of the party of "intellectuals" around the defense of Dreyfus. Following this argument, to refute the accusations of the army meant not only purging France of anti-Semitic poison by publicly proclaiming the truth of the innocent but, above all, teaching people a scientific lesson by criticizing the contradictions of a reactionary discourse.

The Dreyfus Affair and the Change in Mentality

A new term appeared in the public debate to describe such a transformation: to be on the side of the Dreyfusards and to support Dreyfus's innocence was not the result of a solidarity of race or class with a bourgeois Jewish officer, nor was it a conversion from error to truth, but it involved a change in "mentality." If the accusation against Dreyfus produced what Jaurès described as "criminal solidarity between the judges who struck down the innocent and the real culprit who benefited from their error" (Jaurès 1998: 228), demonstrating Dreyfus's innocence produced another form of solidarity around truth and justice. Two types of "mentality" corresponded with these two types of solidarity.

Marcel Proust reported that the term "mentality" appeared in the French public debate on the Dreyfus Affair when he described a conversation about why Robert de Saint-Loup supported Dreyfus to have a retrial. The discussion focused on the ideas and words that circulated between social groups, leading individuals to gather into "mental castes" and not "castes of origin."

> There's a damsel, a fly-by-night of the worst type; she has far more influence over him than his mother, and she happens to be a compatriot of Mister Dreyfus. She had passed on her state of mind to Robert. "You may not have heard, Duke, that there is a new word to describe that sort of mind," said the librarian, who was Secretary to the Anti-revisionist Committee. "They say 'mentality'. It means exactly the same thing, but it has the advantage that nobody knows what you're talking about." (Proust 1988: 235)

In 1899, Zola used the term "mentality" to describe the judge's reasoning during the Rennes trial (Zola 2010: 355). Dreyfus used it in 1904 when he heard a military officer defending Major Hubert-Joseph Henry, who killed himself after forging evidence used against Dreyfus (Dreyfus 2017: 145). Similar to what is now described as plot theory, a mentality was thus defined as a way of thinking that unifies a social group against a criminal despite empirical proof of innocence. While the beginning of the Dreyfus Affair pitted groups against each other based on differing interpretations of a crime, the end of the Dreyfus Affair divided French society between mentalities with different understandings of experience.

Can we say, then, that Lévy-Bruhl's later opposition between "primitive mentality" and "civilized mentality" finds its source in the Dreyfus Affair? If so, this opposition would overcome a conflictual experience by a narrative of progress, since "civilized" is supposedly superior to "primitive." This sheds light on Lévy-Bruhl's 1900 publication, which appeared at the end of the Dreyfus Affair, *La philosophie d'Auguste Comte*. It is striking that Lévy-Bruhl published two books at the beginning and at the end of the Dreyfus Affair but none in the middle—probably because he was too busy with his engagement in the affair and his courses at the Sorbonne. The first book, *La philosophie de Jacobi*, published in 1894, marks his farewell to German philosophy on the grounds that it tends to think about subjectivity in a mystical way. *La philosophie d'Auguste Comte*, in contrast, shows how subjectivity orients forms of solidarity across differences in mentality. The latter marked a shift in the reception of the founder of positivism because it interpreted Comte's philosophy not as the description of a historical progress, nor as the formulation of the criteria of truth, but as an experiment regarding mentalities. The Dreyfus Affair played an important role in this new interpretation of positivism, as it extended Lévy-Bruhl's reflection in his thesis on responsibility.

In the article "Mentality" in his *Dictionnaire de la langue française*, first published in 1863, Émile Littré quoted a member of his positivist group, Hippolyte Stupuy: "The events contrary to the spirit of 1789 could not prevent the change of mentality that was inaugurated by the Encyclopedists from occurring" (Littré 1957: 106). For Auguste Comte, the events of the French Revolution became meaningful through the "law of three stages," asserting that human societies necessarily pass from the theological stage to the positive stage through a metaphysical stage. Littré attempted to justify the colonization of "backward peoples" by a more advanced French society, a position that was implemented by Jules Ferry when he was minister of education, minister of foreign affairs and prime minister between 1879 and 1885. Lévy-Bruhl noted that such an interpretation of the necessary progress of positivism left aside

Comte's praise of the theological stage. For Comte, the human mind makes the first hypotheses by projecting its inner feeling of activity onto things perceived as fetishes. It is a rehabilitation of feeling that Lévy-Bruhl discovered with surprise when reading Comte on the occasion of his hundredth birthday in 1898, for it seemed to him compatible with Renouvier's teaching: in all societies, there are feelings of justice that must find their formulation in positive society.

> If you know Littré and you begin to read Comte, you experience more than surprise: it is almost a revelation. The disciple has brought the master to his own measure. In Comte's philosophy, he especially emphasized the negative aspect and the antagonism that opposed it to theology and metaphysics. But Comte also saw himself as the successor and heir of religions and metaphysics. (Lévy-Bruhl 1898: 395)

In contrast to Littré, John Stuart Mill had criticized Comte for his authoritarian views on family and politics, which he thought were linked to Comte's attempt to rehabilitate the theological stage. Mill borrowed from positivism only the laws of regularity of phenomena, which he codified through psychology. He thus placed two "modes of thought" into opposition with each other: one governed by error and sophistry and the other by truth and logic, respectively following principles of enthusiasm and moderation in the associations of ideas (Mill 1865). But such an interpretation left aside what Lévy-Bruhl considered Comte's real discovery, which he clearly pointed out when editing Comte's correspondence with Mill: the multiple variations of the human mind acting on its milieu were contained in the theological stage and further developed in the positive stage (Lévy-Bruhl 1899a). Whereas Littré and Mill reduced Comte's theological stage to a form of backward superstition, Lévy-Bruhl described it as a mode of thought as consistent as the positive stage.

Yet Lévy-Bruhl refused a third interpretation of Comte's philosophy, defended by his dissertation supervisor Émile Boutroux, who viewed it as a metaphysics close to spiritualism (Boutroux 1902). Indeed, Comte proposed a "subjective method" at the end of his life when he wrote a treatise in the style of a "fetishistic poet." But he was not doing metaphysics, a mode of thought he always described as "mental anarchy." Rather, he was integrating, in the construction of positivism, the subjective feelings developed first by theology and rediscovered by scientific thinking at the level of biological phenomena. Indeed, for Comte, biology is the first science to go from whole to parts, and not, as physics and chemistry, from parts to whole. Lévy-Bruhl thus supported with the history of sciences what Boutroux found in metaphysics. In the vocabulary that Lévy-Bruhl borrowed from Renouvier, biology invents the principle of solidarity later developed by sociology as a specific form of conscious activity. Lévy-Bruhl could, therefore, claim the following as a discovery of his own: "There is only one doctrine of Auguste Comte, not two. From the pamphlets of his twentieth year to the *Synthèse Subjective*, the same thought is developed" (Lévy-Bruhl 1900: 12).

How is such an academic debate in the history of philosophy linked to the political debates of the Dreyfus Affair, and why does it so engage Lévy-Bruhl? Here we can only make hypotheses, since Lévy-Bruhl does not refer to the affair in his 1900 book. But we can notice the parallel between two experiences: that of Comte when he returned to the theological stage and that of Dreyfus when he became a sacrificial victim. In 1824, Comte went through an episode of madness, which he called a "cerebral crisis" and which Lévy-Bruhl preferred to call "mental alienation," a term he had used in his early correspondence with Salomon Reinach. During his stay in the psychiatric clinic of Esquirol, after an episode of overwork related to the writing of the *Cours de philosophie positive*, Comte claimed that he returned rapidly to the theological stage and then gradually to the positive stage, a dramatic experience that he saw as confirming the law of the three stages. If we consider Comte as the founder of social anthropology in France, we can say that his crisis of madness played the same role as "fieldwork" did in British anthropology—that is, as a foundational moment in the authority of the anthropologist (Clifford 1983). According to Comte, if the French Revolution produced a violent discontinuity between the theological stage and the positive stage in modern societies, the foundation of a social anthropology should drive societies that are still in the theological state toward the positive stage, in a continuous and spontaneous path. The sociologist thus presented himself as a "vanguard" of humanity in its march toward the future, helping societies develop without changing their "mental regime."

Dreyfus as a Sentinel of Colonial Violence

We can, then, hypothesize that Lévy-Bruhl saw in the political situation of Dreyfus a similar experience to what he read in the philosophical work of Comte but in the context of the Jewish *émancipation* by the Third Republic. Dreyfus was a modern individual whose mind was divided between two poles: he was attached to his family and the army because of "primitive feelings" such as love and honor, but he reasoned with a "civilized intelligence" when he organized military plans and defended himself in a court of law. This disconnection between feelings and reason in the same mind was criticized by observers of the Rennes trial who expected Dreyfus would use rhetoric to attract public sympathy by narrating his sufferings. It was also criticized by "mystical" Dreyfusards such as Charles Péguy, editor of the *Cahiers de la quinzaine*, who claimed in 1910 that Dreyfus was not strong enough for the ideal of justice formulated in his name. Georges Clemenceau, who had published Zola's "J'accuse" in his journal *L'Aurore*, blamed Dreyfus for accepting a presidential pardon in 1906 after his conviction with extenuating circumstances at the Rennes trial in 1899 and said: "I don't care about Dreyfus, let him be torn to pieces and eaten!" (Harris 2010: 325). But Mathieu Dreyfus pushed his brother to accept the pardon to preserve his physical health as a necessary requisite for his name to be cleared from accusations in later stages of the legal procedure. Here again what is crucial is the separation between the individual body and the ideal of justice, or rather between two ways of expressing this ideal in the same body, through emotions and reason. Julien Benda quoted Dreyfus as saying at the end of the affair: "I am bored with people constantly moaning about my sufferings; what I like is to talk about my case objectively" (Benda 1968: 117). Dreyfus's body was thus divided between the two "mentalities" that, according to Proust's description, divided French society at the end of the century. Hence the eagerness of the public to see his body degraded or rehabilitated at the Rennes trial.

This opposition between emotions and reason was also expressed as a tension between two mentalities within the same body when staged in the public representation of the colonial situation. The *Letters of an innocent man*, sent by Dreyfus to his wife Lucie and published in 1898, made public the conditions of his incarceration (Dreyfus 1898). The Cayenne prisons had been opened in 1852 to establish a settlement in French Guiana on the model of Australia. But death rates were so high (up to 40 percent) that after 1867 French convicts were deported to New Caledonia, while convicts from the colonies were still deported to Guiana. In 1887, deportation to Guiana was again imposed on French convicts considered the most dangerous (Redfield 2000: 51–52). Dreyfus was placed in a hut on Devil's Island, in the middle of the Salvation Islands, opposite Cayenne, under the constant surveillance of a team of keepers.

The books and letters that populated his daily life were eaten away by insects and disintegrated in the humidity. The restrictive measures that were imposed on his movements—a piece of wood to which he was bound by chains after 1896—further enhanced the effects of the heat. His transportation and supervision were managed by the Ministry of the Colonies, whose administrator, Albert Picquier, reported to his superiors in 1896 as follows:

> It is probable that after the tenacious hopes of the first days, the isolation, the nervousness, the vain expectations, and the feeling, which appears day by day more cruel, of the emptiness made around him will cause the resignation and perhaps also the disease of the guilty. The climate of Guiana will then find an easy victim. (Greilsamer 2018: 103)

If Dreyfus did not encounter the diversity of colonial populations sent to the prisons of French Guiana, he did experience the precariousness of colonial subjects. In the letters he sent to Marie Arconati Visconti after his release, Dreyfus described the prison as a state of primitive violence in which colonizers and colonized fall together: "Scratch the veneer of civilization with which centuries have covered us and primitive man reappears. Look at what happens in colonial expeditions" (Dreyfus 2017: 20). Officials of the Ministry of the Colonies told Dreyfus that guards reporting about his constant protests during his nightmares and his episodes of fever convinced them of his innocence (Dreyfus 2017: 253). In 1911, Dreyfus signed a manifesto, published in *L'Humanité*, denouncing the violence of colonial prisons, after two workers were condemned to an infamous prison in Algeria (Kalifa 2009: 39–49): the French media then presented the "Affair Aernoult-Rousset" as the "Dreyfus Affair of workers." We can, thus, presume that the letters exchanged between Lévy-Bruhl and Dreyfus during the deportation, or at least the press articles that Lévy-Bruhl kept from the Dreyfus Affair in the box lost during the Second World War, were about this colonial violence and that they influenced the ethnology of "primitive mentality."

Lévy-Bruhl's reading of Comte's philosophy, therefore, runs as a parallel operation, in the academic field, to Jaurès's political commitment in the Dreyfus Affair. From his position as professor of the history of philosophy at the Sorbonne, Lévy-Bruhl carried out a theoretical critique of the colonial military institution that resonated with the critique developed by Jaurès at the Rennes trial. If Dreyfus returned from the

"civilized mentality" to the "primitive mentality" in his experience of colonial violence, as Comte returned from the positive state to the theological stage in his experience of madness in civilization, philosophers could
express the coherence of this approach in the form of logical arguments.
Lévy-Bruhl was the first to show the unity of Comte's thought after
his thesis on the sentiment of responsibility and after Jaurès publicly
expressed Dreyfus's sentiment of injustice by relying on his own philosophy of "primitive man." In defending Dreyfus against anti-Semitism,
Jaurès embodied the captain's logical reasoning and pushed his critique
of colonialism to the limit, for Dreyfus's dissociation between his surviv-
ing body and his reflecting mind did not allow him to articulate this experience. By giving public expression to his sentiment of injustice, Jaurès
could hold together the two mentalities between which Dreyfus was
torn.

If Jaurès acted as a whistleblower when he gave a public form to
injustice, Dreyfus was a sentinel who survived to bear the signs of injustice. This is what the linguist Jean Psichari meant in the letter to Dreyfus quoted in the introduction of this book: "Every Frenchman must
be grateful to you. You have been there like a soldier at his post. As an
advanced sentinel, you have seen the day of justice finally shine" (Duclert
2006: 571).[2] Unlike the colonial officer who must conquer and manage
a territory by understanding indigenous ways of thinking, as promoted
by Hubert Lyautey (1900),[3] the sentinel shares the experience of the
colonized subjects and returns to the metropole to denounce its injustice

---

2. Jean Psichari (Yánnis Psycháris, 1854–1929) was a French-Greek writer
    born in Odessa who studied and taught at the School of Oriental Lan-
    guages in Paris and married the daughter of Ernest Renan. His research
    on the philology of Greek had a strong influence on the promotion of
    demotic as a modern Greek language. He was one of the founders of the
    League of Human Rights in Paris. His two sons died during the First
    World War.

3. Hubert Lyautey (1854–1934) was an intern student at the army headquar-
    ters in 1876, fifteen years before Alfred Dreyfus, and soon became captain
    after two years of serving the French army in Algeria. In 1891 he published
    a famous article on the "social role of the officer" in the *Revue des deux
    mondes*, where he developed a conception of the alliance between colonial
    officers and local leaders for the construction of infrastructure, one that he
    later implemented in Madagascar and then Morocco. He was in charge of
    the Ministry of War in 1917 and of the organization of the International
    Colonial Exhibition between 1927 and 1931 (see Rabinow 1989).

in the language of the colonizer. In the colonial system, the violence imposed by the colonizer on the colonized turns against the colonizer, so that the sentinel perceives less an actual enemy than the threats for humanity of a fantasized enemy. While the guards keeping Dreyfus at Cayenne fantasized him as a traitor, Dreyfus turned the gaze back on them as a sentinel of the colonial violence that kept them in this degrading position. In contemporary words, we can say that the sentinel turns surveillance into under-veillance: it converts vigilance from a military state of detection of the enemy to a militant state of denunciation of injustice.

Jaurès thus described Dreyfus as a sentinel of the social movement for the conquest of new rights. Against those who accused him of supporting a bourgeois soldier rather than a proletarian worker, Jaurès asserted in *Les preuves* that Dreyfus no longer belonged to the army that degraded him: "He is only an example of human suffering in its most poignant form. He is the living witness of military lies, political cowardice, and the crimes of authority" (Jaurès 1998: 48). The Dreyfus Affair provided Jaurès an opportunity to shed light on the mechanisms of military power through the "socialist ideal." His engagement in the trial at Rennes prepared him to defend social justice because it showed him that the same violence took place in the colonies as in the factories, with an even greater degree of injustice. Jaurès played the role of a whistleblower by transforming the sentiment of injustice experienced by Dreyfus and witnessed by Lévy-Bruhl into a sentinel carrying the signs of new norms of justice. Since Jaurès, as deputy of Carmaux, was concerned with defending the rights of miners, we can even say that he perceived Dreyfus as a "canary in the coal mine," a technique used by coalminers during the nineteenth century who took encaged birds into the mines as these would faint at low doses of sarin gas, thus providing an early warning signal of an impending mine explosion: these birds were not sacrificed to save human lives but cultivated with care to survive this toxic exposure (Burrell and Seibert 1914).

Yet, when he displaced Jaurès's political commitment in the philosophical debate on positivism, Lévy-Bruhl still relied on the narrative of progress that assumed a superiority of the "civilized" over the "primitive." While the sentinel expressed a primitive sentiment of injustice, Lévy-Bruhl still thought of it as an "avant-garde" that must be shaped in the superior forms of civilization. The sense of victory shared by those who supported Dreyfus against what they perceived as irrational attacks brought the ambivalent figure of the "primitive" into the debate on socialism that was to follow this victory.

CHAPTER 4

The Success of Sociology and Socialism

For Lévy-Bruhl, the years following Dreyfus's pardon and rehabilitation were marked by the rise of sociology in the university and socialists in the government.[1] Sociology and socialism were unified and consolidated for a short period because the notion of society as a political reality was widely accepted. As Jaurès had foreseen, the Dreyfus Affair introduced the idea of justice into society and, in return, allowed those who represented society to express their voice in governmental debates. Lévy-Bruhl, because of his position at the crossroads of academic and political networks, could efficiently accompany this movement.

Moral Science: From Ethnology to Microbiology

Lévy-Bruhl's scientific support for Durkheim was the equivalent of his political support for Jaurès. In 1894, when the Dreyfus Affair began, Durkheim was writing *The Rules of Sociological Method* at the University

---

1.   Paula Hyman describes the years 1906–1918 as a "golden age of symbiosis between France and its Jews," interrupted by the arrival of large numbers of Jews from Eastern Europe after the First World War (Hyman 1998: 33). While she identifies the role of Lévy-Bruhl in this "golden age" alongside Durkheim, Bergson, or Blum, she misses the role he later played in the reception of Jewish refugees, perhaps because she restrains her analysis to Jewish institutions.

of Bordeaux, where he taught pedagogy. This book, generalizing the conclusions of his thesis by taking Claude Bernard's experimental method as a model, asserted the possibility of observing social facts from the outside as things independent of the sentiments they arouse in individuals acting in society (Durkheim 1982). Paradoxically, Lévy-Bruhl recommended considering social facts in an objective way when he was most passionately engaged in the political battles of his time, as in this passage of his book on Comte:

> We must detach ourselves from what interests us subjectively in them and consider them in what is "specifically social," in the same way as the physiologist studies the phenomena of the organism as "specifically biological." Mr. Durkheim, as a true heir of Auguste Comte, rightly maintains that this is a *sine qua non* condition of positive sociology. (Lévy-Bruhl 1900: 413)

To de-subjectivize social facts, two methods were available: statistics, which reveal a social trend in the accumulation of figures, and the study of societies distant in time or space, which detects "wild logics" at the heart of industrial societies. In *Suicide*, published in 1897, Durkheim showed that Jews commit suicide less often than members of other social groups because of their greater integration (Durkheim 1897). We have seen that the army's Statistical Office used false evidence to support its accusation against Dreyfus and to drive him to suicide, even if it was not statistics in the sense of strong series of numbers. By contrast, Durkheim mobilized the national statistics of various European countries to explain why Dreyfus did not commit suicide (Karsenti 2017: 189–240). This book on suicide was an opportunity for Durkheim to confront his method with that of Tarde, who had built an alternative sociological theory. While Tarde explained the "suicidal currents" revealed by statistics as stemming from the invention of criminals and the imitation of their followers, Durkheim described them as revealing the action of social groups according to their forms of solidarity. He thus confirmed his thesis, inspired by Kant, according to which society acts in the manner of a "collective consciousness" by imposing representations and categories on individuals from the outside. By contrast, Tarde, in the tradition of Leibniz, defined society as a composition of "monads" that communicate through beliefs and desires.

This methodological confrontation between Durkheim and Tarde on suicide was linked to political commitments in the Dreyfus Affair. Tarde considered writing a book on the Dreyfus Affair, but he ultimately wrote essays on public opinion and crowds. Durkheim published two articles, on militarism and on the individualism of intellectuals. In the first, he emphasized that "the army has ceased to be a profession like any other; it has become something intangible and sacred." In the second, he asserted that "intellectuals"—a new term describing the Dreyfusard scholars— were right to defend the innocence of Dreyfus and to question the honor of the army because, in a modern society, individuals must express themselves according to their social function and not simply out of respect for the sacred (Durkheim 2002: 37). As Durkheim saw it, his central task in the Dreyfus Affair was to oppose the collective form of the sacred put forward by the army with an individualized form of the sacred more appropriate to civilized societies. The distinction he elaborated in his thesis between the mechanical solidarity of primitive societies and the organic solidarity of modern societies was a step toward this operation, accomplished by the ethnology of sacrifice.

Indeed, the ethnological method allowed Henri Hubert and Marcel Mauss at the Practical School of Advanced Studies (École pratique des hautes études) to enter the factory of the sacred, applying the sociological method prescribed by Durkheim to the analysis of religious facts (Fournier 1994, 2007; Karsenti 1997). While Hubert relied on the philology of ancient societies, Mauss discovered the recent works of ethnology carried out in the UK concerning what Edward Tylor had called "primitive culture." In particular, Mauss read James Frazer's vast synthesis on totemism based on Australian and Amerindian facts, published under the title *The Golden Bough*. Around the same time, Durkheim discovered the *Lectures on the Religions of the Semites* published by William Robertson Smith in 1889. These lectures had had a great influence on Frazer at Cambridge, because they described sacrifice as a set of ritual practices of commensality and alliance. Mauss was staying at Oxford in 1898 when he followed the revelations about the false evidence made at the Rennes trial through the reports of Frederick Conybeare, who also wrote an anonymous article and then a book about Dreyfus, where he denounced the lies of the French army (Conybeare 1899).

After Mauss had returned from England, he and Hubert published two major articles in the *Année sociologique*, the journal founded by Durkheim: "Essay on the nature and function of sacrifice" and "Sketch of a general theory of magic" (Mauss and Hubert 1897–98; Hubert and Mauss 1902–03). These articles explored the variations of the religious experience through the polarity between the priest and the magician.

While the former makes up the sacred through the destruction of a ritual victim in the center of social space, the latter does so from the margins by addressing clients with obscure formulas. Such polarity complicated the figure of "collective consciousness" that Durkheim described as the source of categorizations of the sacred. It opened a space for variations of religious experience in individual consciousness, a field that Mauss later explored in the study of linguistic and economic forms of social activity.

This polarity between the priest and the magician can also be read as a diagnostic of the Dreyfus Affair. While the notion of sacrifice may be used to justify the condemnation of Dreyfus—the army asked him to sacrifice himself by committing suicide and staged his degradation as the destruction of an expiatory victim—Mauss's analysis of magical practices showed how experts manipulate waves of beliefs and open spaces to divert them through a form of counter-expertise. If Bertillon thought "like a savage," as Jaurès showed, it does not mean that he was mad but that he used magical practices studied by ethnologists in "primitive societies." The polarization of the scene of sacrifice between the priests and the magicians thus left open a space for the "intellectuals," those individuals who examine obscure economic practices in the clarity of the sacred. The Dreyfus Affair led Mauss to understand the transition from magic to science not as a gradual correction of primitive errors, following the evolutionary anthropology defended by Tylor and Frazer, but as a structural tension in a socially oriented space, which was much closer to the approach developed by Max Weber in Germany. However, by reflecting on the Dreyfus Affair through their scientific articles on sacrifice and magic but without mentioning it, Durkheim, Hubert, and Mauss did not leave space for the point of view of the victim. How does it feel to be a sentinel of expiatory justice and how does it lead to a more reparative justice? This is the question that interested Lévy-Bruhl when he observed the Dreyfus Affair.

Durkheim and Mauss based their ethnology of the sacred on Australian ethnography, which revealed for them the action of collective consciousness. By contrast, Lévy-Bruhl traced his ethnological approach back to an encounter with China. On October 5, 1890, he received a letter from Edouard Chavannes in Peking, who sent him his translation of Sima Qian's (or Se-ma Ts'ien's) *Treatise on sacrifice* (Chavannes 1895–1905). "I do not have the honor of being known by you," Chavannes wrote. "Allow me, however, to send you, elder of the Normal Superior School and, especially, the author of the thesis on responsibility, a small translation that I have made from Chinese. You will find there some facts that are perfectly in line with your theory."[2] The context of the Dreyfus Affair leads to the hypothesis that Sima Qian's texts revealed another version of sacrifice to Lévy-Bruhl than the Indian philology or the Australian ethnography on which Hubert and Mauss relied. Sima Qian was an astrologist at the court of the Chinese emperor Wudi in the first century BCE and was responsible for reworking the calendar that organized all Han ritual life. His recoding of traditional sacrifice according to the polarity between Heaven and Earth is considered a major step in the transformation of religious life in China. According to a Taoist tradition, Sima Qian assigned the function to sacrifice of stabilizing all the beings that make up the universe, especially in times of trouble, such as during a war with foreign tribes or a change of dynasty. This is why he paid attention to the behavior of the sacrificed animal: its reluctance could cause the sacrifice to fail.

Lévy-Bruhl later explained to the French Society of Philosophy (Société française de philosophie) that the letter from Chavannes led him to formulate the hypothesis of a different mentality governed by a specific logic, but that, for lack of being able to learn Chinese, he turned to the more accessible ethnographic data on societies "known as primitive," which, in the same way as China, developed for a long time without any contact with Europe (Lévy-Bruhl 1923b). This letter encouraged him to take an interest in the Chinese tradition, not in the literate version of the various Confucian schools but in its popular version, more deeply marked by Taoism. From 1892 onwards, Lévy-Bruhl read the monumental work *The Religious System of China* by Jan Jakob Maria de Groot, professor at the University of Leiden, which described the complex set of rules by which the Chinese of Fujian buried their dead and the representations of animals and spirits that accompany them (De Groot 1892). This book provided Lévy-Bruhl access to a tradition codified in ancient texts that remained alive in daily practices: "It shows, with the

---

2. IMEC, Lucien Lévy-Bruhl (1857–1939) papers (hereafter Lévy-Bruhl papers), Letter from E. Chavannes to L. Lévy-Bruhl, October 5, 1890, Peking. Edouard Chavannes (1865–1918) went to China in 1889 after passing the *agrégation* of philosophy at the Normal Superior School. On his return in 1893, he was elected to the Collège de France to hold the chair of Chinese language. He is considered one of the founders of French sinology in the tradition of Abel Rémusat. His major work is the translation and annotation of Sima Qian's treatise, *Shiji: The historical memoirs of Sima Qian* (Chavannes 1895–1905).

most perfect evidence, by what social and mental process most of the obligations were introduced and rooted that a Chinese man, today, would not want to miss for anything in the world, even if he is unable to justify them" (Lévy-Bruhl 1903: 88).

In 1903, Lévy-Bruhl published *La morale et la science des mœurs* (translated in 1905 as *Ethics and Moral Science*) to support Durkheimian sociology in its debate with philosophy on the foundations of morality. In the tradition of Voltaire, Lévy-Bruhl took up the concept of *mœurs* to describe the variability of uses and customs as opposed to the universal character of the moral law and took China as a case to relativize the logical and moral rules that apply in Europe. In China, as Voltaire had already noticed, obligations are followed with morality and piety without being founded on a sacred principle that justifies them: the knowledge of ritual rules acquired by education in classical texts is sufficient to hold society together. Lévy-Bruhl was thus looking at modern European societies from the perspective of contemporary China to anticipate how they will be judged by the societies of the future. The shrinking of the world brought all these societies into a common space—that of humanity in the sense of Comte and Jaurès. Lévy-Bruhl's analyses could, thus, be read as a denunciation of the repression of the Boxer Rebellion, which had just taken place in Beijing (then called Peking), and of the burning and looting of the Summer Palace by the British and French armies a few decades earlier, an act that was denounced at the time by Victor Hugo but repeated by the French army when it ransacked the palace of the king of Dahomey (now Benin) in 1892 and by the British army when it looted the palace of the king of Benin City in 1897.

> For the civilized peoples of the Far East, Westerners are barbarians. To our descendants in the fiftieth century, our civilization will undoubtedly appear, in certain aspects, as repulsive as that of the Dahomeans is to us. (Lévy-Bruhl 1903: 27)
> Bombay, and even Peking, are no further from Paris today than Madrid or Stockholm were a hundred years ago. The traditional notion of "man" has to be expanded. (Lévy-Bruhl 1903: 74)

This interest in China may explain why Lévy-Bruhl later supported the career of the young student of the Normal Superior School, Marcel Granet, who attended Durkheim's courses at the Sorbonne, joined Mauss in a group of socialist studies in 1905, and lived in Beijing where he studied Chinese between 1911 and 1913. Granet's studies on matrimonial customs in ancient China, published by Chavannes in the journal *T'oung Pao* in 1912, played a central role in bringing sinology and sociology together. Granet described the seasonal variations of rural life according to the calendar of festivals, the techniques of the body in ritual dances, and the transmissions of gifts and debts from one generation to another (Palmer 2019). The sinological detour of sociology allowed Lévy-Bruhl and Granet to take up the Durkheimian description of sacrifice by insisting less on the clarity of collective categories than on the instability of the beings they stabilize. Granet described emblems, like the Yin and the Yang, not as symbols to represent the social group but as signs to be manipulated in ritual practices. The Chinese tradition thus allowed Lévy-Bruhl—more than the Indo-European or Judeo-Christian tradition projected by Durkheim into the deserts of central Australia— to understand why Dreyfus refused to be a sacrificial victim. The Chinese conception of responsibility, as Chavannes saw it in his letter to Lévy-Bruhl, does not contrast subjective rights and an objective tribunal but manipulates signs so that a new regime of justice emerges on the ruins of an old one.

Another way for Lévy-Bruhl to support Durkheimian sociology was to consolidate his alliance with Pasteurian microbiology in the context of the Dreyfus Affair. Pasteur and Durkheim provided a new conception of contagion as the transmission of affects by contact between bodies. Using the experimental method in microbiology and sociology, they showed that contagion mobilizes relational entities whose compositions must be critically examined.

Lévy-Bruhl was well acquainted with Émile Duclaux, who had succeeded Louis Pasteur in 1895 as director of the institute he had founded in 1888, and defended Dreyfus at his 1898 trial by invoking the forms of proof applied in bacteriology. Born in Aurillac into a Protestant family in 1840, Duclaux entered the Normal Superior School in 1859. There he met Pasteur, the "new Messiah" to whom, in the words of Albert Calmette, he became a new Saint Paul. After traveling with Pasteur throughout France for most of the latter's experiments on diseases affecting vineyards, silkworms, sheep, and chickens, Duclaux was recruited in 1878 by the University of Paris to teach "biological chemistry" following the new principles of Pasteurian microbiology. On January 8, 1898, Senator Scheurer-Kastner, a chemist by training and Alsatian by birth, asked Duclaux, through the intermediary of Paul Appell, dean of the Paris Faculty of Sciences, what he thought, "as a scientist," about the Dreyfus Affair. Duclaux published his answer on January 10 in *Le Siècle*:

"One wonders if the state does not lose its money in its educational establishments, because the public mind is not very scientific" (Moissinat 2015: 193). After the evaluation of Gabriel Monod in November 1897, this was the second one in which a "scholar" asked for the reopening of the Dreyfus Affair. Duclaux read Zola's "J'accuse" while writing *Traité de microbiologie* (*Treatise on microbiology*). The next day he signed the petition published by Lucien Herr in *Le Siècle*. Later, Duclaux wrote three pamphlets on the Dreyfus Affair in the same journal.

In these widely circulated texts, Duclaux showed that a healthy idea—the honor of the army or the defense of the fatherland—can become infectious if it is exercised blindly because it leads to the sacrifice of an individual. He wrote: "Institutions are not sick, but humans are" (Duclaux 1899: 18). In his eyes, the challenge was, therefore, to attenuate the virulence of these ideas by using knowledge of the relations between the living beings that produce them. This meant situating oneself on the right scale: not the level of great principles but the level of individual organisms. If, according to him, the confusion between solidarity and discipline explained the blindness of the French army, Duclaux advised the students of the Pasteur Institute to follow the observations of Elie Metchnikoff on the relationships between the cells of an organism: "It is your task not to try to get together but to be as different as possible from each other so as to find interest and pleasure in getting together. You will see that, while the form remains the same, a new world will appear in you and through you" (Duclert 1993: 24).

Duclaux did not attend the trial in Rennes, but he wrote two letters to Dreyfus. He died five years later, in 1904, after suffering a stroke during a meeting of the committee of the League of Human Rights, of which he was the first vice-president.

The Pasteurian conception of the relations between cells exerted a strong influence on Durkheimian sociology and separated it from the sociology of Auguste Comte. Until the end of his life, Comte refused the biological notion of the cell defended by Lorenz Oken because it privileged the individual over the social. He preferred the notion of tissue supported by François Broussais because it allowed him to think about the phenomena of consensus and interdependence. Pasteurian microbiology thus allowed Durkheim and Lévy-Bruhl to distance themselves from Comtian determinism and to study the contingency of associations. In the section of *The Rules of Sociological Method* devoted to the relationship between the normal and the pathological, Émile Durkheim (1895 [1982]) referred to Louis Pasteur's work on vaccination. He emphasized that collective representations can be considered pathological because they are more intense than individual representations, but, if their degree of contagiousness or virulence is regulated by a principle, they can become beneficial for individuals (Durkheim 1982: 89). We can, therefore, consider the work of Durkheim and Lévy-Bruhl on collective representations to align with the work of Pasteur and Duclaux on microbes, because they involve describing the norms through which invisible entities that emerge in social life affect the bodies of individuals and, in return, the forms through which the state can intervene to regulate interactions between individual bodies and these invisible entities.

If Lévy-Bruhl's books on "primitive mentality" were sprinkled with references to microbes or public hygiene, as we shall see, he also referred to this governmental knowledge transformed by microbiology in *La morale et la science des mœurs* to justify logical and moral relativism. While he quoted ethnological analyses on China or Australia, he also mentioned the sanitary bulletin published each week by the city of Paris because it showed that there were more deaths from infectious diseases in the poor periphery than in the rich center of the capital. The new microbiological and sociological knowledge allowed Lévy-Bruhl to frame moral questions more positively in his engagement toward justice. "One will gradually become accustomed to finding not abstract deductions or the reflections of moralists but ethnographic observations, answers to questionnaires, statistical curves, and columns of figures in works dealing with the science of morals" (Lévy-Bruhl 1903: iv).

We can, therefore, understand how, in his 1903 book, Lévy-Bruhl defended a logical and moral relativism at the same time as a commitment to truth and justice. The Dreyfus Affair showed that if forms of mentality and morality could be compared, it did not mean that all morals were equivalent but that revolutionary transformations shifted society from one mentality to another. Following Durkheim and Jaurès, Lévy-Bruhl thus called for a "common consciousness" to make visible the desire for justice in "modern" society:

> For those of us who are accustomed to the ideas of social progress and even revolution, who have witnessed social and economic changes of capital importance in the last few centuries ... how could we not extend universal relativity to morality? (Lévy-Bruhl 1903: 149)
> After long being considered as normal, inevitable, and even, in a certain sense, providential, today the condition of proletarians in the modern capitalist regime is looked upon in a completely different

light, where the proletariat, aware of its strength, demands and ob-
tains more human conditions of existence. The common moral consciousness begins to regard the claims of proletarians as just. (Lévy-
Bruhl 1903: 218)

In praising the use of the comparative method in the social sciences,
Lévy-Bruhl suggested comparing sentiments of justice rather than legal
organizations, as done by the Durkheimians. He wrote: "The old way of
feeling supports the old notion of justice, while the new notion of justice
has not yet made a new way of feeling prevail" (Lévy-Bruhl 1903: 248).
This insistence on feeling or sentiment comes from his desire to derive
an "art" from social science, comparable to what medicine has become
for the new biological science:

> Just as the physician, before formulating his prescription, takes into
> account both the general indications and the special contraindica-
> tions of his patient's condition, so the social art will not automatically
> apply, so to speak, like an algebraic formula but will take into account,
> in each particular case, all the circumstances peculiar to his case. And,
> like the physician again, if his intervention results in more disadvan-
> tages than advantages, he will refrain. (Lévy-Bruhl 1903: 256)

These pages on "social art" in the 1903 book triggered much discussion:
some have read them as contradicting Lévy-Bruhl's cautious relativism,
others have thought that the political consequences of moral science
should be pursued. After the Dreyfus Affair, the notion of "social art"
was one of the most debated in anarchist and socialist circles to describe
the advent of a society governed by justice. In the wake of the reflections
of William Morris on a popular art opposed to the ugliness of com-
modities, of Jean-Marie Guyau on a morality "without obligation nor
sanction," and of Friedrich Nietzsche on the role of art in the advent of
the "superman," at the turn of the century some journals and associations
proposed uniting artists, art critics, philosophers, and sociologists around
the notion of social art (McWilliams, Méneux, and Ramos 2014). However, Lévy-Bruhl is careful not to speak about artists in his 1903 book:
if he borrows the positivist conception modeling the intervention of the
sociologist from medical prescription, he does not relay the call by Comte
for artists to express the new sociological knowledge for the public. This
is, perhaps, one reason why Lévy-Bruhl coined the inelegant notion of
"rational moral art," after defending the more classical notion of moral

sentiment, as if he feared the forces that this appeal to sentiment might unleash. It should be noticed, however, that Lévy-Bruhl would be one of the first supporters of the surrealist writers in the interwar period who implemented what the movements at the turn of the century had called "social art," based on a new view on the extra-European artifacts.

Participating in the Government: Lévy-Bruhl, Durkheim, and Jaurès

Lévy-Bruhl accomplished the program of a moral science based on Durkheimian sociology, which he announced in 1903, in his next book, *Les fonctions mentales dans les sociétés inférieures*, published in 1910 (later translated as *How Natives Think*). The political contexts of the two books differed significantly. The 1903 book compared a socialist science and a bourgeois morality and was inspired by the political movement that led, in 1905, to the separation of church and state by the government of Émile Combes, a measure supported by Jaurès. The 1910 book seemed to express the superior point of view of a positivist scientist who had triumphed over superstition. Lévy-Bruhl explained his use of the term "primitive" in the book's first note: "By this term, which is improper but almost essential, we simply intend to designate the members of the simplest societies that we know" (Lévy-Bruhl 1910: 11). He then criticized English anthropologists such as Tylor and Frazer who shared the "prejudice" according to which the collective representations of these societies were identical to those of the "white, adult, and civilized" individual. As for the term "mental functions," Lévy-Bruhl clarified that it referred not to faculties mysteriously lodged in the brain but to relations between societies and their environment regulated by operations (memory, abstraction, generalization, classification) and institutions (language, numeration, hunting, war, initiation, funerals, and so forth). By "determining the most general laws that the collective representations in inferior societies obey" (Lévy-Bruhl 1910: 11), Lévy-Bruhl intended to offer an introduction to sociologists who wanted to study their "passage to superior types of mentality"—which is the title of the book's final chapter.

The second chapter of the book identified these "general laws," in the positivist sense of regularities in the observation of phenomena. This chapter has caught the attention of readers because it develops the hypothesis that has made Lévy-Bruhl famous: "primitive mentality" is not regulated by the principle of contradiction, as Western logic has been since Aristotle, but by the principle of participation, which leads "subjects" to hold contradictory beliefs in their relations with "predicates" or "objects." Lévy-Bruhl borrowed an observation from the reports of German ethnologist Karl von den Steinen on his 1884 travels in the Amazonian region of Xingu: a member of the Bororo group says that he is an Ara parrot, which means that he is a human and a nonhuman at the same time. Lévy-Bruhl coined the famous statement "Bororo are Arara" on the model of the classical Aristotelian statement "Subject is Predicate," which explained why he doubled the syllable of "Ara" to make it symmetrical to "Bororo." Lévy-Bruhl solved this logical problem using the Durkheimian conception of Australian totemism. In the ritual context, a thing was perceived, following Durkheim, as duplicated by the collective spirit that manifests itself in it: for instance, the Arunta perceived a caterpillar as the spirit of the clan because it carries within it a principle of growth. Those who eat the caterpillar during a ritual, Durkheim said, "participate" in a collective entity that results from their joint action. Participation is thus the way in which collective representations are experienced by individuals through feelings, sentiments, or emotions.

Lévy-Bruhl took up the concept of participation, which was later highly debated in political philosophy and science studies (Kelty 2020), from Durkheim but in a sense that marked a slight shift. Durkheim showed that participation in sacrifice implies seeing ordinary things through the collective representations that transfigure them into symbols. Lévy-Bruhl did not describe sacrifice through the point of view of the priest who organizes it, what can be called the fabric of the sacred, but through the point of view of ordinary individuals who participate in it, who develop a field of religious perceptions. The concept of participation (*metexis*), in the idealist tradition that extends from Plato to Malebranche, designates the vision of natural things through ideas sent by God. It implies a separation between nature and the supernatural, as opposed to the concept of imitation (*mimesis*), which implies a horizontal relationship to the divine. In the first paragraph of his 1910 book, Lévy-Bruhl made clear the advantage of this concept: it avoided postulating a collective subject—society, which in Durkheim's view takes the place of God or the Cogito in classical philosophy—in order to describe how the action of society is felt by those who participate in it. From then on, Lévy-Bruhl described not society's symbols but the signs of its action on individuals:

> The representations we call collective, if we define them only in broad terms and without going into detail, can be recognized by the following signs: they are common to the members of a given social group;

they are transmitted from generation to generation; they are imposed on individuals; and they arouse in them, according to the case, feelings of respect, fear, adoration, etc., for their objects. They do not depend on the individual to exist. They do not imply a collective subject distinct from the individuals who compose the social group but present themselves with characteristics that cannot be explained by the sole consideration of individuals as such. (Lévy-Bruhl 1910: 10)

This slight difference between Lévy-Bruhl and Durkheim on the notion of participation has consequences for their definition of socialism. For Durkheim, a reader of the German socialists and Saint-Simon, socialism unified economic functions, which were threatened by dispersion and anomia, through a center that regulated them through what Durkheim called "organic solidarity," taking the form of the state in modern societies (Durkheim 1992). For Lévy-Bruhl, who read the English socialists and Comte, socialism consisted in a way of feeling oriented toward the ideal of justice. Lévy-Bruhl was more attentive to the ambivalences and contradictions of participation in society: after the Dreyfus Affair had showed that solidarity can be made a tool of oppression (since there was as much solidarity between the Dreyfusards as between the anti-Dreyfusards), society was no longer considered a pole of clarity where these contradictions could be resolved.

These minor differences between Durkheim and Lévy-Bruhl in the evaluation of the social relate to differing philosophical temperaments—the former was more dogmatic while the latter more skeptical[3]—but also and above all to discussions within the Socialist Party on what participation in the government implies. In his speeches, Jaurès pushed for workers to participate more in the political, administrative, and economic power structure in order to overcome the contradiction between universal suffrage, which theoretically granted them the right to vote, and industrial organization, which in practice

---

3. In a letter to Georges Davy dated 1930, Lévy-Bruhl wrote: "You mark very well what separates me from Durkheim: there are postulates implying a metaphysics and a morality in his doctrine. You rightly say that I am more of an empiricist, more of a relativist, and that I do not have the same idea of science. It must be said that, as I worked, I became aware of my own method, my own objective, and also of what separated me from Durkheim. The reflection on the facts gradually distanced me from the formulas that had initially satisfied me" (Merllié 1989: 445).

excluded them from decision-making and profits (Candar and Duclert 2014: 158, 242). This participation could be facilitated by trade
unions, when they used their right to strike, which Jaurès supported as
deputy of Carmaux, but also by socialist representatives who, as members of the government, could pass laws to improve the conditions of
workers. When, in June 1898, Waldeck-Rousseau proposed Alexandre
Millerand to join him in the government, the Socialist Party debated
whether it could commit itself to a regime that was still tainted by the
repression of the Commune. Jaurès argued for participation, maintaining that the republic owed its salvation to socialism, because the
battles fought in defense of the workers and then in defense of Dreyfus had infused the regime with social justice. According to Jaurès,
participation in the government would allow the French Socialist
Party to support the international socialist movement with the power
of the French state.

Lévy-Bruhl fully supported the position of Jaurès in this debate, not
only because he shared his political diagnosis of the Dreyfus Affair but
also because he sympathized with his philosophical conception of the
manifestation of the ideal in sensible reality, which Jaurès formulated in
his 1892 thesis. It was known in the Socialist Party that Lévy-Bruhl provided financial support for the foundation of the newspaper *L'Humanité*
in 1904—up to 100,000 francs, which was more than a quarter of the
capital of the company that owned the newspaper. Indeed, Jaurès publicly had to pay homage to Lévy-Bruhl during a party congress to put
an end to suspicions about the funding: "Lévy-Bruhl is one of my most
intimate and devoted friends, a professor at the Sorbonne and a man of
honor. He helped me to create *L'Humanité* and I thank him for that"
(Albert 2004: 25). In the text he published in 1915 after Jaurès died,
Lévy-Bruhl emphasized the ideal of humanity that animated his conception of participation:

> Jaurès lived—and died—for an ideal of social justice and liberated
> humanity. ... Escaping misery and all the evils it engenders, the daily
> worry of not knowing whether one will be able, tomorrow, to feed
> oneself, clothe oneself, heat oneself, sleep under a roof: this is still
> only the physical basis of this life. The essential part is the spirit-
> ual part: the intimate contact with the most beautiful part of what
> the past centuries have produced; the participation in the human
> effort to think and understand the world by science and philoso-
> phy; the communion with the mysterious principle of things by the

contemplation of nature; finally, the sentiment of human solidarity released from the hatreds of race, class, nationality, religion. (Lévy-Bruhl 1916b: 40)

How can this Jaurésian conception of socialism fit with the Durkheimian conception of totemism in Lévy-Bruhl's ethnology of participation? I would suggest a hypothesis drawn from the caricatures that bring Jaurès and Dreyfus together through animal figures. The end of the nineteenth century is the moment when animal caricatures of political life experienced their greatest development in France. The freedom of the press proclaimed by the Third Republic after the censorship practiced under the Second Empire encouraged cartoonists' bold attempts, so that this period "is probably the moment in contemporary history when the practice of political insult reaches its peak" (Bouchet 2010: 148). At the time of Zola's trial, the anti-Semitic press used images of pigs to depict Jews and those who supported them, while images of monkeys were used to denounce Darwinian biology. But if these animals aimed at degrading humans by underlining their proximity (physical or intellectual) to nonhumans, the representation of humans as birds was more ambivalent because birds can be a sign of misfortune or of happiness; above all, they form a society parallel to that of humans, arousing both curiosity and suspicion. In *L'Aurore* in 1902, Jaurès was represented as a rooster fighting with Clemenceau in parliament. In *Le Crayon* in 1906, Molynk drew Jaurès as a swallow wearing a spiked helmet with the caption: "It's a bird that comes from Germany." In 1904, Castor depicted Jaurès in the middle of a speech on universal peace with a German imperial eagle. In *Le Frelon* in 1903, Bobb drew two parakeets with the heads of Jaurès and Dreyfus and the caption "The two inseparables" (Perthuis 2003).

These caricatures indicate the political imaginary in which Lévy-Bruhl's logical analysis of the famous statement "The Bororo are Arara" is inscribed. The diversity of social groups identifying themselves with different animal species in the Amazon or in Australia may have led Lévy-Bruhl to reflect critically on the French National Assembly where political parties compared themselves to roosters and others to parakeets to increase their reputation and diminish that of others. Indeed, political life during the Third Republic raised the following question for a philosopher such as Lévy-Bruhl: if participation implies bringing the ideal of justice into political reality, how can one avoid its dispersion into a plurality of animal species or political parties? One can also assume that, for Lévy-Bruhl, bird caricatures referred to another imaginary: that of the *émancipation* of the Jews in a republic that opened the door of the ghetto only to expose its inhabitants to new threats. A 1885 pamphlet kept at the Universal Israelite Alliance, founded in Paris in 1860, thus proclaimed: "When you open a cage full of birds accustomed to slavery, not all of them take flight at the same time" (Vidal-Naquet 1981: 79).

Representing Dreyfus as a parrot, in this moment of sociology's success in the university and that of the socialists in the government, thus displayed the ambivalence of the republican ideal. While Dreyfus was coming out of his social group because he believed in the promise of *émancipation*, he became embroiled in political conflicts about the good way to participate in the republic. The mobilization of the nation during the First World War would manifest this ambivalence even more strongly, leading Lévy-Bruhl to a new conception of participation through his following works on "primitive mentality."

PART II: PARTICIPATION (1914–1939)

CHAPTER 5

Engagement in the War

The First World War marked a rupture in Lévy-Bruhl's thinking, which is hard to perceive when looking at the series of his books on "primitive mentality" between 1910 and 1939. Two of his main interlocutors with whom Lévy-Bruhl had promoted sociology and socialism in the years following the Dreyfus Affair, Jean Jaurès and Émile Durkheim, died during the war. Lévy-Bruhl took up their moral and philosophical heritage to engage in the organization of the war effort in line with the ideal of social justice as it had been defended during the Dreyfus Affair. The First World War can thus be described as an experience of participation for Lévy-Bruhl, not only in the sense that he participated in the war effort as a philosopher, which was the equivalent of doing fieldwork where he could observe social relations, but also that it changed his philosophical views on participation and his analysis of ethnological data. Through this form of collective engagement, one that was much more open than the one he had experienced during the Dreyfus Affair, Lévy-Bruhl realized that participation was not a contradictory and emotional confusion between things that should be separated but a mode of perception and action allowing humans to be prepared for unpredictable events, that is, as a new form of responsibility.

When Jaurès was assassinated on July 31, 1914, at the Café du Croissant in Paris, Lévy-Bruhl was one of the last people with whom he had spoken that day. Since their proximity during the Dreyfus Affair, the two men had been in close contact based on their shared commitment to social justice. This assassination at the entrance of the war led Lévy-Bruhl to engage more actively in the socialist movement. In 1916, he was elected president of the Society of the Friends of Jaurès (Société des amis de Jaurès), thus transforming the burden of mourning and heritage into militant action. After May 1915, Lévy-Bruhl, along with Maurice Halbwachs and François Simiand, two of Durkheim's students trained in economics and statistics,[1] worked for the under-secretary of state for artillery and then for the Ministry of Armaments, directed by Albert Thomas.[2] Another member of this team, Hubert Bourgin, would later describe Lévy-Bruhl's political activities using anti-Semitic connotations, placing Lévy-Bruhl and Léon Blum as coordinators of the socialist network of the Normal Superior School:

> He is one of the high priests of the cult of Jaurès, which the government of the republic has made official. (Bourgin 1938: 228)
> Léon Bruhl [*sic*] has served and serves the men and parties who have used and are using Durkheim's sociology. With his personality and his money, he has contributed to their operations. He is for the Normal Superior School not only a patron but an example and a guide. He is the example of quiet but effective participation. (Bourgin 1938: 230)[3]

---

1. After attending Lévy-Bruhl's courses on Comte, Simiand, who had obtained his *agrégation* in philosophy in 1896, decided to study sociology with Durkheim. Halbwachs, who joined the team of the *Année sociologique* thanks to Simiand, had entered the Normal Superior School five years before him and defended a thesis on Quételet and moral statistics in 1906, with Lévy-Bruhl as a member of the examining committee. Simiand was elected to the Collège de France in 1932 and Halbwachs to the chair of collective psychology in 1945, but both died shortly after being elected.

2. Albert Thomas (1878–1932) had entered the Normal Superior School in 1899 and was awarded the *agrégation d'histoire* in 1902. He was elected deputy in 1910 at the National Assembly for the Seine, founded the *Revue syndicaliste* in 1905 and the *Revue socialiste* in 1909, and was the leader of a variety of socialist networks (Schaper 1960; Prochasson 1993: 122–29; Prochasson and Rasmussen 1996). In 1919, he became the first director of the International Labour Office based in Geneva, from where he supported the reformist policy of Hubert Lyautey in the French colonies (Rabinow 1989: 119, 324).

3. Hubert Bourgin (1874–1955) was a student at the Normal Superior School between 1894 and 1898 and then literature teacher in *lycées* (which

Indeed Lévy-Bruhl was famous for his discretion. He spoke after Blum during the commemoration of Jaurès's death on July 31, 1917; Thomas was not present because he was too visible in the government. Lévy-Bruhl wrote thirty-eight articles in *L'Humanité*, the socialist newspaper he helped fund, under the pseudonym of Deuzelles ("Two L*s*," seeing that "L. L." were the initials of Lucien Lévy) between December 6, 1914, and September 27, 1918. The use of a pseudonym allowed him to circumvent anti-Semitic suspicions about his financial support to *L'Humanité*. His articles translated and deciphered political speeches made in Germany, England, Russia, and the US, thus mobilizing Lévy-Bruhl's linguistic skills in the service of the socialist movement.

Preparing the New Order: Lévy-Bruhl at the Ministry of Armaments

The involvement of former students of the Normal Superior School in the Ministry of Armaments can be explained in part by the trauma of the death of Robert Hertz on April 13, 1915. This disciple of Durkheim, author of remarkable studies on funerary rituals, left–right polarity, and the cults of saints, had justified his participation in the conflict as a sacrifice for the French nation.[4] Lévy-Bruhl, who always avoids the term "sacrifice," instead explained France's entry into the war as an effort to prepare a more just social order. This line of thought takes up a thread put down by Jaurès in his last work, *L'armée nouvelle* (*The new army*), which he had published in 1911 in *L'Humanité* in the context of the

---

provide the last level of secondary education in the French educational system). He was close to socialist and Dreyfusard circles, then moved away from them after the war and became close to the extreme right-wing leagues.

4.   Lévy-Bruhl wrote to Alice Hertz on April 22, 1915: "I am deeply distressed. I had for your husband a very lively affection. I am not speaking only of his high intellectual value and of what could be expected of him. There was something in his nature that drew me irresistibly to him" (Mariot 2013: 301). Robert Hertz (1881–1915), born in a wealthy family to an American Jewish mother and a German father, was in many ways the opposite of Lucien Lévy-Bruhl, which perhaps explains this attraction. Hertz's justification of his involvement in the war as a sacrifice, through his letters to his wife Alice that circulated in the Durkheimian milieu, was both fascinating and repulsive to Lévy-Bruhl (see Hertz 2002).

rising threat of war, particularly after watching the rivalry between France and Germany over Morocco, and which was published as a book after his death (Jaurès 1915). Jaurès's strategy created a division between those socialists, gathered around Thomas, who wanted to prepare for war and those, represented by Romain Rolland, who wanted to suppress it (Prochasson 1993: 243). Halbwachs used the term "prepare" in his description of Thomas's office in a letter to his wife: "War poses a lot of problems that we are not prepared to solve, because it requires a sum of knowledge and a series of reflections that we have not yet been able to gather" (Becker 2003: 79).

The vocabulary of *"préparation"* lay at the center of Jaurès's political thought. "Politics must both effectively protect the present and ardently prepare the future," he wrote in an article from 1889 entitled "The ideal of justice" (Candar and Duclert 2014: 140). In his "Speech to the youth" in 1903, he said: "Courage is to watch over one's spinning or weaving machine carefully so that no thread breaks and yet to prepare a larger and more fraternal social order where the machine will be the common servant of the liberated workers" (Jaurès 2014: 168). According to Jaurès, historical events such as a general strike or a global war were opportunities for socialists to "point out" injustice, not goals in themselves for policies that he calls demagogic or reactionary. "We will point out [*on signalera*] to the workers the vices and disorders of the present social order, while preparing for the realization of the new ideal and the advent of a more just social order," Jaurès wrote in 1890 in *La dépêche du midi* (Candar and Duclert 2014: 149). Preparing a new order for Jaurès meant inserting the social ideal into the problems of the present: it involved a micro-politics of vigilance and not a macro-politics of insurrection.

In 1911, in *L'armée nouvelle*, Jaurès called for the constitution of a national reserve in addition to the active army, renewing the revolutionary conception of a people in arms. It was for him a means to let the people participate in the defense of the nation because he thought that their engagement would vary following one's position in the social space.

> There is no national defense possible unless the nation participates in it with all its heart and mind. (Jaurès 1915: 53)
> If France wants to live truly and be assured of life, if it wants to put a national force that will forever discourage all aggression at the service of its ideal, it must demand a military institution where all able-bodied citizens are supervised, educated, and prepared for war. (Jaurès 1915: 140)

In the eyes of Jaurès, only "a nation that absolutely wants peace and absolutely prepares for war" would be able to guarantee international peace in a context of rising tensions (Jaurès 1915: 145). Since the Dreyfus Affair revealed that the French army was only able to unify the people by the prejudice of anti-Semitism and xenophobia, Jaurès proposed introducing cultural knowledge and social diversity in the army. He recommended that officers learn languages at the university because he saw that the new wars were aimed less at the formation of a nation than at the conquest of new markets through colonization. The French army became, in Jaurès's vision, a sentinel of socialism, integrating human diversity and signaling the transformations of the social order. Jaurès, thus, used the discourse on preparation for war at the intersection of a military vocabulary—designing exercises to train youth and teaching the diversity of languages so that soldiers can better collaborate—and a philosophical vocabulary, since for Jaurès the contradictions of capitalism prepared the advent of a new order whose superior character had been postulated by the dialectics of the class struggle. "The classes that fight each other, the bourgeoisie and the working class, serve each other, even in their fight, and collaborate with each other, by their very battle, in the preparation of a superior order" (Jaurès 1915: 397).

The socialism of Jaurès, close to that of Durkheim, defended the state as an organ that reflects economic activities in order to regulate them and, thus, as the guarantee that a higher principle could be realized in lower realities. *L'armée nouvelle*, though being a treatise of military strategy, rested on the metaphysical principles of the scale of beings, from the sensible individual to the social ideal: "As soon as capitalism begins to reflect on itself, it must admit that it prepares human things to receive the announced social form, claimed by proletarian collectivism" (Jaurès 1915: 424).

After the enthusiasm of the first few months of the First World War and the successful counterattacks staged against the German army's invasion of French territory, the war became mired in the mud of the trenches, which led Lévy-Bruhl to modify his metaphysical conception of preparation and to adopt a more positivist approach. Germany, Lévy-Bruhl argued, was better "prepared" than France because it was better equipped. In his view, having the proletariat serve as a reserve army would not be to introduce a spirit of diversity into a monolithic army, as Jaurès argued, but rather to introduce an industrial activity in military exercise. This change of conception explains Lévy-Bruhl's engagements at the Ministry of Armaments, where he was in charge of coordinating the factories requisitioned to produce weapons. Indeed, this "industrial effort"—when an automobile factory starts to manufacture guns or shells in massive quantities—transformed the course of things. New types of industrial accidents occurred, such as shells exploding during production in the factories (Lévy-Bruhl 1916a). The insurance techniques implemented in the nineteenth century were no longer able to manage these kinds of hazards and it became necessary to draw on the war effort to justify what was no longer the responsibility of workers or employers. In March 1917, the Senate accused Thomas, the director of the Ministry of Armaments, with whom Lévy-Bruhl worked, of not respecting administrative norms in the Roanne arsenal, which the Ministry had built in 1916 on land purchased by the state. Thomas invoked a new form of military government defined by its capacity to insure accidents that were caused by the war effort and seemed unforeseeable, accidents that did not correspond to the risks for which workers were insured through the mutual insurance companies of their unions (Itzen, Metzger, and Rasmussen 2022). The Ministry of Armaments, therefore, set itself the objective of preparing, through statistics on the war industry, for accidents that no probability calculation had up to then considered as possible.

A letter by Alfred Dreyfus to Lucien Lévy-Bruhl in 1916 deals precisely with war factories. Dreyfus thanked Lévy-Bruhl for sending him the *Bulletin des armées* (Bulletin of armies) but added the following:

> You know, indeed, that quantities of factories for the manufacture of explosives have been built, both by private industry and by the state. It is, therefore, necessary to find out now how private industry can use these factories for the manufacture of chemical and pharmaceutical products and how the state can retrocede to private industry the factories that it has been led to build itself.[5]

Dreyfus was a reader of Jaurès's *L'armée nouvelle*, whose views on the preparation of the war he shared. In 1914, Dreyfus was assigned to the Pierrefitte barracks, north of Paris. On September 3, a pilot, who had observed a change of strategy in the German army, came to him, but Dreyfus refused to inform his superiors himself: "Call them yourself! I might not be believed. My name is Alfred Dreyfus" (Jourmas 2011: 25). After refusing to play the role of sentinel because of the stigma attached

---

5.   IMEC, Lévy-Bruhl papers, Letter from Alfred Dreyfus to Lucien Lévy-Bruhl, July 13, 1916.

to his name, he then volunteered in January 1917 to serve in the artillery at the Chemin des Dames and at Verdun. Although he was assigned under the command of Colonel Georges Larpent, who was known for his anti-Semitic and royalist writings (Jourmas 2011: 66–67), Dreyfus showed zeal in combat and care for his soldiers and was promoted to reserve lieutenant-colonel in September 1918. Dreyfus noted in his correspondence: "Here, despite the mud, the rain, the snow, the absolute lack of comfort, I am doing wonderfully. I am getting used to this savage regime" (Greilsamer 2018: 221). In the eyes of Dreyfus, the war was a moment of "savagery" for which he had been prepared by his deportation to Devil's Island in Guiana; but this savage moment transformed the perception of things, since private industries—like that of his father in Mulhouse, by then taken over by his brother Mathieu—had become state factories, an aberration in the eyes of bourgeois rationality. The letter that Dreyfus sent to Lévy-Bruhl in 1916 takes place in this moment when he thinks of returning to the front but still looks at the war effort from a planning perspective.

Lévy-Bruhl tried to justify what Dreyfus described as an aberration—the conversion of private industries into state factories—within the framework of Jaurès's socialism. In April 1916 he transformed the *Bulletin des armées* (*Bulletin of armies*) into the *Bulletin des usines de guerre* (Bulletin of war industries). The aim of this bulletin was to establish constant communication with the worker unions to inform them of the progress of the war. In his personal notes, Lévy-Bruhl gave objective reasons for this transformation ("distrust of workers against prose of official origin") and subjective reasons concerning himself: "1) incompetence; 2) lack of self-confidence; 3) little aptitude for exhortation; 4) lack of contact with the public" (Lévy-Bruhl 1917a). The support of the trade unions allowed him to compensate for his poor ability to address the workers because of his academic training. Lévy-Bruhl received safe passage that allowed him to leave Paris to visit war factories throughout France. On three occasions he accompanied the English trade unionist Ben Tillett, who came to encourage the French troops, as a translator.[6] The visits provided Lévy-Bruhl with the opportunity of describing

---

6. Benjamin Tillett (1860–1943) was an English trade union leader who came to prominence during the London dock strike of 1889. He was a member of the Fabian Society and of the Labour Party. In 1917, he published a pamphlet on the responsibilities of the war and engaged the labor movement to support the British government (see Schnerr 1982).

the landscapes of war: in Messines, there were "clean and dry trenches (which) give no idea of what they were like in winter under the rain: the weather is admirable and we enjoy the view"; in Ypres, he saw destroyed houses, a deserted city "comparable to a modern Pompeii"; in Reims, a "negro village" had been erected next to the burned-down cathedral that reminded him of the African settlements in the Jardin d'Acclimatation, displayed as an exhibition of colonial peoples and their lifeways. Ben Tillett shared Lévy-Bruhl's views on education but became impatient when the philosopher began talking with officers about his courses at the Sorbonne.[7] Ben Tillett and Lévy-Bruhl represented the two sides of Jaurès: the revolutionary unionist engaged in action and the academic philosopher contemplating the landscape. The latter relied on the former to spread the "industrial effort" among the workers. In Lévy-Bruhl's view, the worker on the front line was the outpost of a reserve army working in the background for a social regulation to come.

Who is Responsible for the War? Lévy-Bruhl and Propaganda

During the war, Lévy-Bruhl participated in academic debates on the origin of the conflict. His interest in the question led him to take up again the concept of responsibility that he had analyzed in his thesis and to appraise it in the light of the new set of international relations. In the article "The economic and political causes of the war in Germany," published in the international journal *Scientia* in January 1915, Lévy-Bruhl emphasized that the causes of war were not mechanical but should be sought in "the determining conditions of events as they manifest themselves in the sentiments, ideas, passions, and needs of individuals and peoples" (Lévy-Bruhl 1915: 43). He sought to approach this question with a scientific method to describe how people perceived each other and themselves, in order to understand the chain of misunderstandings that led to war. In particular, Lévy-Bruhl emphasized the economic interests of Germany and Austria, the "advanced sentinel of the German world," in gaining access to colonies along the routes through the Middle East. According to Lévy-Bruhl, the desire to obtain a "place in the sun" gave rise in Germany to a "fear of being tricked by partners who are more malicious and skilful" (Lévy-Bruhl 1915: 53). In a memo that

---

7.   IMEC, Lévy-Bruhl papers, Notes de la mission Ben Tillett, May 29 to June 12, 1915.

Lévy-Bruhl wrote to the French Ministry of Foreign Affairs in 1918 on a postwar Germany stripped of its colonies, he noticed that "a great industrial people cannot live without its colonies. It needs raw materials" (Lévy-Bruhl 1918a).

Lévy-Bruhl's remark that Germany had seen its colonies as an extension of its will to power and not just as source for raw materials for its industry reveals, by contrast, the program he assigned to the French colonial empire. If reliance on its colonies enabled France to stay firm against the German onslaught, Lévy-Bruhl sought to anticipate the future direction of this force by understanding it from within. One can see in these war memos the idea that the colonies are not only material but also psychological resources that must be developed in peacetime by an ethnological science, which will be Lévy-Bruhl's justification for the creation of the Institute of Ethnology in 1925. In his eyes, it was precisely because of Germany's failure to develop the psychology of peoples as a social ethnology of "mentalities" rather than as a natural geography of races that it failed to legitimize its power. In a memo entitled "Reflections on the lessons of war: Force and finesse," Lévy-Bruhl noted that Germany, after exposing its power in the first stages of the war, then showed its "incapacity to enter into the ideas and sentiments of others" because it "believes that it is enough to be able to command. Big mistake: force is only an instrument; everything depends on how it is directed" (Lévy-Bruhl 1917a).

The opposition between German's blind force and France's clear mind was also at the heart of Henri Bergson's patriotic speeches, suggesting how a force becomes durable when it is engaged in action (Soulez and Worms 1997: 151–52). Lévy-Bruhl seemed to echo Bergson when he stated that Germany's weakness was caused by its difficulty of understanding the sentiments of others. If Germany's mechanical force was exhausted when it was confronted by all the events that globalized the war, it was then necessary to analyze how this force persisted in the face of the challenge of the war's unpredictable character. Lévy-Bruhl named it a capacity to prepare for unforeseen events when he wrote: "Unpredictability: 1) the duration of the war; 2) the Marne; 3) the Orient; 4) the achievements of the past: grenades, helmets, etc.; 5) it is part of the likelihood that the implausible will happen. Application: expect the unexpected and prepare everything to channel and direct it" (Lévy-Bruhl 1917a).

Lévy-Bruhl described a convergence between politicians, economic actors, and journalists at the level of moral sentiments in the years preceding 1914, which made war inevitable and acceptable without any conscious intentionality (Clark 2013). His ethnology of the "primitive mentality" appears as a thread in his description of the sentiment of unpredictability that guided his political engagement through the accidents and events of the war. Rather than a conscious justification of war, "primitive mentality" described the entanglement of actions that led to entering and enduring the war in a way that made the unpredictable predictable. Because societies prepared themselves for war through national sentiments, in Lévy-Bruhl's analysis, they could give meaning to the events that followed one another in the conflict.

Ethnology and sociology were called upon in the debate that took place after the war on the reparations imposed on Germany by the Treaty of Versailles in June 1919. The recognition of responsibility for the war implied that the German government should pay the costs of the war for other nations. However, even if it was declared that Emperor Wilhelm II was legally responsible for entering the war, it was not possible, Lévy-Bruhl argued, to declare the entire German people morally responsible, since this would encourage the workers to succumb to revolutionary socialism and ruin Europe's reconstruction efforts.

> The Allies are ready to admit a German nation convinced of its wrongs and willing to make reparation for them as far as possible, providing every guarantee in the future of its respect for the sworn faith and for the law of nations. But the German people, apart from a small minority, are not aware that they have done anything to justify a singular treatment in this respect. They agree to stop fighting, but they do not feel guilty: they admit that it was wrong to brave a world of enemies, but they consider that it was an error of calculation, not a crime. ... It would be in their interest to act on the morale of the German government in order to make it understand, and consequently accept, what otherwise it would have to undergo with a feeling of undeserved humiliation and revolt. (Lévy-Bruhl 1919a)

Here again, Lévy-Bruhl mobilized sentiment to recommend presenting debt to the German people not as the recognition of a fault but as the people's integration into a set of relations. In terms of the Durkheimian sociology of law, the reparations demanded of Germany were not a repressive sanction, which destroys the person responsible for the crime, but rather a restitutive sanction, which returns society to how it was before the event. Germany's entry into the war triggered a chain of unpredictable events that should be redirected by establishing a system of reciprocal benefits. The predictability of the debt would instantiate a sense of obligation that would mitigate the violence of the unpredictable events of the war. Lévy-Bruhl anticipated here the reflections of Marcel Mauss on debt that, echoing the debate on war reparations, would establish a fruitful link between economics, law, and ethnology (Mallard 2019). This engagement toward social reconstruction is also what animated Lévy-Bruhl's governmental action during the war. The unpredictability of the war made it necessary to prepare for a more rational order.

CHAPTER 6

Industrial Accidents

Lévy-Bruhl's second ethnological book appeared in 1922 under the title *La mentalité primitive*. Lévy-Bruhl warns his reader on the very first page: "When *Les fonctions mentales dans les sociétés inférieures* appeared, twelve years ago, it should already have been titled *La mentalité primitive*" (Lévy-Bruhl 1922: i). Such a statement lessens the historical discontinuity by claiming an intellectual continuity, as if these two books were talking about the same thing. Yet the philosophical theses of these books differ radically. The 1910 book asserted that "primitive mentality" ignores contradiction because it is governed by a principle of participation. The 1922 book argues that "primitive mentality" ignores chance because it is oriented toward primary, not secondary, causality. In each case, the thesis takes a negative form ("primitive mentality ignores ...") which inaugurates the search for a regime of positive facts. But from the prewar to the postwar period, this positivity has radically changed because it corresponds to a different engagement of the philosopher and ethnologist. Indeed, the war led Lévy-Bruhl to develop the problem of the unpredictable from new industrial accidents and to reorient his analysis of "primitive mentality" on the notions of chance and hazard, following the philosophical debate of his time.

"Primitive Mentality Ignores Chance": Lévy-Bruhl and Cournot

What does it mean to assert, in 1922, that "primitive societies ignore chance"? This statement implies a whole history of statistics in Europe, which was profoundly disrupted by the First World War. When he worked at the Ministry of Armaments with sociologists trained in the statistics of their time, such as Maurice Halbwachs and François Simiand, Lévy-Bruhl erased the bad memory of the Statistical Office, an intelligence agency based on the false expertise of Alphonse Bertillon during the Dreyfus Affair. Statistics, indeed, has the capacity to cancel or "tame" chance, because it reveals social tendencies behind the accidents of life, through mathematical tools such as the calculation of probabilities and the law of large numbers (Hacking 1990; Desrosières 1993). Bertillon, following Quételet, wrongly believed that these social tendencies were those of a biological race or of an average type, but Durkheim showed that they were rather collective representations organizing the social body (Lécuyer 1987). Lévy-Bruhl's 1910 book on "primitive mentality" was an attack on Bertillon and the anti-Dreyfusards who ignored the principle of contradiction when they asserted that Dreyfus was both here and elsewhere, or that his writing was double. His 1922 book is a reflection on the war, which multiplied accidents and produced new collective representations unifying the social body (Itzen, Metzger, and Rasmussen 2022). Between these two books, the role of statistics in French society had changed and Lévy-Bruhl began to see it as a technique that could bridge the gap separating the socialist ideal from everyday life by using social representations as means to anticipate the future.

Lévy-Bruhl's experience in Albert Thomas's ministry appears in an article entitled "Primitive Mentality and Gambling," which Lévy-Bruhl published first in English in 1924 and then in French in 1926 (Lévy-Bruhl 1924b). It described the similarities between the reasoning of military generals, financial speculators, and "primitive societies," emphasizing that military generals think on two levels at once: as moderns when they measure chance or calculate risk and as "primitives" when they invoke their lucky stars or their fatherland.

> In warfare, the most certain strategies and the most shrewdly, meticulously prepared operations may suddenly be compromised or paralyzed by an unforeseeable mishap: a poorly transmitted order, a sudden change of weather, and so on. Napoleon said that, in military matters, chance intervenes 25 percent of the time. Among certain

generals, as among certain politicians, the gambler's mentality is pro-
nounced. They have a taste for risk and a sense that success depends
on imponderables, over which they think they exercise some sort of
mysterious influence, having faith in their "star." (Lévy-Bruhl 1924b
[2020: 422])

Arguing that "primitive mentality ignores chance," beyond the negative
aspect of the formula, joins two historical observations: non-European
societies have not developed the mathematical concept of chance; and
European societies have invented statistics, by which they secularized
the primary causes other societies invoked to explain accidents. The concept of chance indeed implies the ability to distinguish between second
and first causes, for instance between the parts of a machine and its
external impulse. Antoine-Augustin Cournot gave a famous definition
in his *Exposition de la théorie des chances et des probabilités* (*Theory of chance
and probabilities*) in 1843: chance is the encounter between independent
causal series (Cournot 1843). This definition of chance echoed a debate
that took place in France in 1842 on the causes of train accidents. At the
time, as accidents were increasing in this promising industry, it was necessary for railroad companies to show that they were not responsible but
that these accidents resulted from the unpredictable encounter between
heterogeneous causes, such as the heat of the rails and the speed of the
train (Fressoz 2012: 272). Once industrial accident legislation was introduced at the end of the nineteenth century, the new insurance schemes
began to attribute the responsibility for accidents that affected workers
to the factory owners (Ewald 2020). The reasoning behind no-fault liability is that the factory owner is the primary cause of the accident,
even if the worker is the secondary cause: the reason is that, although it
was the worker who put his hand in the machine, it was the owner who
made him work in the factory. With the multiplication of industrial accidents in mechanized societies, new forms of primary causality had to
be invented in order to attribute responsibility.

Such a transformation in the social use of statistics implied epistemological shifts in the conception of chance, which Lévy-Bruhl closely
observed. If the philosophy of Cournot, who died in 1877, had become
marginal under the Third Republic, Lévy-Bruhl gave it an important
place in his *History of Modern Philosophy in France*: "Chance is not a word
invented to hide our ignorance, as some philosophers have claimed; it is
a positive factor in the sum total of reality; it includes all the results of
the competition of an independent series of causes" (Lévy-Bruhl 1899b:

458). Working closely with the mathematician Denis Poisson, Cournot held administrative positions in French public education, even though he never taught, and wrote a series of works developing the philosophical consequences of the calculus of probability (Martin 1996). Cournot objected to Aristotle's definition of chance, which distinguished between events that happen without being expected (*automaton*) and those that signal a favorable intention or good fortune (*tuché*). The development of the calculation of probabilities introduced rationality in the interplay of mechanical causes and secularized the idea of a favorable intention by mathematically measuring the expectation of an event (Hacking 1975; Daston 1988; Brian 1994).

The calculation of probabilities was the weak point of Auguste Comte's philosophy, which provided an ideological foundation for the Third Republic. When Comte proposed replacing metaphysical causes with positive laws on the regularity of phenomena, he did not go so far as to recognize that certain events occur by chance, since he viewed all events as resulting from the determined course of biological or social organization. In his thesis on responsibility, Lévy-Bruhl opposed this deterministic conception and mobilized the neo-Kantian philosophy of Boutroux and Renouvier to recognize that there is an irreducible unpredictability and contingency in human action. It seems, then, that reading Cournot led Lévy-Bruhl to elaborate a nondeterministic version of positivism in his book on Comte in 1900, which allowed him to reflect on the transformations of industrial societies.

Cournot saw the foundation of a reconstruction of knowledge in the calculation of probabilities and posed the critical question after Kant: how can the human mind know an external world that presents itself as indeterminate? Whereas, for Comte, each set of phenomena was constituted by regularities that can be transcribed into laws, Cournot postulated the indeterminacy of phenomena and saw a tool for progressively reducing this indeterminacy in the calculation of probabilities. Such a philosophical difference stems from the fact that Comte and Cournot did not classify the sciences in the same way for their contributions to the history of the human mind. In Comte's classification of the sciences, mathematics came first as a model of the invariability of laws and was progressively applied to fields of increasing complexity: astronomy, physics, biology, sociology. Cournot introduced mechanics as a science and situated it between mathematics and physics. Taking into account all the forces that apply to a body, mechanics requires calculating probabilities, since the number of forces at play is so great that one can only predict a probable movement without being able to show how it is determined by the other movements. On the contrary, for Cournot, social life makes the actions of individuals more predictable because it is governed by the law of large numbers, as revealed by statistics. Cournot's classification of the sciences proceeds like an inverse hourglass: complexity increases from mathematics to biology but decreases from biology to sociology (Vatin 1998).

Cournot's philosophy thus reformulated the Kantian distinction between subjectivity and objectivity with the scientific vocabulary of the nineteenth century, which informed Lévy-Bruhl's thesis on responsibility. Cournot's contribution to the debate on probabilities is, indeed, the distinction between subjective and objective probabilities: the former measure human ignorance, the latter describe an indeterminacy internal to things themselves. This philosophical distinction can be grasped in the ordinary difference between chance and hazard: the first term describes a human belief based on past experiences, the second describes orders of causalities that intersect in reality. According to Cournot, the progress of scientific knowledge consists in formulating statements with increasing probability until they become equivalent to a physical certainty. But determinism is not so integral that we could know all the elements from a single one, because each element acts on the others in a different way. Even a superior intelligence knowing all possible relationships would not abolish hazard and would have to think in terms of probabilities. One must, according to Cournot, imagine a God who plays dice knowing only the rules of construction of the dice and the table and rejoicing in the unpredictability of His creation.

Lévy-Bruhl wrote a preface for the 1911 republication by Hachette of Cournot's *Treatise on the sequence of fundamental ideas in science and history* (Cournot 1911), which had first appeared in 1861. He pointed out that Cournot was more interesting for future generations of students because he knew the sciences of his time more than his contemporary Victor Cousin, who dominated the teaching of philosophy at the Sorbonne in the mid-nineteenth century: "While the discussions that fascinated the Eclectic School are now of historical interest to us, most of the problems on which Cournot focused have become actual problems. In this sense, he was a pioneer and a precursor" (Lévy-Bruhl 1911: ix).

Just before his death in 1903, Gabriel Tarde paid tribute to Cournot's social philosophy for its indeterministic arguments. But in 1911, Lévy-Bruhl rather likened Cournot to Henri Bergson, whose fame had eclipsed that of his predecessor at the Collège de France, Gabriel Tarde (Azouvi

2007). In Lévy-Bruhl's eyes, Bergson was taking over the philosophical work of Cournot in the same way that Durkheim was continuing the sociological work of Comte: "If a metaphysician like Mr. Bergson carefully delineates what is, according to him, the proper field of science and that of philosophical speculation, he teaches at the same time, by his example, that a true philosopher must be in a position to criticize the principles and results of the positive sciences" (Lévy-Bruhl 1911: ix).

"We Do Not Endure Alone": Lévy-Bruhl and Bergson

In 1890, Bergson had asked Lévy-Bruhl, who had been his senior by two years at the Normal Superior School, to publish a review of his first book, *Essai sur les données immédiates de la conscience* (*Essay on the immediate data of consciousness*), in the *Revue philosophique*, then edited by Théodule Ribot. Though altogether laudatory, Lévy-Bruhl's review concluded with a criticism. Bergson opposed the interior duration of the "deep self," which he described as "continuous creation of unforeseeable novelty" (Bergson 1888: 57), to mathematical science, which makes the world measurable and predictable. He thus described the illusion of free will as a projection of stable representations of social life on the individual's states of consciousness. Lévy-Bruhl objected to this: "I confess that I have, according to Mr. Bergson's own expression, an incredible difficulty in representing duration in its original purity. According to him, that is because of the fact that we do not endure alone. ... Does not a succession without distinction, which is a mutual penetration of elements, escape our thought?" (Lévy-Bruhl 1890c: 529). Such an objection anticipated the difficulties that Lévy-Bruhl himself would have to fit "primitive mentality" into the frameworks of "civilized mentality." But it also announced that Bergson's individual psychology should be enlarged to collective representations to understand how human action mitigates the unpredictability of future events. Indeed, Lévy-Bruhl's first book on ethnology, published in 1910, borrowed many analyses from Bergson's *Matière et mémoire* (*Matter and memory*), published in 1896, in which the latter discussed Ribot's psychology in some detail (Bergson 1896). But Lévy-Bruhl's preface to Cournot in 1911 came in the context of a new debate that pitted Bergson against scientists after the publication of Bergson's *L'Évolution créatrice* (*Creative evolution*) in 1907.

The Bergsonian analysis of intelligence as measurement was, indeed, contested by one of the greatest mathematicians of the time, Émile

Borel, who had just developed a theory of chance. A former student of the Normal Superior School who was close to the Dreyfusards, Borel launched the *Revue du mois* (*Journal of the month*) in 1905, in which he intended to disseminate the advances of scientific research to a literate public (Pinault 2017). He published his own articles on probability and statistics, which he collected in a book entitled *Le hasard* (*Chance*) in 1914 (Borel 1914), with several reeditions after the war. Since the work of Cournot half a century earlier, the calculation of probabilities and statistical methods had indeed been applied to a wider range of phenomena, such as the kinematics of gases and the experimental study of microbes. Borel proposed reducing the indeterminacy that Cournot had introduced to his classification of sciences through the mechanics of shocks by the calculation of chance. The new techniques of chance calculation, applied in particular to gases, led Borel to discuss Bergson's analyses in *L'Évolution créatrice*. In 1907, Borel published an article in the *Revue de métaphysique et de morale* that challenged Bergson's opposition between geometric intelligence and philosophical intuition. According to Borel, Bergson had attached intelligence to the ancient Greek geometry and had ignored the capacities of modern intuition to produce new geometries. Bergson replied that his conception of evolution, on the contrary, accounted for the transformations of geometry, which provoked an article by Borel in return. The debate remained limited to the pages of the *Revue de métaphysique et de morale*, but the liveliness of the tone—Borel accused Bergson of anti-intellectualism—created a division between science and philosophy at a time when philosophical journals were seeking to bring them closer together (Bergson 1907 [2013: 589–618]).

Lévy-Bruhl knew Borel before the war through the French Society of Philosophy and met him again at the Ministry of War when it was headed by the mathematician Paul Painlevé. Their paths crossed many times after the war in groups entitled La politique républicaine and L'Union rationaliste. Borel was a member of the board of the General Statistics of France and succeeded in attaching this entity, founded in 1833 within the framework of the Ministry of Trade, to the prime minister. In 1922, he created the Institute of Statistics at the University of Paris and in 1928 the Henri Poincaré Mathematical Center (Desrosières 1993: 193; Pinault 2017: 328). Borel played an institutional role for mathematics similar to what Lévy-Bruhl did in the humanities. Lévy-Bruhl never quoted Borel, probably because their commitments were different: Lévy-Bruhl was a Jewish socialist and Borel a Protestant radical (in the sense of the Radical Party, considered as more conservative than the

Socialist Party). But this silence also has an epistemological significance: by paying homage to Bergson in his preface to Cournot and then by asserting that "primitive mentality ignores chance" because it privileges the visions seen in dreams and the memories of tradition, Lévy-Bruhl sided with Bergson, whom he called "the prince of philosophers" (Lévy-Bruhl 1928a) in the quarrel in 1928 about the human meaning of scientific activity, which pitted him against Borel.

It was, therefore, surprising that Bergson criticized Lévy-Bruhl around the notion of chance in his last book, *Les deux sources de la morale et de la religion* (*The two sources of morality and religion*), published in 1932. If each of Bergson's books confronted his metaphysical method of intuition with a positive science—mathematics, then psychology, then biology—this time "the prince of philosophers" targeted Durkheim's sociology. But Bergson's most intense discussions concerned Lévy-Bruhl's thesis that "primitive mentality ignores chance." Against Cournot's distinction, Bergson asserted that the notion of chance (*hasard* in French) is not radically different in its use from that of luck (*chance* in French), conceived as a force that acts behind things. Thus, Bergson wrote, the gambler waits for luck to push the ball he has chosen at the roulette wheel, even if he knows the probabilities that his number will come up, just as the hunter accompanies the movement of his arrow by invoking the spirit of the game, even if he knows the strength of his bow (Bergson 1932 [1935: 139]). Bergson, thus, took up Aristotle's analysis of chance by adding a new element. Chance is what explains the gap between the forecast and the result of human action because some catastrophic effects of this action are unforeseeable. When a roofing tile falls on a passerby's head, the passerby imagines that his intention to walk collides with an equivalent intention coming from the tile (Bergson 1932 [1935: 147–48]). Similarly, William James says he perceived the San Francisco earthquake as a familiar person because he could not conceive of such an event as real before it happened, even if he vaguely knew it could happen (Bergson 1932 [1935: 153–58]). In the same way, Bergson says, the war with Germany was, for his generation, an event "at once probable and impossible," which suddenly became real with the declaration of war in 1914, "an invisible presence which all the past had prepared and foretold, as a shadow may preceded the body that casts it" (Bergson 1932 [1935: 159]). Trust in action prevents humans, according to Bergson and James, from calculating risks by introducing virtual entities in their perception. Bergson, thus, described chance as "mechanism behaving as though possessing intention," "a shadow where the shape is there even if the matter is not," "an intention emptied of its content," "the phantom of an intention" (Bergson 1932 [1935: 148-49]).

Bergson then made a distinction between "static religion" regulated by obligation in "primitive societies" and "dynamic religion" regulated by the call of "mystical heroes."[1] In this second form, metaphysical intuition seizes complete personalities, by contrast with the partial and ghostly entities of the first one, endowing nature with intentionality as a "vital impulse" (*élan vital*). Bergson's thesis can be qualified as evolutionist because it opposes the great scientific and moral inventors with primitive societies as two steps in a "creative evolution." The ignorance of chance is, here, the sign of a delay, of an intention that did not go as far as it can, of a vital impulse that falls on itself in exhaustion.

> To pass from this "primitive mentality" to states of mind which may well be our own, more often than not we have to do two things. First, we have to make a clean sweep of all our science. Then we must abandon ourselves to a certain laziness, turn aside from an explanation which we surmise to be more reasonable but which would call for a greater effort of intelligence and, above all, of will. ... So let us not talk of minds different from our own. Let us simply say that they are ignorant of what we have learned. (Bergson 1932 [1935: 150–51])

In the vocabulary of contemporary sociology, we can say that Bergson analyzed the normative dynamics of whistleblowers who launch public causes leading to the invention of new forms of risk from their perception of environmental problems; but he then dismissed the sentinels as whistleblowers who have failed to translate their perception into the language of risk. Lévy-Bruhl's conception of "primitive mentality" is, then, closer to the experience of sentinels when they perceive signs of danger that cannot be reduced to the form of the calculation of probabilities.

---

1.   Bergson here develops a conception of mysticism that is closer to that of Péguy, in the sense of a preparation of the divine city, than to that of Lévy-Bruhl, who defines it as "belief in forces imperceptible to the senses and yet real" (Lévy-Bruhl 1910: 22). Bergson kept himself apart from the Dreyfus Affair, which left him "indifferent," and his authority was claimed by the Dreyfusards as well as by the anti-Dreyfusards (see Soulez and Worms 1997).

In asserting that "primitive mentality ignores chance," Lévy-Bruhl emphasized that "primitive societies" do not mobilize statistical knowledge because, in the absence of a centralizing state, they use other techniques to anticipate the future. Lévy-Bruhl repeatedly quoted the observation of a missionary in South Africa who reproached the inhabitants of the Northern Transvaal for wasting their time on "games of chance" when they threw the bones for each important decision. They replied: "But this is our book; we do not have any other. You read your book every day because you believe in it; we do the same because we have faith in our book" (Lévy-Bruhl 1922: 214). Lévy-Bruhl made the following comment on this scene:

> Can the missionary do better than talk to God? God speaks to him in the Bible. (A book has, for the natives, a very pronounced magical character.) Well, the ancestors "speak" to the natives through the bones. Or, rather, the Bible speaks and the bones speak too. To consult them is, therefore, not to practice an absurd art or to have fun like children; it is to be wise enough not to risk anything without the ancestors' acknowledgement. (Lévy-Bruhl 1924b [2020: 424])

Lévy-Bruhl's analysis was astonishingly visionary because it criticized the split between societies without writing and societies with writing; or, rather, it problematized the effect of writing in the perception of the hazards of social life. The missionary who interrogates the "natives" relates all events to a written totality, the Bible, while the players do not need to transcribe the rules in a book to play since the bones "speak" through an implicit knowledge of the game (Goody 1977). Playing with divinatory bones is, therefore, a real institution in societies where the outcome of hunting or war is determined by the way the bones fall to the ground, because this distributes "luck" or "fortune" in advance as a collective good (Hamayon 2016). Calling them "games of chance" is a mistake that projects onto one institution the rules of another that functions differently. Lévy-Bruhl thus managed to reconcile Durkheim and Cournot in a way that escaped Bergson: chance does exist in technical things, but it is the result of a social construction that has become constitutive of modern reality. If we look at it from the point of view of "primitive mentality," it ceases to appear as real and becomes a simple belief. "Chance does not exist at all. It is an institution, in the Durkheimian sense of the term, that is to say, the lasting result of an impersonal force that exceeds individuals" (Héran 1987b: 160).

New Risks of the Postwar Period: Divination, Ordeal, and Public Health

This ethnological view of statistical probabilities explains why Lévy-Bruhl became interested, through his students and sons, in several institutions that were to occupy a central place in the human sciences: divination, ordeal (an archaic form of trial), and public health (a modern form of hygiene). His work on "primitive mentality," which first concerned the ethnology of colonial societies, shed light on the new risks resulting from the transformations of industrial societies.

Auguste Bouché-Leclercq had studied techniques of divination in Greek and Roman antiquity (Bouché-Leclercq 1879–82) and Edouard Chavannes those in Chinese antiquity (Chavannes 1895–1905). But Lévy-Bruhl opened a vast field of comparison with his 1922 book, where he proposed to study divinatory practices in Africa, America, and Oceania, inspiring future research in that field (Guiart 1962; Holbraad 2012). This empirical field of enquiry could be oriented by the logical question that was at the heart of Lévy-Bruhl's philosophical reflection. Techniques of divination do not rely on the Aristotelian logic, which attributes a predicate to a subject following the principle of noncontradiction, but rather follow a Stoic logic linking events together. Thus, the famous statement "The Bororo are Arara" is contradictory only in an Aristotelian logic, but it ceases to be so if it links two events, the flight of a flock of parrots and the hunting of a Bororo individual, because one of the events is a sign of the other (Hamelin 1902). Since his first work on Seneca, where he analyzed the conception of God as a providence that makes the signs of the world legible (Lévy-Bruhl 1884b), Lévy-Bruhl kept this Stoic logic in mind as an alternative to the logic of representation. He was, moreover, assisted, when he edited the *Revue philosophique*, by a specialist in Stoic philosophy, Émile Bréhier, and by a specialist in Asian philosophy, Paul Masson-Oursel, two of his former students who would take over the direction of the journal after his death (Bréhier 1907; Masson-Oursel 1938).

Lévy-Bruhl's interest in ordeals opened up another field of empirical research: that of legal forms in stateless societies. The notion of the ordeal, which describes ritual trials aimed at settling a dispute or an accusation, comes from the German term *Urteil*, which designates judgment. Gustav Glotz, a Hellenist close to Durkheim, devoted his thesis to this practice, claiming that "there is perhaps not a country in the world where, in order to repel an accusation and to claim a right, one has not submitted to the test of cold or hot water, fire, or poison" (Glotz 1904). Lévy-Bruhl explained the universal belief in the legal value of this archaic form of trial by the fact that poison, water, or fire were not perceived as mechanical causes but as vehicles of mystical forces. Glotz showed that this primitive practice survived in the oath, by which individuals invoked the protection of the gods and symbolically placed themselves in water or fire and which is transformed in the Christian rituals of baptism and the Eucharist. In this genealogy, ordeal is considered a prelegal form of the modern contract through the intermediary form of the oath.

Lucien Lévy-Bruhl's second son, Henri, spent his life developing this legal genealogy. Born in 1884, he studied law at the Faculty of Paris, where he defended a thesis in 1910 on instrumental testimony in Roman law. For three years during the war, Henri fought at the front, where he met Robert Hertz in the spring of 1915 and where he was wounded in March 1917. Appointed associate professor of law at the Faculty of Lille in 1919 and then at the Faculty of Paris in 1930, he published articles in the interwar period on the forms of the oath in ancient Roman law but also on the rights of the shipwreck or bills of exchange in early French modernity (Chevreau, Audren, and Verdier 2018). These works on ancient Roman law and modern commercial law came in the wake of the sociologists of law such as Georges Davy, Paul Fauconnet, Paul Huvelin, and Marcel Mauss, who collaborated in Émile Durkheim's *Année sociologique*.

Through a meticulous analysis of legal sources that he was sometimes the first to exhume, Henri Lévy-Bruhl described how the law moved from public oaths validated by mystical tests to the written codification of obligations, in a way that modified the concept of moral personhood. Following his father's work on "primitive mentality," he showed that, when individuals had to engage in uncertain actions such as war between Roman tribes or the exploration of the seas by European sailors, they resorted to imaginary entities that did not follow the modern form of risk calculation but prefigured it, such as the belief in chance or fortune. Therefore, the modern notion of enterprise, seen from the broad angle of an ethnology of law, is a legal construction that makes it possible to limit uncertainty as much as to invoke invisible spirits. Here we see how Henri Lévy-Bruhl combined Durkheim's evolutionism (ordeal prefigures contract, the spirit of enterprise prefigures risk calculation) and his father's relativism (these archaic forms are irreducible to modern forms and should be understood in their own terms). The family memory of the Dreyfus Affair was decisive in Henri Lévy-Bruhl's work: for instance, he showed that trade liberated modern individuals from the arbitrary accusation of crime. Because the Jews had long been considered by the Catholic Church as the only social group that could engage in trade and because this made them easy targets for popular forms of lynching in crisis situations, the modern legal framework of banking activity guaranteed, according to Henri Lévy-Bruhl, the access of all men to a moral and legal personality (H. Lévy-Bruhl 1933). This meant that, for Henri Lévy-Bruhl as for his father, modern law was better than archaic law and yet always threatened by its return, which justified the study of archaic law to fight against it on its own terms.

Before the war, Henri Lévy-Bruhl was strongly involved in socialist circles, in particular the Group of Socialist Studies (Groupe d'études socialistes) run by Robert Hertz at the home of François Simiand. In 1909, he wrote a booklet on "the economic organization of the commune" for the *Cahiers du socialiste*, which inspired Albert Thomas during the electoral campaign for the mayor's office in Champigny in 1913. This commitment was confirmed and reinforced by Henri Lévy-Bruhl's marriage in 1917 to Hélène Rauh, daughter of the philosopher Frédéric Rauh who was both a friend of Jean Jaurès at the Faculty of Toulouse and the interlocutor of Lucien Lévy-Bruhl in the debate on morality in 1903. In 1922, Henri Lévy-Bruhl published a short piece in *L'Humanité* to express the support of his father, then on a trip to the US, for the liberation of André Marty, a communist militant imprisoned in Odessa for his participation in a mutiny on a French ship three years earlier (H. Lévy-Bruhl 1922). Henri Lévy-Bruhl thus presented himself in the aftermath of the First World War as both the political and the scientific successor of his father, roles that he took on even more clearly after the Second World War.

In the interwar period, Lucien Lévy-Bruhl thus analyzed divinatory and juridical practices as ways to tame chance and mitigate uncertainty that could return to modern societies by calculating risk following deterministic laws. This may explain why, after the First World War, Lucien Lévy-Bruhl was also attentive to the new forms of public health through his two other sons, Marcel, born in 1883, and Jean, born in 1890, as they introduced new forms of indetermination in the interventions on human lives. The older one studied medicine at the Faculty of Paris, graduating as a doctor in 1914. He served as a physician during the war and received the Croix de Guerre (a military reward) in August 1916; by 1918 he ended up as a bacteriologist in an army laboratory. While a student, he joined the Pasteur Institute in 1912, where he met his wife Berthe Marchand, and later, between 1921 and 1941, worked as an assistant researcher with the two Nicolle brothers while heading laboratories in several hospitals in Paris. Maurice Nicolle, a member of the Imperial Institute of Bacteriology in Constantinople and author of *Éléments de microbiologie générale* in 1900, had to stop his scientific activity because of two strokes in 1920 and 1926 that left him paralyzed. His brother Charles Nicolle, who directed the Pasteur Institute of Tunis from 1903 until his death in 1936, received the Nobel Prize in Medicine in 1928 for his work on typhus before being elected to the Academy of Sciences in 1929 and then to the Collège de France in 1932 at the chair of physiology and experimental medicine (Pelis 2007). In the shadow of these two giants of Pasteurian medicine, Marcel Lévy-Bruhl continued his father's commitment, inventing a new form of solidarity with living beings through the methods of microbiology.

Marcel Lévy-Bruhl's first publication was in 1915 on chicken spirillosis, following the research conducted on immunology by Elie Metchnikoff at the Pasteur Institute. This article demonstrated that hens whose thyroid had been removed retained immunity to this bacterial disease, whereas hens whose spleen had been removed lost it. Marcel Lévy-Bruhl then published articles on bacterial infections from food sources in the journal *Paris médical*, worked as an expert on intoxication for the Commercial Court of the Seine department, and introduced micro-cinematography in biology courses, supporting the diffusion of Jean Comandon's films at the Pasteur Institute. In 1938, he published an article on "human pasteurellosis" in line with Nicolle's reflections on new infectious diseases. The term "pasteurellosis" had been coined in 1900 by Joseph Lignières to generalize the observations Pasteur had made in 1880 on chicken cholera. Commenting on the discovery of these microorganisms in many species (rabbit, fish, etc.), Marcel Lévy-Bruhl wrote:

> One is thus led to adopt a conception of pasteurellar viruses as unique and to consider that the different varieties come from a single microbe. This microbe easily acquires or loses its virulence and, by its passage through the organism of certain animals and its adaptation to a given species, it causes a pasteurellosis special to that species. (M. Lévy-Bruhl 1938: 411)

Marcel Lévy-Bruhl's article continued with observations of cases either in the medical literature, such as an officer wounded by a panther and treated in Dakar, or in his own hospital practice, such as a forty-eight-year-old miner treated after being scratched by a cat. Lévy-Bruhl observed that these cases were most often due to unfavorable climatic or hygienic conditions but that they remained rare, the "pasteurellose virus" finally proving to be "refractory" in humans, who have only benign diseases when infected by it, whereas it is "ubiquitous" in other animal species, causing ravages in birds and mammals (M. Lévy-Bruhl 1938: 431). Marcel Lévy-Bruhl's clinical experience thus led him to rethink the variations in solidarity between humans and other animals in the face of mutations in pathogens, but it also lead him to politically engage in the protection of workers exposed to these diseases. In an article published in November 1940, Marcel Lévy-Bruhl reported the first case of fatal pyobacillosis in a sixty-four-year-old shepherd treated at the Hôtel-Dieu hospital, noting that this disease, common in cattle, goats, sheep, and pigs, had never been observed in humans. He concluded his article with the following statement: "The occupational origin of this disease can hardly be doubted" (M. Lévy-Bruhl 1940). Such an expert judgment may have served to support the right of the shepherd's widow to compensation for a work-related injury.

Marcel Lévy-Bruhl took from Nicolle the idea of a solidarity not only among humans but among all living beings in the face of a disease that reveals, through the mutations of pathogens, the similarities and differences between species. However, Nicolle himself borrowed from Lucien Lévy-Bruhl the idea that human intelligence can access biological causality if it makes an effort to imagine the logic of life without projecting on it the logic of intelligence. Nicolle thus justified the Pasteurian research with sheep, cows, and lice in the colonies of North Africa: diseases bring humans and animals back to a "primitive" state where they are all "brothers."

> The knowledge of infectious diseases teaches men fraternity and solidarity. We are brothers because the same danger threatens us and we are in solidarity because the contagion comes to us most often from our fellow men. From this point of view and regardless of our feelings towards them, we are also in solidarity with animals, especially domestic animals. (Nicolle 1930: 13)

> Whatever problems our minds tackle, the surest weapon we possess to force them is reasoning, logic. It is the awareness of the value of such an instrument and its practice that have made civilized man and that distinguish us from primitive or uncultivated people. ... We are astonished to note, with Lévy-Brühl [sic], that peoples have ignored

this discipline and that, among the non-civilized, effect and cause do not appear linked together, one resulting from the other. ... How many errors we commit when we seek this intelligence where it is not and, first of all, in our primitive brothers, the animals, whom we consider intellectual brothers without inquiring whether their senses inform them as ours do, if they do not have others that we ignore. (Nicolle 1930: 34)

For Nicolle, the logical imagination should be combined with the experimental method to follow the mutations of microbes in animal reservoirs. As these mutations are unpredictable, it was necessary, in his view, to prepare for them as for bacteriological warfare or a gas attack. While Nicolle argued that microbiology served peace rather than war and considered the occurrence of a microbial attack unlikely, he used the microbiological imagination as a strategic tool to anticipate these unpredictable events. Nicolle thus brought together the two threats that emerged during the world conflict.

Let us not conclude that microbial warfare is impossible. Under certain conditions, it could, perhaps, create a few epidemic outbreaks, but these would be quickly stopped. The task would be more difficult in the case of the transmission of certain contagious diseases to animals and this could cause serious damage to supplies. Perhaps this was tried during the last war? But all in all, next to artillery and gas, this work would be of little importance! (Nicolle 1930: 159)

Historians have showed that the industrialization of war led to the emergence of new diseases among humans who gathered in the trenches, such as pandemic influenza and chemical poisoning. Some even assume that the use of gas as a chemical weapon was a factor in the weakening of the respiratory tract and the transmission of the so-called "Spanish flu" (Crosby 1989; Webster 2018). Lucien Lévy-Bruhl's third son, Jean, a chemical engineer, was both a victim of this new weapon, gas, and a researcher on it. Poisoned at Verdun on June 24, 1916, while serving as a lieutenant, he was sent to Salonika in October 1917 to participate in a course on the military use of gas, in order to train the French soldiers on the eastern front who had not yet been exposed to it.[2] At the end of the

---

2. Daniel Lévy-Bruhl personal collection, Letters from Jean Lévy-Bruhl to his military superiors dated 1917 and 1941.

war, he took courses at the Pasteur Institute; there, his brother Marcel introduced him to Odette Dreyfus-Sée,[3] who was also studying chemistry. Jean and Odette married in 1921 according to the rabbinic rite and afterwards Jean wrote a letter to thank his father for this departure from his principle of secularism. This letter reveals that Lucien Lévy-Bruhl had moved from taking distance from Judaism to actively rejecting it after the debate on the secularization of morality and religion.[4] Jean founded a chemical company that prospered between the wars selling ambrelite, a product extracted from resins and used in the manufacture of objects of ordinary modern life.

Jean Lévy-Bruhl thus took part in the military effort to prepare for a gas attack by Germany. The novelty and effectiveness of this new weapon, developed by German scientists, worried the French military authorities during the interwar period (Lepick 1998). In December 1930, rumors reached Maurice Halbwachs, who was then a visiting scholar in Chicago, about clouds of gas afflicting the population in Belgium and being blown towards Paris. "Why are you not close to me, far from this Europe where miasmas and wars still linger?" wrote the sociologist to his wife who had remained in France (Halbwachs 2012: 197). Indeed, in France, toxic pollutants were considered more a problem of public hygiene than of environmental health and the hygienists did not distinguish clearly between the "miasmas" of natural origin and the pollution caused by industry (Murard and Zylberman 1996; Sellers 1997; Bourdelais 2001). The philosopher Michel Alexandre, who was Halbwachs's brother-in-law, reported that twenty-three workers at the Lyon slaughterhouses were punished in November 1933 for refusing to take part in a gas attack simulation exercise in which they were expected to escape to shelters wearing masks and in the dark. As this military exercise had been organized by the mayor of Lyon, Edouard Herriot, Alexandre called for the mayor to be excluded from the League of Human Rights for this breach of pacifism (Zimmer 2016: 203).

While his sons Marcel and Jean prepared for new epidemics and gas attacks, Lucien Lévy-Bruhl reflected on contagion in his work on "primitive mentality." The last chapter of his 1922 book, which appeared in prepublication on December 25, 1921, in the *Revue de Paris* under

3. Odette Dreyfus-Sée had no relation to Alfred Dreyfus. Her grandfather was Léopold Sée, the first French Jew to reach the rank of general in the French army.
4. Viviane Lévy-Bruhl personal collection, Letter from Jean Lévy-Bruhl to Lucien Lévy-Bruhl, 1921.

the title "La mentalité primitive et les médecins européens" (Primitive mentality and European physicians), underlined the misunderstandings caused by French public health policy when it was applied in the colonies. Lévy-Bruhl quoted the observation of Reverend Father Trilles in the French Congo. The therapeutic situation, Trilles explained, implies mutual gifts: the patient offers his body for observation to the doctor who provides treatment.

> Many times, Europeans have been surprised and scandalized to see the natives they had treated not being being grateful to them for this but asking them for payment. The doctor, with our European and Christian ideas, is rightly shocked to see his devotion, almost always disinterested, thus disregarded; the patient, for his part, is also right: he believes that he was, in the circumstances, a simple subject of experimentation. (Lévy-Bruhl 1922: 494)

In *L'âme primitive* (Primitive soul), published in 1927, Lévy-Bruhl analyzed the beliefs reported by observers according to which "death is felt as contagious," asserting that the members of the family of the deceased "participated" in his or her spirit, which connected them in a mystical way. Lévy-Bruhl thus showed that what the colonial physician explained as the action of microbes was perceived by his patients as the intervention of mystical forces:

> The primitive, however, does not think of contagion as we do. He has no idea of the pathogens that produce infection, nor of the way in which contact can communicate it. He believes—one might as well say, he feels—that death is contagious, for reasons both physical and mystical, inseparable in his mind. The contact of the corpse makes "impure" those who touch it, who make its funeral toilet, who transport it, who bury it. Men and women who have taken a more or less active part in the funeral rites and who have undergone this contact must go through a series of purifications—we would say disinfection. However, the most formidable danger of contagion lies not in this impurity, a stain often easy to remove by the appropriate rites, but in the dead man himself, who exerts an attraction on his own. (Lévy-Bruhl 1927: 275–76)

Lévy-Bruhl's work on "primitive mentality" thus analyzed the system of "mystical" obligations in which the doctor unknowingly entered with a therapeutic gesture that he conceived as mechanical. Since the work of

Villermé on the spread of cholera in cities and of Tarde on the contagion of crime, this kind of analysis of the collective reaction to public health measures had come under the heading of "moral statistics"; but it had not yet taken the scientific form of an "epidemiology." At the time when the first accidents in vaccination campaigns in France were reported (Bonah 2007), Lévy-Bruhl emphasized that the patients to be enrolled in these campaigns should not be considered only as objects of experimentation but should be respected as social subjects.

These three fields of phenomena—divination, ordeal, and public health—radically separate the analyses that Lévy-Bruhl made in 1910 concerning dreams, memory, and numeration from his works following *La mentalité primitive* in 1922, where the question of contagion and infection became central. In 1932, Bergson misunderstood this when he wrote that the author of the works on "primitive mentality" had missed the meaning of human action in situations of uncertainty. To understand the gap between the political diagnoses of Lévy-Bruhl and Bergson on what uncertainty meant in the interwar period, we can analyze what they said of the president of the US. Woodrow Wilson fascinated them equally because he embodied the ideal of international justice at the end of the war. Bergson made a diplomatic mission in 1917 to convince Wilson to enter the European conflict and this mission played an important role in the genealogy of his analysis of "mystical heroes" fifteen years later (Soulez and Worms 1997). That same year, Lévy-Bruhl wrote four articles in *L'Humanité* in which he argued that the American president was pursuing the same goals as the French socialists:

> The entry of America into the conflict, with disinterested disposi-
> tions so continuous with the noblest French traditions, completes the
> picture of the present war: it is the war of democracies united against
> autocratic imperialism. It is no longer possible to doubt that the ideas
> expressed by Mr. Wilson have the full approval of the American peo-
> ple. ... The consciousness of the civilized world proclaims, through
> the voice of America, that the cause of the Allies is merged with the
> cause of justice and humanity. (Lévy-Bruhl 1917c)
> It will be the eternal honor of President Wilson to have put forward
> the League of Nations and of the United States to have entered the
> war to realize it. This ideal is also that of the people of France. (Lévy-
> Bruhl 1917d; see also Lévy-Bruhl 1917e, 1918b)

These statements, whose emphatic tone was appropriate for wartime propaganda literature, are striking today for their lack of foresight.

Neither the US nor the Soviet Union would join the League of Nations, whose principles Wilson defined in his January 1918 speech. When Wilson arrived at the Versailles Conference in January 1919, he was stricken with influenza and unable to defend his principles against the political realism of Clemenceau and Lloyd George (Crosby 1989). On his return, the American Congress refused to ratify the Treaty of Versailles and voted for an intervention against Bolshevik Russia.

In the years following Wilson's failure, Bergson became involved in the League of Nations, chairing the International Commission on Intellectual Cooperation, a forerunner of UNESCO. He thus responded to Wilson's appeal in the field of education. Lucien Lévy-Bruhl instead supported Albert Thomas, who directed the International Labour Office from 1920 until his death in 1932, because this organization seemed to him to fulfill Jean Jaurès's political vision: the participation of workers in the world war should be followed by an improvement in their working conditions. This divergence of orientation in international politics between Bergson and Lévy-Bruhl makes it possible to formulate a hypothesis on their diagnoses of Wilson's program. For Bergson, Wilson was part of a theological history of justice, because he inserted transcendence into immanence, or openness into enclosure, whereas for Lévy-Bruhl, Wilson's failure was an accident in the history of industrial societies that could be illuminated by comparison with the ethnology of "primitive societies."

One could, then, generalize Lévy-Bruhl's thesis to measure its scope: all events carry an apparently transcendent meaning that can be described, through the distant gaze of ethnology, as accidents that give rise to mystical phenomena of participation, because they mobilize invisible entities and collective representations in order to stabilize their uncertainty. Does not the Dreyfus Affair itself appear in retrospect as an accident—the random encounter between a document written by a traitor and a slightly overambitious Jewish captain, which gave rise to the constitution of a party of intellectuals? Wilson's failure can, indeed, be interpreted either as an accident of history or as an ordeal (Freud and Bullit 1966). If the mystical hero is interrupted in his impetus to invent new norms of justice by a flu virus, how is it possible to reorganize an international policy that prepares industrial societies for new threats? Lévy-Bruhl's reflection on industrial accidents through the detour of "primitive mentality" led him to set up a policy of vigilance in a world transformed by the war and the first signs of decolonization. The gap between Dreyfus and Wilson thus distinguishes the sentinel from the

whistleblower: the former outlines new forms of justice from within colonial violence whereas the latter formulates it in an emancipatory way
that can lead to its failure due to the multiplication of threats. A politics
of vigilance based on the observation of sentinels allowed Lévy-Bruhl to
be attentive to this diversity of threats in a changing world.

CHAPTER 7

Colonial Sentinels

After the war, Lévy-Bruhl made a series of trips that marked a new inflection in his ethnological thinking. On his return from one of these trips, he gave a lecture at the Sorbonne in 1921 entitled "Le tour du monde d'un universitaire" (A scholar travels around the world) in which he talked about the global character of the war that had drawn into the conflict first the African colonies, then the Asian empires and, finally, the US. In an article published in 1917 under the title "The new aspects of war," Lévy-Bruhl wrote: "The conflagration, now universal, covers both hemispheres. May the peace that will end it found a universal League of Nations, too, and make a single body of all civilized humanity, animated by the same spirit of justice" (Lévy-Bruhl 1917b: 141).

Travels for the Alliance Française in East Asia and South America

While he participated in the establishment of the International Labour Office, directed by Albert Thomas in Geneva under the framework of the League of Nations created by the Treaty of Versailles, Lévy-Bruhl organized his travels within another framework, as he became vice-president of the Alliance française in 1914. Founded in 1883 by Paul Bert to "propagate the French language in the colonies, the protectorate countries, and abroad" (Chaubet 2006), the Alliance française brought together academics, diplomats, and colonial officials to organize the network of French citizens living abroad. Based in Paris with the status of an association, it linked a set of foreign committees under local law and endowed with their own sources of financing. Jaurès had supported this creation in 1884 in Albi in a speech that carried a clear colonial tone:

> A few very simple notions of French language and history, of trade, of a somewhat vague Christianity is all that can be introduced into these minds and there is nothing to be confused about: these people are children. As for the French living in the colonies, in spite of their attachment to France, they cannot have the same preoccupations as we do. Their life is not the same as ours: it is more primitive, more exterior, less concerned by speculative problems. The Alliance is right to think above all about the diffusion of our language: our colonies will only be French in their intelligence and in their heart when they understand a little French. For France, language is the necessary instrument of colonization. (Jaurès 2009: 443)

After the death of Jaurès, Lévy-Bruhl organized with Albert Meillet, professor of comparative grammar at the Collège de France, the publication of ninety-five issues of the *Bulletin de l'Alliance française* between November 1914 and the summer of 1919, in order to tell "the whole truth about the causes of this war, about France's will to avoid it, about the methods of our enemies, about the suffering of the innocent populations of France and Belgium, about the attacks on the most respected wonders of human art" (Hertz 2002: 112). When traveling around the world after the war to open offices of the Alliance française in countries where it was not yet represented, Lévy-Bruhl's mission was not only to contribute to the spread of the French language but also to explain why France had entered the conflict under the Jaurésian ideal of a war for justice. He defended the French language as an alternative to other imperial languages (English or German) because it was supposed to carry more peaceful and universalist ideas.

Lévy-Bruhl's first trip after the war was organized with the intention of opening an office of the Alliance française in Manila, the capital of the Philippines. A letter he received from the French vice-consul in Manila explained it in the following way:

> There are the elements necessary to ensure the success of an office of the Alliance française in the American and Spanish colonies and among the Filipinos. The difficulties will come from the French

community, too small and divided. We can, however, count on the financial support of one person and the activity of two or three others. A good building and a beautiful library would be very important factors and for books we rely heavily on Paris.[1]

One may wonder why Lévy-Bruhl chose to go to the Philippines, which was not part of the French zone of influence. This mission was inscribed in a longer journey that led him, first, to Harvard, Beijing, and Tokyo, and, after Manila, to Saigon and Jakarta. Manila was, therefore, a stop in a world tour, but it was where he stayed the longest, between February 6 and 27, 1920.

A note dated November 18, 1919, provides a context for this mission. During his stay at Harvard, where he was invited to lecture on moral philosophy, Lévy-Bruhl met William Cameron Forbes, who had been governor general of the Philippines between 1910 and 1913. The US had colonized the Philippines in 1898 as a result of the war against Spain in Cuba, because the conquest of Manila provided them with a gateway to the China Sea and a training ground to practice the military techniques they used against Native Americans. In fact, the war to conquer the Philippines was especially violent because the US army was up against a pro-independence elite trained at Spanish universities. If the US army used techniques of repression that had been employed in the "pacification" of the American West, it also invented techniques of torture to force well-organized and often educated enemies to talk. The US strategy was to ally itself with the indigenous populations (called Negritos) against the Christianized mestizo elites of Luzon Island (called Filipinos) and the Muslim royalty of Mindanao Island (called Moros). This strategy of division, carried out through public health campaigns and the construction of infrastructure, aimed at rallying the Negritos and Moros against the Filipinos. The territory of the Philippines was, thus, considered by the American governors as their outpost in the control of infectious diseases in Asia, notably plague, smallpox, and cholera, and also as an alternative colonial model to that of the British and the Dutch in the same region. Dean Worcester, the Philippine secretary of the interior between 1900 and 1913, thus pledged his colonial policy as a model: "Never before in the history of the world has a powerful nation assumed toward a weaker

---

1.   IMEC, Lévy-Bruhl papers, Letter from Henri Aymé Martin to Lucien Lévy-Bruhl, February 26, 1920.

nation an attitude like the one we have adopted toward the Philippines"
(Worcester 1914: 931).

Lévy-Bruhl knew the Philippine independence movement through
Jean Jaurès who was attentive to its meaning. Jaurès had published in
L'Humanité reports written by the journalist Henri Turot, who had
stayed in the Philippines in the aftermath of the Spanish-American
War. These reports presented positively the political project of Emilio
Aguinaldo, who was then leading the provisional government ignored
by the US. In his preface to these reports, Jaurès wrote:

> There is not a man in the world who is conscious of the rights of hu-
> manity and does not wish that the United States would not abuse its
> power. They can make amends for many things by providing the Fili-
> pinos with a regime of civil liberty and political freedom, by develop-
> ing among them education, science, economic activity. Will blind and
> selfish capitalism allow it? (Jaurès 1900: xi)

Jaurès declared that mankind was interested in the cause of the Philippines because this cause had found a particularly strong literary expression through the writings of José Rizal, considered today the precursor
of other revolutionary figures in Asia (B. Anderson 2007; Harper 2020).
Educated at the Jesuit University of Manila, Rizal traveled to Europe
and Cuba, where he frequented anarchist and socialist circles, before returning to the Philippines in 1896, where he was executed by the Spanish government. If Jaurès often criticized Aguinaldo for his naive trust
in the American government and his dictatorial tendencies, he always
praised Rizal for launching the independence movement through his
sacrifice: "The life and death of Rizal leave in the souls a kind of sacred
shiver" (Jaurès 1900: ix). In the eyes of Jaurès, Rizal was, like Dreyfus, a
victim of a clerical and military power that oppressed individuals in the
name of racial difference. Since Rizal's works *Noli Me Tángere!* (Rizal
1887) and *El Filibusterismo* (Rizal 1891) were circulating in Europe in
socialist circles at the beginning of the twentieth century, we can assume
that Lévy-Bruhl was familiar with these works, even if he does not quote
them; indeed, they report Filipino myths very similar to those Lévy-
Bruhl analyzes in his books on "primitive mentality." Rizal wrote in *El
Filibusterismo*:

> It seems that formerly the river, as well as the lake, was infested
> with caymans, so huge and voracious that they attacked pirogues

and upset them with a slap of their tail. Our chronicles relate that one day an infidel Chinaman, who up to that time had refused to be converted, was passing in front of the church, when suddenly the devil presented himself to him in the form of a cayman and upset the pirogues, in order to devour him and carry him off to hell. Inspired by God, the Chinaman at that moment called upon St. Nicholas and instantly the cayman was changed into a stone. (Rizal 1891 [1912: 26])

In Rizal's anticlerical view of the Philippines, the beliefs of indigenous people about the active presence of invisible spirits were intertwined with those of the Malay and Chinese traders and the Spanish colonizers. This justified his call for the enlightened minds of the world to fight against the colonizers. The Filipino independence movement claimed Rizal as its advocate for the right of mestizo elites to self-government and for the education of the people to achieve a form of Asian enlightenment. Thus, physician Pardo de Tavera, a member of the Manila Public Health Office, criticized his fellow citizens "infected with the leprosy of superstition" and encouraged them to attain "a regime of freedom, industry, labor and logical mentality" (W. Anderson 2006: 186).

Lévy-Bruhl's mission in the Philippines led him to question this evolutionary framework from a "prelogical" mentality to the "logical" mentality, which he had contributed to spread with his 1910 book. While the elites of the colonized societies could claim they were governed by the colonizer's "mentality" in a way that made them seek autonomy and independence, the "primitive" societies were increasingly described by the colonial authorities as governed by norms that were radically different from those of Europe or the US, so as to maintain them in a state of subjugation (Conklin 1997). This insight is what Lévy-Bruhl retained from his conversation with Cameron Forbes. As a former governor of the Philippines, Forbes was part of a commission in 1921 that concluded that it was impossible for the US to grant independence to the Philippines. While power had gradually been handed over to the Filipino elites since 1913, in the eyes of the American colonizer, they had not managed to maintain roads or control disease and corrupt officials had squandered public money. Lévy-Bruhl wrote in his notes: "The native municipalities (numbering about eight hundred) no longer feel supervised by independent American inspectors; abuses occur, and complaints, once seriously investigated, now remain without effect if the abuser is influential" (Lévy-Bruhl 1919b).

In the US, ethnology, which until then had studied people from North America or Africa, found in the Philippines a figure of the "primitive" which broadened its field of scientific investigation. At the 1904 St. Louis World's Fair, the presentation of the indigenous people of the Philippines was a subject of contention between President Roosevelt, who wanted to show civilized or civilizable subjects to justify colonization, and American anthropologists, who emphasized the otherness of these colonial subjects (Baker 1998: 71). A compromise was found by presenting, side by side, Negritos and Igorots from the island of Luzon, the latter being described as lighter-skinned and more intelligent. Henry Otley Beyer "discovered" the populations of the Philippines during this exhibition. After studying anthropology at Harvard, he was appointed as ethnologist at the Manila Science Office and then, in 1914, as professor of anthropology at the University of the Philippines (Zamora 1967). He invited Lévy-Bruhl to Manila in February 1920 and accompanied him on his expeditions to the island of Luzon, first among the Negritos, then among the Igorots. Lévy-Bruhl transcribed a conversation he had with Otley Beyer in his notes:

> From the ethnographic point of view, the Filipinos are furious about the importance given to the "savages" with whom the mass of opinion easily confuses them. [They] protested violently against the exhibition of Negritos in St. Louis if they were taken for inhabitants of the Philippines. In Manila [they] destroyed the photographs of the natives. [It was a] very beautiful collection of which a copy fortunately is in the museum of Harvard. The question is whether they will let the Bureau of Science continue the ethnographic work. (Lévy-Bruhl 1919b)

Lévy-Bruhl bought more than two hundred anthropological photographs of the Philippines, probably through Otley Beyer. On his return, he gave them to the Musée d'Ethnographie du Trocadéro in 1924, from where they joined the Fonds Lévy-Bruhl, first at the Musée de l'Homme and then at the Musée du quai Branly, where they are kept today. With the captions "Negrito," "Igorot," "Ifugao," "Mangyan," "Tinguian," and, in some cases, the names of the individuals represented, these photos are always in pairs, front and side, according to the anthropometric method applied in France to criminals; but the people represented do not look captive under the photographic device and the quality of the images is good. This collection also contains about a hundred objects from the

Philippines, particularly weapons (arrows and clubs), as well as an album containing photographs of the Philippines and Indonesia, an image of Lévy-Bruhl in front of the Great Wall in China, and around ten images of Lévy-Bruhl among the "Negritos."

It is surprising that Lévy-Bruhl never mentions the Philippine societies or Otley Beyer's work in his books on "primitive mentality," although this encounter seems to have made a great impression on him. However, the last chapter of *La mentalité primitive* on "Primitive mentality and European physicians," prepublished upon his return from his mission, implicitly attested to his discussions with Cameron Forbes and Otley Beyer. The development of public health by American physicians, supported by local elites, indeed produced numerous conflicts with the indigenous populations. Measures such as vaccinations, quarantines, and changes in hygiene and diet were justified by health authorities in the name of strengthening the population against climate-related diseases, but they conflicted with indigenous systems of explaining disease (W. Anderson 2006: 69).

In many ways, then, the Philippines as seen by Lévy-Bruhl in February 1920 can be considered a sentinel: a vanguard of the contestation of colonialism in Asia, because of the long-standing presence of Spain, and of an independence movement inspired by international socialism; but also an outpost of disease control, because of the American government's significant investment in public health. For these two reasons, Lévy-Bruhl accepted the invitation of Cameron Forbes and Otley Beyer to visit the indigenous societies of the Philippines, although he brought back only a few photographs and objects rather than ethnological data that he could publish in his books. The discussions in the federal capital of Washington about the possibility of granting independence to the Philippines were, indeed, closely followed by the diplomatic authorities in Paris, because the proclamation of independence by the Filipinos would have shaken the entire Asian balance and, potentially, led to the independence of Indochina. Therefore, it was important to Lévy-Bruhl, echoing the efforts of Minister of the Colonies Albert Sarraut, former governor of Indochina, to understand the motivations of the independence movement and the constraints that could slow it down. Lévy-Bruhl saw the creation of scientific ethnology as a way of highlighting the value of the local populations against both the colonial authorities and the Filipino elites.

On his return, Lévy-Bruhl drew lessons from this mission in an article he published anonymously in the *Revue de Paris* under the title

"L'ébranlement du monde jaune" (The shaking of the yellow world). While Western powers remained focused on the resolution of the world conflict in Europe, Lévy-Bruhl encouraged them to look to the Far East to "measure the strength of the ideas propagated there and the feelings of the crowds" (Lévy-Bruhl 1920: 871). Because Japan had recovered the German colonies in China at the Congress of Versailles, Lévy-Bruhl compared the position of Japan in Asia to that of Prussia in Germany and he predicted the unification of the "yellow race" by the military power that had defeated Russia in 1905. To this threat he added that of Soviet Bolshevism, which he described as *socialismus asiaticus* because it contained elements "foreign to the European mentality." Lévy-Bruhl thus observed the rise of egalitarian movements operating through strikes and attacks in Java, the Philippines, and Indochina with skepticism: for him, the natives "understand more or less well the principles on which the demands are based" (Lévy-Bruhl 1920: 881). Hence the need for instruction, which he strongly affirmed at the end of his article, to provide a period of transition to independence. Defined here as the teaching of scientific culture, instruction did not include principles of moral, social, or religious life, which for him were framed by "civilization." France, according to Lévy-Bruhl, recovered its role as a universal nation ahead of Japan since the latter instrumentalized scientific culture in order to expand its power. Thus, Lévy-Bruhl justified the series of lectures he gave in Beijing by the need to bring the principles of the European Enlightenment and of French rationalism to those Chinese students who demonstrated against the Treaty of Versailles and the Japanese occupation after May 4, 1919.

In this respect, Lévy-Bruhl's trip to Asia can be compared to those of John Dewey and Bertrand Russell, who arrived, like he did, in Beijing in the wake of the May 4 movement, to teach a new generation of Chinese thinkers fascinated by Western intellectuals. While John Dewey, invited for several months by the philosopher Hu Shi, found in the Chinese thought of nonaction the ferments of democratization that he described in an article entitled "As the Chinese Think" (Wang 2007), Bertrand Russell, invited by the reformist thinker Liang Qichao, wrote in *The Problem of China* that China needed a Western scientific education (Argon 2015). Lévy-Bruhl's position was closer to that of the pragmatist philosopher than to that of the analytic philosopher; but because he did not spend as much time in China as Dewey, it could only be based on quick observations. By contrast with Dewey, who valued forms of collective action from an inside understanding of Chinese thought, and Russell, who analyzed the structures of the individual mind from a distanced observation of the problems of Chinese society, Lévy-Bruhl highlighted the dynamics of imitation and contagion that occurred throughout the Asian continent.

Lévy-Bruhl's trip to Asia in 1919–20 was followed by a trip to South America in 1922, which led him successively to Brazil, Paraguay, Bolivia, Argentina, Peru, and Chile. Lévy-Bruhl attended the International Congress of Americanists in Rio de Janeiro from August 20 to 30, on the occasion of the one-hundredth anniversary of Brazil's independence, gave lectures on French sociology, and met with members of socialist parties to discuss with them the role of the International Labour Office. But the decisive event during this trip was his meeting with General Cândido Rondon, who founded and directed the Indian Protection Service of Brazil (now called the National Indigenous People Foundation) from 1910.[2] Born to a Portuguese father and a Bororo mother in Mato Grosso in 1865, Rondon entered the Military School of Rio de Janeiro and was among the officers who overthrew the imperial regime of Pedro II in 1889. The government of the Republic of Brazil sent him to Mato Grosso to make peace both with the border states (Bolivia and Paraguay) and with the indigenous tribes. Following the teaching of the Positivist Church of Brazil, which he joined in 1898, and in accordance with the anti-colonial orientation of its director, Teixeira Mendes, Rondon wanted to substitute trade for war to constitute a humanity enlightened by scientific principles of development. He is known for "pacifying" the Nambikwara, an indigenous tribe feared by adventurers set on exploiting the abundant resources of the region, particularly wood and rubber. His army built a telegraph line connecting Rio to the Amazon, crossing a state that today bears his name, Rondonia. Rondon's policy of protecting indigenous populations and helping them access land was opposed to the policy of extermination then advocated by Hermann von Ihering, the director of the Museum of Ethnology of Sao Paulo (Museu Paulista). Today Brazilian historians and anthropologists often critique Rondon's policy as one of assimilation aimed at transforming rebellious hunter-gatherers into farmers subjected to the Brazilian state within the

---

2. A letter from General Rondon dated February 19, 1923, allows us to date this trip. In it General Rondon expresses his thanks for a letter Lévy-Bruhl sent him from Buenos Aires on October 22, 1922, and wishes him a good trip to Peru and Bolivia. Rondon promised Lévy-Bruhl to visit the sites of positivism in Paris, but he never made the trip.

framework of its deforestation policy (Diacon 2004). If, in his letters to his wife Alice, Lévy-Bruhl borrowed the paternalistic terms for which Rondon is reproached today, it may be that he distanced himself from them with humor:

> He inaugurated a completely new policy toward them. Instead of waging a war of extermination against them, of hunting them down, of destroying the tribes that had responded to the encroachments of the whites with assassinations or massacres, he made it a rule never to shoot at the Indians—big, irresponsible children—and to return good for evil. Even when attacked by them with arrows, he did not retaliate; on the contrary, he left, at the place of the encounter, objects that could seduce them: iron, axes, provisions, etc. After a while, the Indians' distrust disappeared, their hostility turned into affection, and General Rondon found in them faithful companions. Thus he lived for six months with 500 Bororo (men, women, and children) who followed him to a certain point in the forest. His principle is to let the Indians live as they please, without enslaving them or forcing them to work, but educating them little by little, teaching them to cultivate the land, to look after the livestock, giving them schools where they learn to read, write, count, etc., and, finally, civilizing them little by little without violence. He obtained, by this means, remarkable successes and he formed a corps of officers capable of continuing his work.[3]

Lévy-Bruhl met Rondon in Sao Paulo on September 10, 1922. A French photographer from the Havas agency took a photograph of the professor and the officer. Rondon was famous for traveling, in 1914, with the US president Theodore Roosevelt to explore the river that today bears the president's name, located in the north of Mato Grosso. Lévy-Bruhl dined with "the French colony of Sao Paulo," which he described as "strongly Semitic. They are good people, very devoted to France, and, a rare thing, united among themselves."[4] The next day he and Rondon took the train to Corumba in the south of Mato Grosso, on the border with Bolivia and Paraguay. For six days he traveled by boat and train with Rondon and marveled at the landscape: plains, coffee plantations, bush,

---

3. Daniel Lévy-Bruhl personal collection, Letter from Lucien Lévy-Bruhl to Alice Lévy-Bruhl, Asuncion, September 20, 1922.

4. Daniel Lévy-Bruhl personal collection, Letter from Lucien Lévy-Bruhl to Alice Lévy-Bruhl, Asuncion, September 20, 1922.

mountains. He saw an "arara" parrot, a bird he had mentioned in his 1910 book, quoting the ethnologist Von den Steinen who had traveled in the region thirty years earlier, but also ostriches, parakeets, and deer. On the last day he met with indigenous societies who had been connected to the outside world by the construction of the telegraph line: Terinas, Guayacurus, and Terenas. Lévy-Bruhl commented on the scene thus:

> Needless to say, these quick visits did not teach me anything at all—no more than the Negritos of the Philippines or the Moïs of Indochina: it is a satisfaction of pure curiosity and still, as in the Philippines, we were only shown the Indians wearing clothes that did not fit them very well. The most interesting thing was the attitude of General Rondon in the presence of the Indians and that of the Indians towards him. He was paternal, kind, caressing the children, chatting with the men in their language, with the air of a big brother and a natural protector. They crowded around him, with all the signs of the most lively affection, familiar with respect, happy to be recognized personally by him, having eyes only for him, visibly ready to do whatever he would wish of them.[5]

On his return, Lévy-Bruhl wrote a letter to Bronislaw Malinowski, who is considered the founder of long-term ethnography in the UK because he stayed in the Trobriand Islands for two years during the First World War, after having traveled along the great oceanic expeditions of Haddon and Seligman, and subsequently published his masterpiece, *Argonauts of the Western Pacific* (Malinowski 1922; Kuper 1973). Contrasting himself to Malinowski, Lévy-Bruhl acknowledged that his ethnographic experience was short:

> I, indeed, saw natives in the state of Mato Grosso in Brazil (in the company of the General Rondon) on the edges of the High-Paraguay, in the region of Chaco and on the edges of Bolivia. Unfortunately, I only saw them. I passed too quickly for a study to be possible—especially given my ignorance of the language. … It is no longer completely useless to have seen the people with one's own eyes and to have realized the environment in which they live.[6]

5.   Daniel Lévy-Bruhl personal collection, Letter from Lucien to Alice Lévy-Bruhl, Asuncion, September 20, 1922.

6.   Bronislaw Malinowski papers, Yale University, Letter from Lucien Lévy-Bruhl to Bronislaw Malinowski, July 3, 1923.

How did Lévy-Bruhl's trips to East Asia and South America in the early 1920s determine the direction he prescribed in ethnology within the French colonial empire? In what ways did the philosopher of responsibility reach an understanding of the societies he described under the term "primitive mentality"? Probably because the letters that Lévy-Bruhl sent during these journeys share intimate convictions and not public arguments, they give an ambivalent feeling about his position toward the societies he observed. If he criticized the violence of American colonization, he also took up its prejudices about the corruption of the officials and the beliefs of the Negritos. If he praised a mestizo general, he also seemed to take up his paternalistic view of the Amazonian societies. This ambivalence may be explained by the long intimate reflection he had on the Dreyfus Affair as a trial of colonial violence and on the emergence of new accidents during and after the war, as both profoundly shook the positivistic schema of *émancipation* by the French civilization in which he had been raised. It also sheds light on the broad political spectrum of those who read the author of *La mentalité primitive* during the interwar period.

Supporting Ethnology in the Colonial Context (Africa, Indochina, New Caledonia)

In the letter quoted earlier, Lévy-Bruhl did not reject the method of participant observation taught by Malinowski at the London School of Economics as "useless"; but, in light of his own age and training, he thought it more reasonable to rely on mediators like Otley Beyer or Rondon. Edward Evans-Pritchard, considered the second founder of British ethnography, recognized the philosophical effort Lévy-Bruhl prescribed to set aside his prejudices in order to enter into other habits of mind. Evans-Pritchard was opposed to the evolutionary anthropology of E. B. Tylor and James Frazer, which Lévy-Bruhl and Durkheim had radically criticized (Kuper 1973). In 1934, the young Evans-Pritchard visited Lévy-Bruhl in Paris after delivering a paper on the theory of "primitive mentality" at a conference in Cairo (Evans-Pritchard 1965). He found in Lévy-Bruhl a form of reflexivity that he thought was lacking in Malinowski's empiricist ethnography. In Evans-Pritchard's view, ethnographic participation implied not only "taking part" in the ordinary life of individuals but also understanding the gap between the values of indigenous societies, based on ritual sacrifice, and those of colonial societies, based on administrative writing. Writing, according to Evans-Pritchard, imposed quests for totalization on forms of collective action that should remain partial and fragmentary to function, such as witchcraft, oracles, and magic (Evans-Pritchard 1937). That is the reason for Evans-Pritchard's interest in Lévy-Bruhl's distinction between "mystical" first causality and "ordinary" second causality and in the philosopher's statement that "primitive mentality ignores chance." Evans-Pritchard even confirmed Lévy-Bruhl's attention to contradictory statements when he noted that, for the Nuer living on the Nile, "twins are birds" (Evans-Pritchard 1940). This may explain why Evans-Pritchard asked Lévy-Bruhl for a letter of support for his application to the Department of Anthropology at Oxford, where he was finally appointed in 1946. In a letter to Lévy-Bruhl from Sudan, where he was conducting research on witchcraft and divination in 1935, Evans-Pritchard wrote:

> You have not touched this delicate subject: the ethics of ethnological fieldwork. If you read carefully the work of professional anthropologists like Malinowski, you will not get a picture of native life and thought except through his glasses—which are tainted and do not fit all eyes.[7]

This reflection on the ethnographic method launched by Malinowski in 1922 led Lévy-Bruhl to found the Institute of Ethnology in 1925. He did so with Paul Rivet, a physician who specialized in South American societies at the National Museum of Natural History (Laurière 2008: 348), and Marcel Mauss, who taught "the history of religions of non-civilized peoples" at the Practical School of Advanced Studies. Maurice Delafosse played an important role in this institute; after his retirement from the colonial administration in 1919, he took up teaching African languages at the School of Oriental Languages and at the Colonial School (Sibeud 2002; Singaravélou 2011). While Lévy-Bruhl, the dean of the triumvirate, was appointed president of the institute's governing council, Rivet and Mauss were its general secretaries. The aim of the institute was to coordinate the teaching of ethnology at the University of Paris on the model of the chairs of ethnology that existed in a large number of European countries. Lévy-Bruhl justified this creation by the practical needs of the administrators of the colonies, whose decisions

7.   IMEC, Lévy-Bruhl papers, Letter from Edward Evans-Pritchard to Lucien Lévy-Bruhl, April 15, 1935.

were met by the local populations with incomprehension. According to him, ethnology should contribute to the "development" of the colonies because it studied the languages, religions, and social frameworks of the populations in order to better adapt the colonial policies. Lévy-Bruhl thus added mental resources, which should become the object of ethnology, to the natural resources (forests, mines, etc.) and biological resources (populations) of the colonies, which were under the responsibility of engineering and medicine:

> When a colony includes populations of inferior civilization or that are very different from ours, good ethnologists can be as necessary as good engineers, good foresters, or good doctors. ... Everyone recognizes that to achieve a development [*mise en valeur*] of our colonies that is as complete and economical as possible, not only capital is needed. We also need scientists and technicians who will draw up an inventory of their natural resources (mines, forests, crops, etc.) and indicate the best methods of exploitation. But is not the first of these natural resources, the one without which the others can do almost nothing, the indigenous population? Is it not in our interest to study them methodically, to have an exact and thorough knowledge of their languages, their religions, their social frameworks, the thoughtless destruction of which is so very reckless [*qu'il est si imprudent de briser à la légère*]? (Lévy-Bruhl 1925: 2)

It is remarkable that Lévy-Bruhl never went to Africa, even though nearly half of the ethnographic facts he quotes come from that continent. His correspondence with Jules Brévié, lieutenant governor of Niger from 1922 to 1929 and governor general of French West Africa from 1930 to 1936, is instructive in this respect. Brévié was a fervent supporter of a colonial administration based on science: he created the French Institute of Black Africa (Institut Français d'Afrique Noire) in Dakar in 1936 and the Office of Overseas Scientific Research (Office de la recherche scientifique et technique outre-mer) in 1942 when he was minister of overseas France and the colonies in the Vichy government (Bonneuil and Petitjean 1996). After reading *La mentalité primitive*, Brévié wrote to Lévy-Bruhl:

> From now on, the way is open. I do not doubt that the good pioneers of science will follow this path. Proceeding immediately to meticulous and coordinated investigations, and with an infallible criterium, they will soon fill the gap that has weakened this order of research

in the French colonies. I give you the assurance that, as far as the colony I administer is concerned, I will do my utmost to ensure that the most qualified civil servants and officers devote themselves to these fascinating studies before the last vestiges of such an interesting mentality have disappeared or been modified by contact with our rising civilization.[8]

In December 1931, Lévy-Bruhl for the third time canceled a planned trip to Africa, invoking health reasons. Brévié, after expressing his regrets, invited him to reschedule his trip a year later and imagined what it would have been for a "professor at the Sorbonne" to meet the people he was writing about.

Your letter telling me that you were unable to make the trip to West Africa, in which I had placed so much hope, caused me real disappointment. I would have been so happy to see you cross our immense federation to make contact with our races so curious and diverse, some of which have remained so close to nature. Your appreciation, your impressions would have been of unique value to me.[9]

When Brévié was appointed governor general of Indochina between 1936 and 1939, Lévy-Bruhl contacted him to express his concern about the situation of Nguyễn Văn Huyền. Nguyễn, who had arrived in France from Vietnam in 1930, had defended a thesis under Lévy-Bruhl's supervision at the Sorbonne in 1934, where he studied the gender alternance in songs in rural Vietnam, following the model of Granet and Mauss. Nguyễn valorized a popular form of "spirit" which escaped the codified models of Confucianist elites and oriented matrimonial practices. He returned to Vietnam in 1936 and taught at the high school of Hanoi while trying to enter the French School of the Far East (École Française d'Extrême-Orient). He would finally become the first permanent native member of the school in 1941 and the first minister of national education of the Democratic Republic of Vietnam between 1946 and 1975 (Nguyen 2012: 157–94). In the first books he published when he returned to Vietnam, Nguyễn used Lévy-Bruhl's methods to describe how

---

8. IMEC, Lévy-Bruhl papers, Letter from Jules Brévié to Lucien Lévy-Bruhl, October 15, 1923.

9. IMEC, Lévy-Bruhl papers, Letter from Jules Brévié to Lucien Lévy-Bruhl, December 4, 1931.

rural populations used divination and gambling to attenuate the precarity of their social life. He recommended including native conceptions of prevention in a more conscious politics of development, thus combining French republicanism and Chinese Marxism. "Nothing will be done if we do not modify the rural mentality, if we do not prepare generations more aware of their real interests" (Nguyen 1944: 29). The obstacles that Nguyễn encountered to find a place in the colonial education system led Lévy-Bruhl to fear that he would join the independence movement. Brévié's answer to this concern reveals the widening gap between the colonial official, who placed the "primitive mentality" in opposition to the social movement, and the socialist philosopher, who alerted the colonial authorities as early as 1920 to the rise of independence movements.

> Do we not see here, dear Master, an example of the anxiety that is at the bottom of the Asian soul? I am slowly discovering this people; even the best are infinitely enigmatic. Those who complain have received the best share, the petty bourgeois, the workers, more than the peasants. Led by communist leaders with orders from abroad, they have brought the fever of the country, even recently, to a dangerous degree. The mystique of the strike is in all minds. Overwhelmed, the administration finds it difficult to undertake its great task of developing the country, of solving the dreaded problem of hunger, of overpopulation, of conducting, in a word, the human policy that is necessary. Where is my good Africa, so simple, so direct, so frank, and which knew how to be grateful?[10]

We can contrast Brévié's trajectory with that of Léopold Sabatier, a French resident in the province of Darlac, who also maintained a correspondence with Lévy-Bruhl. Born in France in 1877, Sabatier arrived in Indochina in 1903 and spent many years alone in this mountainous province of Laos, administratively attached to Annam, whose language and customs he learned. In 1923, he was appointed governor of the province of Darlac and convinced the administrator of Annam to stop using the pejorative term *moï* to name the populations of his province and rather to adopt *rhadé*, the term by which they designated themselves. In the "Palaver of the oath of Darlac," a text that circulated widely in reformist colonial circles, Sabatier addressed the Rhade chiefs in their own

---

10. IMEC, Lévy-Bruhl papers, Letter from Jules Brévié to Lucien Lévy-Bruhl, September 2, 1937.

language to justify the development of their territory by building roads, sending children to school, and planting coffee. This bold policy attracted the disapproval of the French colonial authorities, who forced him to return to France, where he died in 1931. We can, thus, understand the poignant tone with which he addressed Lévy-Bruhl in a letter of August 12, 1925, which might remind us of the tone that Dreyfus used in his letter from prison. The colonial sentinel requested the philosopher's help to express his feelings when he returned to the "primitive" and collected its signs to improve "civilization." In contrast to the evolutionary model of the education of "our races" that Brévié defended, Sabatier promoted a relativistic model of the protection of "primitive tribes," thus revealing how Lévy-Bruhl's books could be interpreted in radically opposite directions.

> In the isolation of the forest, I opened this book: *La mentalité primitive*. From the introduction to the conclusion, it was for me more than joy but a relief, the end of an anguish. Do you understand me well? Everything you say was a lived experience for me. Your book is the expression of the purest, most luminous truth. I, an obscure administrator, grasped this and said it in vain. But when you speak, as a French scholar, a member of the Institute, a professor at the Sorbonne, one is obliged to believe you. It is necessary that the parts of the high region of the south of Annam, which are inhabited by the most primitive tribes who are untouched by the virus of civilization, become national reserves. All the civil servants who are sent to the high region should read it [your book] and become familiar with it so that the mistakes that destroy a society and kill a people are no longer committed.[11]

Lucien Lévy-Bruhl also cultivated friendly colonial relationships in New Caledonia with the pastor Maurice Leenhardt and the adventurer Georges Baudoux. Born in Montauban in 1883 to a family of Alsatian Protestants, Leenhardt wrote a theology thesis on the Ethiopian movement in southern Africa before going to New Caledonia in 1902 as a missionary, evangelizing and publishing texts on the "Canaques" (today spelt as Kanak) in missionary journals until 1920. He met Lévy-Bruhl in 1921 at the home of his father-in-law, André Michel, curator at the

---

11. IMEC, Lévy-Bruhl papers, Letter from Léopold Sabatier to Lucien Lévy-Bruhl, August 12, 1925.

Louvre, and asked the philosopher to encourage the minister of the colonies to finance his future missionary trips between 1923 and 1926 (Clifford 1982). At the request of Lucien Lévy-Bruhl, Leenhardt published the *Notes d'ethnologie néo-calédonienne* for the Institute of Ethnology in 1930. Lévy-Bruhl wrote to Leenhardt's wife about her husband's first book:

> It is a work of extraordinary interest. I do not know if an ethnological study of comparable value has ever appeared in one of our colonies. I congratulate myself more than ever for encouraging him in this kind of work. He was wonderfully prepared for it. He knows his Canaques thoroughly—their character, their beliefs, their language. All this will be saved for science by the publication of his book.[12]

Leenhardt introduced Lévy-Bruhl to the *Légendes Canaques* published by Georges Baudoux in Caledonian journals, which the philosopher read with admiration and quoted extensively in *La mentalité primitive*. The son of a jail overseer, Baudoux had met Leenhardt during the trial of Kanak rebels in Nouméa in 1917 (Bensa 2015). After making a fortune in mining, he devoted himself to writing poems and stories about his discovery of nature and the Kanaks (O'Reilly 1950). Lévy-Bruhl wrote a preface for *Légendes Canaques* in 1928, warning the reader of their sensationalist character. If the accidents of daily life reveal unpredictable reactions in all societies, wrote Lévy-Bruhl, the astonishment of the observer is even stronger among peoples "who have behind them a thousand-year-old past of which we know nothing and whose civilization has almost nothing in common with ours" (Lévy-Bruhl 1928b: 7). Lévy-Bruhl inscribed this book in the genre of the "colonial novel" and underlined its danger: whereas, for the realistic novel, the reader can discern what is plausible, Lévy-Bruhl said, this is not the case when an author speaks about distant populations, so that "the informed public quickly becomes suspicious of his inventions and disgusted at the exoticism" (Lévy-Bruhl 1928b: 13). According to Lévy-Bruhl, Baudoux escaped these criticisms because "his work as a geologist and prospector provided him with the opportunity to participate in the daily life of tribes that still had few relations with whites," which brought his book

---

12. Archives de la Nouvelle-Calédonie in Nouméa, New Caledonia, Maurice and Raymond Leenhardt papers, Letter from Lucien Lévy-Bruhl to Mrs André Michel, September 29, 1929.

closer to "documentary film" (Lévy-Bruhl 1928b: 13). Just as, according to Lévy-Bruhl, the Caldoches (Caledonians of European descent) "saved the Canaques" by writing about their mentality, one can say that Lévy-Bruhl saved Baudoux from colonial literature by inscribing him into ethnological science with the help of Leenhardt. Lévy-Bruhl's admiration for Baudoux, despite the sensationalist character of his writing, perhaps stems from the parallel between his trajectory and that of Dreyfus, since both experienced "primitive mentality" in the incidents of daily life after their experiences of colonial prisons.

Literary Critiques of the Colonial System

If colonial administrators often read Lévy-Bruhl's books in a paternalistic way, travelers found resources for a critique of the colonial system in his description of the misunderstandings between the administrators and the natives. The gap between science and literature in the reception of Lévy-Bruhl is exemplary of the situation of French ethnology during the interwar period (Debaene 2014). André Gide's *Voyage au Congo*, written on his return in 1926, denounced the failure of French colonial officers. Upon his arrival in Brazzaville in 1925, he attended the trial of Henri Sambry, a colonial administrator accused of mistreating forced laborers. The reading of *La mentalité primitive* enlightened him on the reasons why the natives could not enter into the framework of legal rationality.

> In general, the word "why" is not understood by the natives; and I even doubt if some equivalent word exists in most of their idioms. During the trial in Brazzaville I had already noticed that the answer to the question "Why did these people desert their villages?" was invariably, "How, in what way ..." It seems that the brains of these people are incapable of establishing a relation between cause and effect. Note: This is confirmed, commented on, and explained very well by Lévy-Bruhl in his book *La mentalité primitive*, which I did not know yet. (Gide 1927: 106)

Between 1933 and 1939, *La nouvelle revue française*, the journal Gide had founded, published extracts from the works of Lévy-Bruhl. Jean Paulhan, who directed the journal at the time, asked Lévy-Bruhl to supervise a thesis he planned to write on the Malagasy proverbs he had studied before the war, even though he would later be critical of the idea of a "prelogical mentality" (Paulhan 1945). It is undoubtedly through *La nouvelle revue française* that Michel Leiris became aware of Lucien Lévy-Bruhl's work, since he declared the following in 1948 during a stay in Haiti: "I tried to escape from this European mentality, which bothered me like a badly made garment, by reading works on 'primitive mentality,' a mentality that—if one believes Lévy-Bruhl and other theorists—implies a play of affective powers and imaginative capacity much freer than the so-called civilized mentality" (Leiris 1995: 879).

Leiris participated in the Dakar-Djibouti mission organized by Marcel Griaule in 1931 with the scientific support of the Institute of Ethnology and funding from the National Assembly. He saw a confirmation of Lévy-Bruhl's analyses of participation in the phenomena of ritual possession that he observed in Gondar, Ethiopia, since it seemed to him that, through trance, an individual could be both himself or herself and another self. Lévy-Bruhl also followed the work of Denise Paulme and Deborah Lifchitz in Mali through the Institute of Ethnology. He wrote to them on July 12, 1935:

> It is very kind of you to give me news of your work and to tell me that reading *La mentalité primitive* is not useless to you. The people you are studying are much more "evolved" than those mentioned in the book; but there are many common features in their ways of thinking and feeling. (Paulme and Lifchitz 2015: 256)

When *La nouvelle revue française* published selected writings from Lévy-Bruhl in 1937, Paul Nizan wrote an article in *L'Humanité* that highlighted Lévy-Bruhl's contribution to a Marxist analysis of the colonial situation. Nizan compared the notion of "mentality" to the Marxist concept of "superstructure" and requested a study of modes of production in "primitive societies." The young communist philosopher, who had published a strong criticism of colonialism in his book *Aden Arabie* in 1931, found confirmation of his own observations in Lévy-Bruhl's analyses of the violent contacts between colonizer and colonized:

> A considerable body of work has been established and a Marxist revival can bring it the new dimensions it lacks. One will read the chapter of the *Selected Writings* concerning the primitives and the Europeans with particular interest. The problem of their contact is not only important for the study of the primitive mentality confronted with a different mode of thought. Contact, whether with merchants,

colonizers, or missionaries, is almost always disastrous for primitive populations. Mr. Lévy-Bruhl notes well that even the most "harmless" relations are dangerous. … Where the violence of the white man is not exercised, the native gradually loses his "will to live." While the research of Mr. Lévy-Bruhl remains on a strictly scientific ground, it leads to a hard criticism of colonization. (Nizan 1937: 8)

On Nizan's advice and with Lucien Lévy-Bruhl's "blessing," Claude Lévi-Strauss went to Brazil in 1938 for his second mission (Lévi-Strauss 2008: 243). This double tutelage subverts the idea that Lévy-Bruhl and Lévi-Strauss were "armchair anthropologists" building a gap between "primitive societies" and modernity. Following Nizan's footsteps in Arabia and those of Lévy-Bruhl along the Rondon telegraph line in the Mato Grosso, Lévi-Strauss was aware he was observing societies that had been profoundly impacted by their contact with Europeans. Indeed, the Nambikwara, estimated at 20,000 individuals when Rondon met them in 1907, were only 1,500 when Lévi-Strauss observed them thirty years later. Nevertheless, following Nizan's advice, Lévi-Strauss managed to analyze the modes of production of this "primitive society" by describing their forms of kinship and exchange. Marxism brought Lévi-Strauss the tools to analyze what was missing in Lévy-Bruhl's ethnology, namely a dialectical conception of contradiction and a linguistic conception of signs, but he kept answering the same political question. This question came to Lévi-Strauss through the memory of the Dreyfus Affair, transmitted by his family. Lévi-Strauss was born in Belgium in 1908 into a Jewish family that he described as

a good bourgeois family that had seen better days, with a conservative temperament, except, probably, in the youth of my father and his brothers at the time of the Dreyfus Affair. They told me they had been to a demonstration for Dreyfus where Jaurès was speaking. They approached him at the end to thank him and Jaurès gave them an equivocal answer: "I hope," he said, "that you will remember this." Which meant as much as: "You might be joining us and supporting our cause today, but you'll desert us quickly again afterwards." This was the truth. (Lévi-Strauss 1988: 17)

Indeed, Lévi-Strauss's parents were not engaged in the socialist movement, but in 1925 one of their friends introduced Lévi-Strauss to the writings of the Belgian socialist thinker Henri de Man, who aimed at organizing Marx's revolutionary ideal through collective planning. In 1926, Lévi-Strauss published an essay entitled "Gracchus Babeuf and Communism" at the press of the Belgium Workers Party, paying tribute to a major figure of the French Revolution. By 1928, Lévi-Strauss was secretary general of the Federation of Socialist Students (Fédération des étudiants socialistes) and secretary to the socialist deputy Georges Monnet, which allowed him to participate in the parliamentary life of the socialist party (Stoczkowski 2008). In 1930, he studied law and philosophy at the Sorbonne and wrote a thesis on "the postulates of historical materialism" under the direction of Célestin Bouglé, a student of Durkheim and director of the Normal Superior School; during this time he also published articles in the Franco-Belgian journal *L'Étudiant socialiste*. In 1932, Lévi-Strauss was teaching philosophy in Mont-de-Marsan, where he was campaigning for the cantonal elections, when he received a phone call from Bouglé proposing that he go and teach sociology in Sao Paulo. Arriving in the Brazilian metropolis in 1935, Lévi-Strauss began developing a plan to travel to Mato Grosso, despite his colleagues telling him that there were no more natives.

Lévi-Strauss's observations regarding the Bororo and Caduveo during his first expedition aroused the interest of ethnologists such as Lévy-Bruhl and Rivet in France but also Robert Lowie in the US. Lévy-Bruhl wrote to Lévi-Strauss on April 24, 1937: "And this was your first fieldwork experience, you were born to do ethnology, and you have a beautiful scientific future ahead of you" (Loyer 2015: 193). Without doubt, Lévy-Bruhl's interest came from the fact that Lévi-Strauss, a reader of Karl von den Steinen, was bringing new elements to solve the enigma of the famous statement analyzed by Lévy-Bruhl, "Bororo are Araras," by bringing to light, in particular, the use of the colors of the birds for the names of the clans and of their feathers in the manufacture of objects. After reading his article on the dualist organization of the Bororo, Robert Lowie invited Lévi-Strauss to New York in 1941 as part of a rescue program for French academics during the war. The fact that Lévy-Bruhl had organized a similar program for academics from Central Europe in Paris suggests a political transition from Lévy-Bruhl to Lévi-Strauss.

To trace this political transition, let us return again to the figure of Dreyfus as we follow its transformations in the ethnology of Lévy-Bruhl. It can be said that Lévy-Bruhl encountered "sentinels" during his travels around the world, in the sense that this term was used to describe Dreyfus returning from Cayenne to bring about a new norm of justice. Rizal in the Philippines, Rondon in Brazil, Nguyễn in Vietnam, and

Baudoux in New Caledonia lived on the border between two worlds, the "primitive" and the "civilized," and perceived in advance the signs of their encounter, which cannot be reduced to the linear scheme of progress but should rather be seen as a series of accidents punctuating the colonial adventure. Just as Dreyfus experienced the precariousness of colonial living conditions on Devil's Island while maintaining the intellectual demands of a cultivated European, so Rizal, Rondon, Nguyễn, and Baudoux returned to the frontier between "civilization" and the "savage world" to find in this conflictual space possibilities of mutual learning. While Rondon formulated this process in a positivistic and paternalistic schema of progress inherited from Auguste Comte, Lévy-Bruhl criticized this schema after the Dreyfus Affair and Lévi-Strauss drew all the consequences of this criticism when he observed the political and ecological ravages of "Western civilization" in Brazil.

Many years after his expeditions in Brazil, reflecting on the despair he felt during his ethnographic experience, Lévi-Strauss confided: "I felt like Dreyfus in Cayenne."[13] Such a confession undoubtedly comes from the circulation of Dreyfus's Cayenne notebooks among the circles of French Judaism at the beginning of the twentieth century. But it also sheds a singular light on the end of *Tristes tropiques*, especially the play entitled "L'Apothéose d'Auguste" (The apotheosis of Augustus), which Lévi-Strauss had left unfinished on his return from Brazil and which he transcribed twenty years later (Lévi-Strauss 2008). This play features Augustus, about to accede to the emperor's throne, and Cinna, his childhood friend, who has explored nature and returns to bring back the lessons he has learned. Cinna's warning about the emptiness of power takes the form of an eagle, not the symbol of Jupiter but a fierce, smelly animal. Power, according to this fable, comes from the ability to approach wild beasts without fearing their bad smell. We can, thus, compare the experience of Dreyfus in Cayenne, whose books were devoured by humidity and insects and whose body was ravaged by humiliation and ill-treatment, with the experience of the ethnographer who confronts the wild world in order to convey its meaning, which the logic of the sacred or of sovereignty fails to capture. The ethnographer, Lévi-Strauss claimed strongly against the universalistic theses of Roger Caillois, "does not circulate between the country of the savages and the country of the civilized: in whatever direction he goes, he returns from the dead" (Lévi-Strauss 1955: 1217).

---

13. Monique Lévi-Strauss, personal communication, September 24, 2015.

In the 1950s, Lévi-Strauss was struggling to be acknowledged in the French academia because of a strong anti-Semitism among the established academics who had been appointed during the Vichy regime. His defense of the role of the ethnographer during this time sheds light on Lévy-Bruhl's position in the 1930s, when he seemed to enjoy the greatest academic power in the context of the Popular Front that appointed the socialist party to head the French government under the leadership of Léon Blum. As a moral witness to the Dreyfus Affair and a global observer of the flaws in the colonial system, Lévy-Bruhl anticipated the wave of anti-Semitism that swept through Europe between the wars.

CHAPTER 8

The Politics of Vigilance

After the First World War, Lévy-Bruhl gained a dominant position in
the French academic field. From 1925 he presided over the Institute of
Ethnology and helped found the Society of French Folklore in 1929
under the patronage of Sir James and Lady Frazer. He became something of a French version of James Frazer, with his series of six books on
"primitive mentality" that seemed to mimic the twelve volumes of the
Golden Bough, for which he wrote a preface in the French edition. He
was a member of the Academy of Moral and Political Sciences, a part of
the French Institute, where he wrote reviews of books on ethnology. This
central role in the new science of ethnology coincided with a key position in philosophical circles. From 1917 onward, Lévy-Bruhl was the
director of the *Revue philosophique* that ruled the academic field along
with the *Revue de métaphysique et de morale*. At the time of their respec-
tive foundation in 1876 and 1893, these two journals represented the
positivist and spiritualist poles of philosophical activity, but the direction
that Lévy-Bruhl gave to the *Revue philosophique* blurred this opposition
(Clark 1973; Fabiani 1988). Xavier Léon contacted Lévy-Bruhl during
the war in 1915 asking him to participate in the revival of the *Revue de
métaphysique et de morale*, but Lévy-Bruhl informed Léon a year later,
on December 14, 1916, that Théodule Ribot had asked him to edit the
journal Ribot had founded forty years earlier (Merllié 1992: 95). Because
he appeared to be a neutral figure in the philosophical debates that were
playing out, Lévy-Bruhl was able to edit the *Revue philosophique* while

publishing an important article on the philosophy of Hume in the *Revue de métaphysique et de morale* (Lévy-Bruhl 1909).

International Congresses of Philosophy

At the *Revue philosophique*, Lévy-Bruhl mobilized the skills he had shaped at the *Bulletin des armées* and the *Bulletin de l'Alliance française*, asking for regular updates on the list of copies distributed free of charge and on the list of subscribers, developing the image of the journal among English-speaking universities and teachers of philosophy classes in high schools. In 1925, while the journal's publisher Félix Alcan faced a difficult financial situation, Lévy-Bruhl reorganized the typographical presentation of the journal (Tesnières 2001: 221). If he refrained from publishing reviews of his own works in the *Revue philosophique*, he made sure that important authors published them in other journals, like Léon Brunschvicg in the *Revue des deux mondes* (Meyerson 2009: 421).

Together with Léon, Lévy-Bruhl also headed the organization of the two great events that marked French philosophical life: the meetings of the French Society of Philosophy and the international congresses of philosophy. Lévy-Bruhl participated as a discussant in the first sessions of the society in 1902, which launched the project of the *Vocabulaire de la philosophie* directed by André Lalande, and presented talks by Émile Boutroux on "Comte and metaphysics" and by Émile Durkheim on "the determination of moral fact." Léon organized two sessions of the French Society of Philosophy around the books of Lévy-Bruhl, in 1922 on *La mentalité primitive* and in 1929 on *L'âme primitive*. Their correspondence shows their concern to include members of all the disciplines in the discussion: "linguists, ethnologists, sociologists, missionaries" (Merllié 1992: 93). For the 1929 session, Lévy-Bruhl wanted Frazer and Granet to be present, but ultimately the two could not attend. The session began with a humorous exchange of courtesies between Léon and Lévy-Bruhl in which they pointed out to the audience the supposed differences in style between the *Revue de métaphysique et de morale*, more oriented toward arguments, and the *Revue philosophique*, more oriented towards facts:

> Léon: You know that our friend does not have much faith in the virtue of philosophical discussions and I will not withhold from you that I had to overcome his resistance to convince him to come.

Lévy-Bruhl: Ladies and gentlemen, while I keep writing books on primitive mentality, for which you might condemn me, Mr. Xavier Léon insists to an equal measure, and very kindly, that the Society of Philosophy discuss them. (Lévy-Bruhl 1929b: 108)

Preempting the objections against his term "prelogical mentality," Lévy-Bruhl admitted with the candor of a philosopher recognized within the academy: "The more I persevere in these studies that I have pursued for nearly thirty years, the more I see distinctly the difficulties with which they are bristling" (Lévy-Bruhl 1929b: 109). In fact, apart from Marcel Mauss, who revived Durkheim's objections to Lévy-Bruhl's deliberate ignorance of social morphology, the other speakers offered testimonies to their interest in the study of "primitive mentality" rather than raising objections.

Many of Lévy-Bruhl's readers and interlocutors came from a Catholic background, which may be surprising in the light of the vigorous reactions that his 1903 book on morality received, becoming a milestone in the debate on the law of secularism. In 1931, Lévy-Bruhl was to place the notion of the supernatural at the center of the title of his fourth book on "primitive mentality," *Le surnaturel et la nature dans la mentalité primitive* (*Primitives and the Supernatural*) (Lévy-Bruhl 1931). In 1903 this theological notion of the supernatural played a central role in the modernist crisis, which shaped Catholic debates on secularism (Poulat 1962). As the theologian Alfred Loisy and the philosopher Maurice Blondel had taken up this notion to think how Christ's action inserted the supernatural into nature, the Vatican placed their works on its *Index Librorum Prohibitorum* (List of Prohibited Books). Lévy-Bruhl noted in his little book on Jean Jaurès that Jaurès "followed with passionate interest the efforts of Abbé Loisy" (Lévy-Bruhl 1915: 53). He asked Maurice Blondel, who was then retired in Aix-en-Provence, to write a letter to the French Society of Philosophy for its session on "*L'âme primitive.*" In 1923, Lévy-Bruhl proposed to Léon a conference on "Renan's religion," at a time when Loisy's detractors were questioning the possibility of his teaching the history of religions at the Collège de France as a priest. One can then suppose that Lévy-Bruhl's books contributed to attenuate the gap between *catholiques* (Catholics) and *laïques* (seculars) by staging, through the detour of colonized societies, the contrast between "primitive mentality" and "civilized mentality." Lévy-Bruhl himself hinted at this possibility when he conceded multiple times that a "primitive mentality" persisted through the contradictory dogma of the Trinity supported by the Christian church. In fact, the philosophers who were to contribute to the philosophical renewal of Catholicism by returning to the Thomistic system, such as Étienne Gilson or Jacques Maritain, found in Lévy-Bruhl a source of teaching and recognition.

It is, therefore, surprising that Lévy-Bruhl is not one of the "watchdogs" denounced by Paul Nizan in 1932 in his attack on the dominant philosophers of the spiritualist pole, such as Boutroux, Brunschvicg, Bergson, and Maritain (Nizan 1971). Indeed, Lévy-Bruhl remained strongly attached to the socialist party through the figure of Jaurès, whose message he carried on his travels throughout the world. Rather than using the figure of the "watchdog" who protects the bourgeoisie from a social movement by drawing on an idealistic discourse, it is better to use Jean Psichari's term of the "sentinel," brought into the debate on the Dreyfus Affair, to describe Lévy-Bruhl's international commitment as an attempt to recognize the signs of the social movement in advance so as to amplify and organize it.

We can, thus, understand why, within Léon's multiple institutional activities, Lévy-Bruhl was more involved in the international congresses of philosophy, the first of which, organized by Léon in Paris in 1900, was followed by large-scale events in Geneva, Heidelberg, and Bologna, until the war interrupted the series. When the congresses were resumed after the war, their aim was to organize in philosophy the same effort for peace that the League of Nations made in the diplomatic field or the International Labour Office in social relations. After a smaller event that took place in Oxford in 1920, Léon and Lévy-Bruhl launched a meeting of national philosophical societies, with the exception of that of Germany; it took place at the Sorbonne in 1921. Lévy-Bruhl presided over a session on the "History of Philosophy" where Gilson presented a paper on Auguste Comte. The success of the event convinced Lévy-Bruhl, at Léon's insistence, to participate in the congress planned for Harvard in 1926, where he had already been a guest professor in 1919 (Merllié 1992: 101). Paul Lapie and Célestin Bouglé also attended the congress at Harvard, representing respectively the Sorbonne and the Normal Superior School. Gilson presented a conference paper on Thomism that was highly appraised. Following the thesis he defended at the Sorbonne in 1907 under the direction of Lévy-Bruhl, Gilson showed the gap between the philosophical ideas of Descartes and the theological system of Thomas Aquinas.[1] Medieval scholasticism was the object of an entire

---

1. Gilson described the influence of Lévy-Bruhl in his acceptance speech at the Académie française in 1947: "At the time when, as a young student, I

section at the Harvard congress, which thus marked the formation of neo-scholasticism, in which Gilson would participate when he took refuge in the US during the war (Michel 2018: 148). Lévy-Bruhl, more modestly, talked about the role of sociology in dealing with the study of morality. By inviting Gilson to this international congress, Lévy-Bruhl answered a question that the young Catholic philosopher had asked him in 1918:

After the war, will the history of medieval philosophy, or any other, but especially medieval, not be an inappropriate luxury? ... I would simply like to have your opinion in order to focus on the definitive task of my life and to prepare myself for it. I believe that something has changed in the problem since 1914. I have reread and burned my philosophy essays; this sub-Bergsonism has disgusted me.[2]

During the Harvard conference, Lévy-Bruhl sent a letter to his wife, in which he confided to her the satisfaction he had felt at the warm reception of his works.

The spirit of Locarno is also blowing between Europeans on this side of the Atlantic and we French people [*nous Français*], we are doing everything we can to make it last. The Germans are pleasant and tactful. I am also on best terms with the Italians, the Czechoslovakians, the Belgians, the Poles, and, in general, the representatives of all

---

was looking for a subject for my thesis on Descartes, I went to consult my master Lucien Lévy-Bruhl. ... Heir to the pure rationalism of the Age of Enlightenment, this great mind remains in my memory and my affection to this day as the least medieval man I have known. Not only did he consider, with Auguste Comte, that metaphysics are not worth refuting and that it is enough to let them fall into disuse, he also thought that, among so many dead, none is more irrevocably dead than the scholasticism of the Middle Ages, which can well be said to be so by universal consent. By advising me to seek in medieval thought the possible origin of certain doctrines taken up by Descartes, it was he, however, who made me open the *Summa Theologica* for the first time—and neither he nor I doubted that, once I had opened it, I would never decide to close it again. Thus, in the middle of the twentieth century, the author of *Primitive Mentality* recruited a new disciple for Saint Thomas" (quoted in Michel 2018: 55).

2. IMEC, Lévy-Bruhl papers, Postcard from Émile Gilson to Lucien Lévy-Bruhl, April 16, 1918.

nations. The only people missing are the "primitives," who obviously would have no better friend than me.[3]

In this personal letter, Lévy-Bruhl humorously described the spirit of the international philosophical congresses, in which the representatives of the different nations enacted the ideal of universal peace through a regulated discussion. German philosophers were indeed invited again to participate in discussions on pragmatism or religion. But Lévy-Bruhl also pointed out that a large number of peoples were not represented and that he could serve as their spokesman, or at least as a facilitator, because of his work on "primitive mentality." At a time when the League of Nations did not represent colonized societies, this joke, which might seem a cavalier way of speaking for those who were silenced, marked above all a desire to introduce extra-European points of view to the changing game of philosophy. Lévy-Bruhl saw his role as that of a diplomat, who, because he was not attached to a "mentality," can bring these different points of view together.

Supporting Jewish Intellectuals in Exile

After attending the Harvard Congress, Lévy-Bruhl met Franz Boas, the founder of American cultural anthropology. Born into a German-Jewish family that had been involved in the revolutions of 1848, Boas had attended the anthropology courses of Bastian and Von den Steinen in Berlin before leaving for North America to study native societies on the Northwest Coast. After a brief stay at the Museum of Natural History in New York, he gathered around him Columbia University students who shared his interest in Native American societies and his commitment to anti-racism (Stocking 1974). In his role as the founder of the Institute of Ethnology, Lévy-Bruhl met Boas on September 9, 1926, and described their discussion in New York to his wife as follows:

> I went to see an American anthropologist, the first of them, whose name was Boas. We had lunch at the Faculty Club and I was pleased to have a serious talk with him about my work and his. When I first came here, I had not seen him and even avoided him; I had been told

---

3. Daniel Lévy-Bruhl personal collection, Letter from Lucien Lévy-Bruhl to Alice Lévy-Bruhl, September 16, 1926.

that he was very Germanophile (he is of German origin; he also has cousins in Paris, who I believe are in the diamond business and whom we must have known at the office). Now he is in excellent relations with Rivet and Mauss and he welcomed me quite as a friend. He does not entirely agree with what I am arguing, but he understands and is not decidedly hostile either.[4]

Boas had indeed reacted negatively to Lévy-Bruhl's early work, in which he perceived echoes of the racialist theses he was fighting. When read from Boas's side of the Atlantic, where racism had very direct effects on education, the assertion that "primitive mentality ignores contradiction" resembled the racist idea of a congenital incapacity to think in an intelligent way. Through his work measuring the skulls of American immigrants, Boas had showed that cognitive abilities changed rapidly as individuals moved from one society to another. For this reason, Boas took up the concept of culture from German philosophy to describe the totality of activities of a social group that characterize the behavior of individuals. In his work entitled *The Mind of Primitive Man*, published in 1911, Boas discussed the thesis that Lévy-Bruhl had just supported in *Les fonctions mentales dans les sociétés inférieures*. The central chapter of this book, entitled "The Physiological and Psychological Functions of the Races," is followed by another chapter showing that variable forms of language have a greater correlation with the culture of individuals than do biological determinations of race, language playing the role of a model for the totalization of culture. In Boas's view, the notion of "inferior societies," which was close in his views to the thesis of the superiority of certain races in the biological anthropology of his time, was contradicted by the diversity of cultural and linguistic phenomena. However, Lévy-Bruhl always refused to use the notion of race that was the central notion for physical anthropologists such as Charles Letourneau; he spoke of "mental functions," following positivist psychologists such as Ribot, to describe all the cognitive operations developed by the social environment. If he knew the origins of the notion of culture in German Romanticism, Lévy-Bruhl never went as far as the radical relativism that it implies, namely to affirm that each culture is an equally valid expression of the potentialities of humanity. Lévy-Bruhl's notion of mentality implied a pattern of development in which a "superior mentality" turns to

---

4.   Daniel Lévy-Bruhl personal collection, Letter from Lucien Lévy-Bruhl to Alice Lévy-Bruhl, September 16, 1926.

an "inferior mentality" in order to understand it in its own principles, but failed to reach it because of the superiority postulated at the beginning. Just as the notion of race was a way to exoticize other human beings by classifying their bodies, the notion of mentality exoticized them by trying to access their mind. This is what Boas clearly reproached Lévy-Bruhl for in his book in 1911:

> Lévy-Bruhl developed the thesis that culturally primitive man thinks prelogically, that he is unable to isolate a phenomenon as such, that there is rather a "participation" in the whole mass of subjective and objective experience which prevents a clear distinction between logically unrelated subjects. This conclusion is reached not by a study of individual behavior but by the traditional beliefs and customs of primitive societies. (Boas 1911 [1938: 135])

Boas opposes the method of "armchair anthropology" adopted by Lévy-Bruhl, starting from the observations of travelers and missionaries, with his own field method, which led him to work in collaboration with indigenous people to record their mythological narratives, their songs, their dances, their ceremonies. These ritual performances differed from intellectual systems in that they engaged bodily emotions; but Boas also noticed that the war had showed that intellectuals could be enrolled by collective emotions. He wrote to Lévy-Bruhl on April 24, 1922, following the reading of *La mentalité primitive*:

> You will find an attitude of ignorance in our civilization as well as among the primitives. My own point of view is largely determined by personal contact with so-called primitives, and I have never been able to discover that they think differently from us in any way. It is only in cases where a highly emotional dogma affects them that they act differently from modern intellectuals, and if ever we doubted that modern intellectuals could be influenced in the same way, I think the events of the last eight years should have removed this error.[5]

Lévy-Bruhl and Boas set up their debate publicly during the session of the French Society of Philosophy organized in Paris in 1929 around *L'âme primitive*. Boas abruptly reaffirmed that what Lévy-Bruhl

---

5.   IMEC, Lévy-Bruhl papers, Letter from Franz Boas to Lucien Lévy-Bruhl, April 24, 1922.

explained by a prelogical mentality was rather a tendency of the human mind to think in a traditional or dogmatic way when struck by strong emotions. Lévy-Bruhl answered him laconically to preserve a budding friendship:

> FB: I conclude, basing myself on the experience of my personal relations with primitive peoples, that we are not dealing with a simple phenomenon, but that a great diversity of conditions can contribute to explain the apparently prelogical approaches of primitive man, and that it is necessary to seek the source of these approaches in a certain general trait of human nature: man is made in such a way that, in moments of intense emotion, logical thought sinks, and traditional forms of thought take over. ...
> LLB: I thank Professor Boas again for kindly bringing us the fruit of his long experience and his reflections. As for the objections he makes to the very position of the problem I am trying to solve, I already knew them from the conversations I found so interesting that we had in his office in New York. I confess that they did not convince me. (Lévy-Bruhl 1929a: 114–15)

To raise the problem of cultural diversity otherwise than setting up a hierarchy of mentalities, Boas explained, it would be necessary to think of "human nature" outside of Hume's psychology, which Lévy-Bruhl had taken up to understand how different mental habits can coexist in a broad experience. In the more pragmatist version proposed by Boas, "human nature" is a set of potentialities that actualizes itself according to the crisis situations that the individuals encounter within the collective traditions that they find at their disposal. In this conception, experience is an investigation into the troubles of perception and not an association of ideas by imagination. Lévy-Bruhl could have discussed this question with John Dewey, who participated in the Harvard congress in 1926 and who was elaborating, in discussion with anthropologists, a philosophy of human nature in which the notion of participation took on a new meaning (see Dewey 1925).[6] The absence of discussion between Lévy-Bruhl and Dewey is all the more striking as *Les fonctions mentales dans les sociétés inférieures* was translated in 1926 with a title, *How Natives Think,* that

---

6. Dewey had dinner with Lévy-Bruhl in March 1920 in Beijing where they were both invited professors, as can be found in a letter sent by Dewey to his family on April 1, 1920.

referred to a book published by Dewey (1910), *How We Think,* and reissued in 1966 with a preface by a student of Boas, Ruth Bunzel. It seems, however, that the meeting between Boas and Lévy-Bruhl at Harvard was an opportunity for a discussion on pragmatic philosophy. In a letter he sent him on June 12, 1926, in preparation for his lecture at the Harvard Philosophy Conference, Boas criticized the notion of universality that Lévy-Bruhl assumed he represented when he addressed his listeners as "children." Instead, he encouraged him to describe the conditions of work in the university, so as to make his audience reflect about what it means to think in modernity. In fact, the lectures that Lévy-Bruhl gave in the US were later published with the title "Research as it is Today" (Lévy-Bruhl 1926). Boas wrote to him:

> The speech must not smell of propaganda. You must not talk about the French soul, Lafayette, our brave soldiers and the superiority of French science, and all that. Americans, as you well know, do not think they are as childish as they are. I would love to hear the thoughts of a French philosopher and academic on the role of a university in modern society.[7]

After their meeting in 1926 and their public confrontation in 1929, the correspondence between Lévy-Bruhl and Boas became more friendly, as if a solidarity developed between the two men in the face of the troubles of the present. The German-Jewish anthropologist switched from English to French when he wrote on October 20, 1931:

> I often ask myself if I am not having a nightmare from which I will wake up at dawn. Unfortunately, dawn does not come, and I fear that a cannon shot will replace the crowing of the rooster. Nightmare or reality, it is now heard by people who whisper softly the possibility of invigorating the business by a small war. In the meantime, I study music.[8]

Together with Rivet, Lévy-Bruhl tried to publish in the major French newspapers Boas's open letter of March 27, 1933, to Marshal

---

7. IMEC, Lévy-Bruhl papers, Letter from Franz Boas to Lucien Lévy-Bruhl, June 12, 1926. Archives.
8. IMEC, Lévy-Bruhl papers, Letter from Franz Boas to Lucien Lévy-Bruhl, October 20, 1931.

Hindenburg. This poignant letter, which circulated in international circles fighting against anti-Semitism, challenged the Marshal who had just named Hitler chancellor: "Do I not know that good men, simply because they are Jews, lost their jobs and positions? Do I not know that defenseless Jews are exposed to insult at every step, that venom foams from the mouth when the word Jew is uttered?" (Laurière 2008: 501).

In a letter dated 1936, Boas asked Lévy-Bruhl about the chances of Léon Blum's Popular Front government, and said he was preparing for an imminent war. Boas died of a stroke on December 21, 1942, three years after Lucien Lévy-Bruhl, during a dinner where he was seated next to Claude Lévi-Strauss, exiled in New York.

This particular relationship between Lévy-Bruhl and Boas, which sets aside other figures of the American academic scene such as Dewey, can be explained by the following hypothesis: sensing the war rising in Europe, Lévy-Bruhl discovered in the US a space in which French anthropologists could find refuge. Certainly Lévy-Bruhl did not think of settling there nor of sending his children there, but nieces of his wife Alice settled in the US after 1940. In Lévy-Bruhl's eyes, the US did not offer Europeans a new philosophy, like Dewey's pragmatism, but a publishing market in which European science could spread, and academic institutions where it could find allies. Two surprising indications in Lévy-Bruhl's correspondence with his wife suggest this hypothesis.

Here is how he relates to his wife his meeting with Robert Lowie at Berkeley, with whom he visited San Francisco on November 5, 1926: "He is Austrian by origin, and it seems to me that he might as well write his name Loewy or Lévy. His nose suggests it."[9] The use of anti-Semitic stereotypes to describe a fellow Jewish intellectual is troubling: no doubt there is a form of humor here as in the rest of the correspondence between Lévy-Bruhl and his wife, but one can also see in this relation between the two "Levys" a prefiguration of the encounter between Lowie and Lévi-Strauss, since it was at the invitation of the former that the latter took refuge in New York. If we want to play with Lévi-Strauss's joke quoted at the beginning of this book, we could say that ethnology was founded in France and the UK by scientists with double names, such as Lévy-Bruhl and Evans-Pritchard, and that it was founded in the US by Lowie-Boas.

The second indication is the encounter between Lévy-Bruhl and the Jewish anthropologist Edward Sapir at the University of Chicago on

9.   Letter from Lucien Lévy-Bruhl to Alice Lévy-Bruhl, November 5, 1926.

November 4, 1930, through the intermediary of Maurice Halbwachs, who was there as a visiting professor (Marcel 1999). Lévy-Bruhl recounted this event to his wife in these terms: "Halbwachs ingeniously confessed to me that he had no idea of the influence of my works in the United States."[10] Halbwachs, an Alsatian Catholic married to the daughter of Victor Basch, an important Parisian secular Jewish family, saw Chicago as an open-air experiment for a sociology of the city, and observed Jewish resistance to assimilation in the dominant culture. He described Lévy-Bruhl's visit to his wife Yvonne on November 8, 1930, in the following terms: "Talking about the sacred race, I now come to Lévy-Bruhl" (Topalov 2006: 575). The affinities of destiny between European and American Jews were thus evoked between Durkheimian sociologists by humorously diverting the racial stereotypes that they criticized in their work.

The hypothesis that Lévy-Bruhl's travels in the US prepared the refuge that French scientists found there during the war is attested by another correspondence, between Lévy-Bruhl and Émile Meyerson. Born in Poland in 1859 into a Jewish family, Meyerson studied chemistry in Germany and arrived in France in 1882. After working in the chemical industry and in journalism, he entered the service of banker Edmond de Rothschild in 1899 to organize the settlement of Jewish emigrants in Palestine (Kaspi 2010: 200–201). He made many trips to Eastern Europe and Palestine until his retirement in 1923. At the same time, he published works on the philosophy of science, which he taught at the School of Advanced Social Studies, and participated in the work of the French Society of Philosophy. Lévy-Bruhl contacted him in 1921 after reading his last book, *De l'explication dans les sciences* (*Explanation in the Sciences*). It marked the beginning of a singular friendship that deepened until Meyerson's death in 1933. Their correspondence goes quickly from "dear Sir" to "dear friend," and ends with passionate formulas such as "See you soon then, although this 'soon' seems to me still very distant" or "I miss you terribly" (Meyerson 2009: 411). Lévy-Bruhl indeed visited Meyerson weekly in his apartment in the rue Clément Marot, and phoned him regularly. One can assume that their discussions were as much about international politics as about the philosophy of science. Meyerson's last book, *Du cheminement dans la pensée* (*Paths in Thinking*), published in 1931, is a philosophical dialogue with Lévy-Bruhl on the tendency of scientific thinking to identify apparently contradictory

---

10. Daniel Lévy-Bruhl collection, Letter from Lucien Lévy-Bruhl to Alice Lévy-Bruhl, November 5, 1926.

entities. Meyerson seems to have taken in Lévy-Bruhl's discussions the place of Moisei Ostrogorski, who died in 1921, the year when Lévy-Bruhl began his correspondence with Meyerson. Both informed the Sorbonne professor about the political situation of the Jews in Eastern Europe, and enabled him to anticipate the coming threats to the whole of humanity.

Indeed, Lévy-Bruhl began his series of journeys when Meyerson stopped his for health reasons, and their trajectories came to be reversed. Meyerson, after traveling extensively in support of Jewish settlement in Palestine, sought to put down roots in the Parisian academic system, while Lévy-Bruhl, after attaining a central position in that system, traveled the world to defend French universalism. Lévy-Bruhl wrote to Meyerson from San Salvador on September 11, 1928: "I have seen beautiful countries, especially coming up here by the Pacific coast, and my instincts as a 'wandering Israelite' have been satisfied" (Meyerson 2009: 410). When he was invited to Cairo for a series of lectures in October 1932, Lévy-Bruhl followed the advice given by Meyerson to visit Palestine. "Thank you for the recommendations you sent me. I did not go to Tel Aviv and could not make use of it. I was, however, able to visit a number of settlements, going from Jerusalem to Tiberias, and what I saw, in the company of an English Zionist, made the deepest impression on me" (Meyerson 2009: 423).

Meyerson always expressed reservations about the Zionist project of a national state of Israel, as his correspondence with Bernard Lazare attests (Meyerson 2009: 308–34), but he shared with Lévy-Bruhl the idea of a Jewish home as a space for education. In a speech he gave at the Salle Pleyel on May 25, 1935, for the tenth anniversary of the University of Jerusalem, Lévy-Bruhl defended the project of the Universal Israelite Alliance:

> When I heard ten years ago that a university was being founded in Jerusalem, I said to myself: in a new country such as Palestine, are there not more important things than a university? I now believe, after speaking with Émile Meyerson, that a people with this deep need for education, who succeeds in achieving its national existence, should immediately seek to give its national consciousness a concrete intellectual form.[11]

---

11. This speech was quoted after Lévy-Bruhl's death in the journal of the Zionist Organization of France, *Terre retrouvée*, on April 1, 1939.

The Jewish identity that shaped itself through the enduring friendship between Lévy-Bruhl and Meyerson was described in an earlier article published by Meyerson in 1891 and republished in 1936 by Lévy-Bruhl in a posthumous work, under the title "Cupellation among the Ancient Jews." Here Meyerson argued that the purification of metals was practiced in antiquity as a political ritual, with the quality of the metal obtained auguring future happiness and misfortune, in a way that anticipated Lévy-Bruhl's thinking on divination in *La mentalité primitive*. "In the cup of adversity, most friendships go up in smoke," wrote Meyerson. "There remains little gold left but it is pure" (Meyerson 2008: 257). Jewish identity, in the light of these analyses, appears not as a biological race nor as a linguistic culture—notions that Meyerson and Lévy-Bruhl equally criticized (Meyerson 2009: 157)—but as a set of trials through which friendship is tested, like the quality of a good metal.

By combining his central position in the academic field with the role of intermediary played by Meyerson, Lévy-Bruhl became a privileged interlocutor for Jewish scholars from Central Europe who settled in Paris and often shifted their exile to the US, whom he took under his academic protection. This was the case of Alexandre Koyré, born in Russia in 1892, who arrived in Paris in 1912 after studying philosophy in Göttingen. Koyré placed himself under the protection of Meyerson, who helped him to obtain a chair in "History of Religious Ideas in Modern Europe" at the Practical School of Advanced Studies. After reading with enthusiasm *L'âme primitive*, he wrote a review for the German translation in 1930 and confided to Meyerson: "I am increasingly convinced how much the primitives think like us. They are unconscious Hegelians who do not admit the irrational: everything has a meaning, everything must have a reason" (Meyerson 2009: 241).

Koyré's work in the history of science shows, in the wake of Edmund Husserl and Meyerson, a mystical tendency among the founders of scientific thought (Zambelli 1995). Lévy-Bruhl published in the *Revue philosophique* his review of a work on Meyerson and supported him in the creation of the journal *Recherches philosophiques*, which introduced in France the new trends of phenomenology and pragmatism (Meyerson 2009: 408). Koyré proposed to translate into French Maximilian von Schwartzkoppen's *Notebooks*, which Lévy-Bruhl prefaced by emphasizing that these documents of the German general officer in Paris provided the definitive proof of Dreyfus's innocence (Lévy-Bruhl 1930). When the Second World War broke out, Koyré taught at the University of Cairo, and then went, via a long trip in Asia, to the Free School of

Advanced Studies, a section of the Practical School of Advanced Studies, based close the New School for Social Research in New York.

The fate of Koyré, whose international fame has eclipsed that of Lévy-Bruhl and Meyerson, can be contrasted with that of Hélène Metzger. A daughter of Alice Bruhl's brother, and therefore niece of Lucien Lévy-Bruhl, and a war widow, she published an important series of books on the history of science in discussion with Meyerson on what the study of "primitive mentality" entailed, but she suffered from her lack of position (Metzger 1930; Freudenthal 1990; Chimisso 2001). Lévy-Bruhl never mentioned her, except to thank her for making the index of his books on "primitive mentality." She died in Auschwitz in 1944.

The contrast is also striking between the tragic life of Hélène Metzger and the happier trajectory of Ignace Meyerson. Born in 1888 in Warsaw to cousins of Émile Meyerson, often presented as his nephew, he joined him in Paris in 1906 where he worked at the Laboratory of Physiological Psychology and the *Journal of Normal and Pathological Psychology*, founded by Henri Piéron. Meyerson published a review of *La mentalité primitive* in the *Année psychologique* in 1925 (Meyerson 1925), and Lévy-Bruhl supported him in 1926 to succeed Lucien Herr as director of the Musée pédagogique. During the war, he left Paris for Toulouse where he joined the Résistance alongside Jean-Pierre Vernant, with whom he developed at the Practical School of Advanced Studies a historical psychology of images that had a great influence on the human sciences, until his death in 1983 (Fruteau 2007).

Lévy-Bruhl also supported Léon Chestov, who was born in 1866 into a family of Jewish merchants in Ukraine, where he studied law. He moved to Paris in 1921 and published texts in the *Nouvelle Revue Française* and then in the *Revue philosophique*, notably an article on Martin Buber in 1933, as well as a review of *La mythologie primitive* (Chestov and Schloczer 1933; Chestov 1938). The poet Benjamin Fondane, born in Romania in 1898 into a family of Jewish merchants and intellectuals, arrived in Paris in 1923 where he considered Lévy-Bruhl and Chestov his two masters in philosophy. In 1934, Chestov told Fondane: "It is fortunate that I met Lévy-Bruhl, who published me thanks to some misunderstanding. It is probable that he does not read my articles." Lévy-Bruhl told Fondane a year later: "I disagree completely with Chestov, but he is a talented man, and he has the right to express his thoughts" (Fondane 1982: 71, 82). At the death of Chestov in 1938, Fondane published an article on his work in the *Revue philosophique*. The following years, Fondane published in the *Cahiers du Sud* a review of Lévy-Bruhl's book,

L'expérience mystique et les symboles chez les primitifs, and in the *Revue philosophique* a text on his "metaphysics of knowledge" (Fondane 1938, 1940). Arrested by the Vichy police in March 1944, Fondane died at Auschwitz seven months later.

Besides these historians and poets, Lévy-Bruhl also spoke with prominent German-Jewish scientists who wished to go into exile in France. He became acquainted with Albert Einstein in 1928, when they both gave the inaugural lecture of the first Davos University Course. After Einstein's visit to France in 1922, this university course, which would have four sessions until 1931, marked the warming of Franco-German relations in the scientific field. Following this meeting, Lévy-Bruhl asked Einstein to write an article on Meyerson's philosophy in the *Revue philosophique* (Meyerson 2009: 194–95). The discussions with Einstein accompanied Lévy-Bruhl in his reflections on chance, as he wrote down ideas for a forthcoming book:

> In front of the at least relative unintelligibility of the mythical world, our mind experiences a trouble, an embarrassment, a perplexity: what is a world that is not rational, intelligible? … Here Einstein's reflection crosses ours. For he shows that this intelligibility of the sensible world ordered and regulated by science is itself forever unintelligible. It is a fact, which imposes itself on us. … Would there not simply be a difference of degree? a transfer of the unintelligibility of the detail to the world as a whole? (Lévy-Bruhl 1949: 71–72)

The thesis of generalized relativity thus led Lévy-Bruhl to change his frame of reference or point of view, in order to describe the emergence of science from the experience of contingency. Similarly, Lévy-Bruhl took seriously the Freudian hypothesis of the unconscious, even if it was still contested by a large number of French psychologists. Lévy-Bruhl went to Davos in 1928 with Charles Blondel, who taught psychology in Strasbourg and had developed comparisons between psychoanalysis and the ethnology of "primitive mentality" (Blondel 1914). Lucien Lévy-Bruhl met Sigmund Freud on February 6, 1935, during his visit to Vienna.[12] In his posthumously published notebooks, Lévy-Bruhl explained his abandonment of the term "prelogical mentality" as follows:

---

12. Daniel Lévy-Bruhl personal collection, Letter from Lucien Lévy-Bruhl to Alice Lévy-Bruhl, February 7, 1935; Letter by Sigmund Freud to Marie Bonaparte, February 9, 1935 in Bonaparte and Freud (2022: 804).

I do not have an adequate vocabulary. The vocabulary transmitted to me by tradition was formed by reflections on the psychic phenomena of sensitivity, perception, memory, reasoning, effort, will, etc., as they present themselves in the consciousness where they can be observed. It is only recently that the existence and importance of the unconscious has been recognized (Freud). (Lévy-Bruhl 1949: 104)

Einstein found refuge in the US and Freud in England, but it can be guessed, though not proved, that they discussed their possible exile in France with Lévy-Bruhl.[13] But we do have two letters showing that Ernst Cassirer and Edmund Husserl approached Lévy-Bruhl to ask for his help. Cassirer is famous for having opposed Martin Heidegger on Kantian philosophy during the second university course in Davos in 1929, a year after he and Lévy-Bruhl inaugurated the course. He developed a positive assessment of the Enlightenment movement and tried to understand mythology as a force that resists it (Cassirer 1946). His wife, Tomi, wrote to Lévy-Bruhl on April 19, 1933: "How sweet it would be to be able to walk the streets of Paris again. As German Jews, today we are no longer guests abroad. And yet there will be a country that will want us."[14]

Husserl wrote a long letter to Lévy-Bruhl in 1935 in which he told him about his reading of *La mythologie primitive* and the manner in which it echoed with his own reflections on "the crisis of European sciences" (Husserl 1998). While Lévy-Bruhl was confused by the obscurity of the phenomenological vocabulary, this letter became the object of many comments in the 1960s when French phenomenologists discussed the philosophical stakes of ethnology (Merleau-Ponty 1975). It attests, indeed, that a method that starts from the criticism of the presuppositions of consciousness can join a set of affective connections below consciousnesses, or what Husserl called "the world of the life" (*Lebenswelt*). In the end, Husserl remained in Germany, but Cassirer found refuge in the US.

Both Cassirer and Husserl perceived in *La mythologie primitive* echoes of the political situation in Germany. The project of this book,

---

13. It is said in the Lévy-Bruhl family that Lucien interceded with Léon Blum to help Einstein settle in France, but that Blum, who was then prime minister, considered it too sensitive.

14. IMEC, Lévy-Bruhl papers, Letter from Tomi Cassirer to Lucien Lévy-Bruhl, April 19, 1933.

published in 1935 (Lévy-Bruhl 1935), goes back to the summer of 1933. On June 21, Lucien Lévy-Bruhl participated in the meeting against fascism organized by the Federation of Trade Unions of the Paris region to warn them of the "lightning success of Hitlerism." On August 4, his son Henri alerted the public to the "death or suicide sentence" of German Jews by comparing it to those of the Armenians "exterminated in Turkey" during the First World War (Hirsch 2016: 243–44). In February 1936, Lucien Lévy-Bruhl himself published a text in the *Nouvelles littéraires* in which he contrasted "a European spirit," which he defined as "common ways of thinking and feeling" developed by "philosophers, writers, artists," with "the explosion of nationalist passions in the aftermath of the Great War." "Despite all that separates us from primitive societies," Lévy-Bruhl wrote, "quite often, today, we are led to recognize in myth a function that is not without analogy with that of primitive myths" (Lévy-Bruhl 1936: 1). As an example, Lévy-Bruhl quoted "the myth of race," in which Nazi Germany found "a source of strength." In this context, "when combating the mystical form of nationalist passion," the role of intellectuals was "to help to 'understand,' that is to say to discover, the causes of the evil from which our societies suffer and, if possible, to remedy them" (Lévy-Bruhl 1936: 1). The last books published by Lucien Lévy-Bruhl thus seemed to answer the criticisms formulated by Boas, showing how collective emotions orient the intellectual forms of mythology or how the "mystical experience" is expressed in symbols that mobilize a society. The participation in the social ideal, in this context, appears through a multitude of forms of participation that enclose the individual and shape his personality: it is no longer what opposes the contradiction, as at the time of the Dreyfus Affair, but what conditions its expression. At the end of his life, Lévy-Bruhl, following Einstein and Freud, described how a clear consciousness emerges from a set of affective links that make sense of contingent events. While colonial sentinels had given him a sense of disaster to come, Lucien Lévy-Bruhl and his son Henri acted as whistleblowers when they analyzed the new threats in Nazi Germany. For the first time in his life, Lucien Lévy-Bruhl departed from his legendary cautiousness and spoke as a public intellectual.

The young philosopher Emmanuel Levinas attended the Davos conferences and took courses with Husserl and Heidegger in Freiburg before teaching at the University of Strasbourg. He published two articles on Heidegger and Husserl in the *Revue philosophique* and described the resonance of Lévy-Bruhl's philosophy with the latest trends in German philosophy (Levinas 2001). While he sought a way to resist Nazism in phenomenology, which was nevertheless supported by his master Heidegger, Levinas found in the notion of "primitive mentality" the description of a dependent and vulnerable relation to the world that, for him, existed before individual consciousness.

> The notion of mentality consists in affirming that the human mind does not depend solely on an exterior situation—climate, race, institution, even contracted mental habits that would pervert the natural illumination. Mentality is *in itself* dependence; it emerges from an ambivalent possibility of turning toward conceptual relations or of remaining in relationships of participation. *Prior* to representation it is strikingly engaged in Being; *it orients itself* in Being. (Levinas 1957, quoted in Wolff 2011: 40)

After the war, Levinas described what Lévy-Bruhl had qualified as participation in collective life through the affective modality of horror and insomnia. "In a way, horror is a movement that will strip consciousness of its very subjectivity. Not by appeasing it in the unconscious, but by precipitating it into an *impersonal vigilance*, into a *participation*, in the sense that Lévy-Bruhl gives to this term" (Levinas [1963] 1998: 98). Levinas placed this collective attention for threatening events in contrast with the absolute responsibility for others that constitutes the personality. The term "vigilance," however, captures well the theoretical and political line that unifies Lévy-Bruhl's works, from his thesis on responsibility to his books on "primitive mentality," including his cautious engagement against anti-Semitism during the Dreyfus Affair and his public commitment against fascism in the interwar period. In 1934, Lévy-Bruhl was a founding member of the Vigilance Committee of Anti-Fascist Intellectuals (Comité de vigilance des intellectuels anti-fascistes) together with the philosopher Émile Chartier, known as Alain, the physicist Paul Langevin and the ethnologist Paul Rivet. A pamphlet entitled "Vigilance" specified the meaning of the notion of vigilance as a struggle against fascist irrationality through a collective rationality:

> Our vigilance is exercised over armaments, over propaganda, and over fascist pressures. Our intellectual struggle is waged against the fallacies that the avowed or camouflaged fascists and those who serve the cause, consciously or not, are spreading in the nation. Fascism

appeals to the passions of men to disregard their critical intelligence; it disguises facts; it blurs ideas. Our aim is to restore the reality of facts and the clarity of ideas. (Bensaude-Vincent 1987: 186)

The notion of vigilance was used by Jaurès when he created the Socialist Party in 1898 during the Dreyfus Affair and it was promoted by the Communards to describe their fight against the reactionary armies (Candar 2008). Lévy-Bruhl signed the Vigilance Committee's first manifesto on March 5, 1934, and, together with Langevin and Prenant, wrote a preface for S. Erckner's book *Germany as a Field of Maneuver: Fascism and the War.* The Vigilance Committee's president, Rivet, had met Lévy-Bruhl at the French Institute of Anthropology before the First World War and had invited him to a "socialist dinner" with Jean Jaurès, Alfred and Mathieu Dreyfus on July 28, 1914 (Laurière 2008: 487). After the two of them, together with Mauss, founded the Institute of Ethnology in 1925, all three participated in a demonstration against the extreme right-wing leagues organized by the unions at the Manège Jappy on June 21, 1933, and Lévy-Bruhl supported Rivet's socialist candidacy in the municipal elections in Paris on May 12, 1935. During the Second World War, Rivet made the Musée de l'Homme a place of resistance against the Nazi occupation before he went into exile in South America. After the war, his politics of vigilance unfortunately led him to support the Socialist Party in the fight against the independence movement in Algeria.

Lévy-Bruhl also participated in a vigilance committee that met every two weeks at the home of Robert de Rothschild to share information on questions of religion, Jewish literature, and anti-Semitic threats in Europe. On February 1, 1938, when Rothschild proposed publishing a text against anti-Semitism, Lévy-Bruhl asked that this committee be kept secret and not reported on in the media, because he did not want to be seen as being a member of a committee that was brought together by a Jewish identity:

We are not only a religion (I belong to those who are defined as being without a confession). If Jews are attacked, they are not only attacked because they have a different religion from others, because they go to a synagogue while others go to church or the temple; they are attacked in a deeper way. They are attacked in the name of race. If there is no disadvantage for the Protestant or the Catholic to defend himself or herself as a Protestant or a Catholic, there may be one for the

Jews to form an association to defend themselves as Jews: they will not only defend themselves as having a religion (the Jewish religion that is distinct from the Christian religion) but, by force of circumstance, will show or will appear as if they belonged to a different race that needs to protect itself against other races. (Gottlieb 1939)

By opposing religion and race, personal choice and biological identity, as two public forms of personal identity, Lévy-Bruhl here explores a third and more discrete way to engage oneself in the public space: an "impersonal vigilance," to borrow Levinas' description of "primitive mentality," shared between members of the same community exposed to a threat, who rely on the invisible presence of tradition without making it visible in collective representations. Such impersonal vigilance cannot be declared publicly but must be constituted horizontally and anonymously, in the sharing of affects of fear in the face of the coming danger and of acts of attention to the signs of the threat. We can, thus, understand Lévy-Bruhl's politics of vigilance in the 1930s by following the philosophy that Levinas developed after the Second World War. This politics of vigilance is not a new form of Enlightenment philosophy exposed in the public space but operates as a return to "primitive mentality" to find the affective and intellectual resources against fascism in a common tradition. In Lévy-Bruhl's writings in the 1930s there is, indeed, a real ambiguity, which is that of the historical period itself: "primitive mentality" is no longer opposed to "civilized mentality" like shadow to light; rather, it becomes a game of shade and light in which humans must learn to orient themselves through a multiplicity of forms of participation. As Levinas writes in his Heideggerian prose: it is an orientation in Being that seeks a pole of responsibility. The clear contrast Lévy-Bruhl drew between the two mentalities in 1910 gave way in the interwar period to a blurring that became more and more accepted as political events became more alarming, leaving only generalized vigilance as a resource. But vigilance could not constitute a politics if it remained impersonal: hence the call by all intellectuals, including Lévy-Bruhl himself, for regrounding the discourse of the human sciences, which would take place after the war. But Lucien Lévy-Bruhl would no longer be part of it; he died in 1939.

Figure 1. Photograph of the 1876 cohort of the École normale supérieure. Salomon Reinach is sitting second from right in the front row. Lucien Lévy-Bruhl is second from left in the third row. Lévy-Bruhl has the rebellious look described by some of his fellow students.
(École normale supérieure bibliothèque Ulm-Jourdan, Fonds photographique, ENS01_PHOD_2_1876_1.)

Figure 2. Photograph of the 1876 cohort of the École normale supérieure. Salomon Reinach is first from the right and Lucien Lévy-Bruhl third from the right in the front row.
(École normale supérieure bibliothèque Ulm-Jourdan, Fonds photographique, ENS01_PHOD_1_1_18.)

Figure 3. Alfred Dreyfus, his wife Lucie and his two children Pierre Léon and Jeanne, around 1900. (Library of Congress, Prints & Photographs Division, George Grantham Bain collection.)

Figure 4. Alfred Dreyfus at the prison rue du Cherche-Midi, 1894. (PVDE/ Bridgeman Images.)

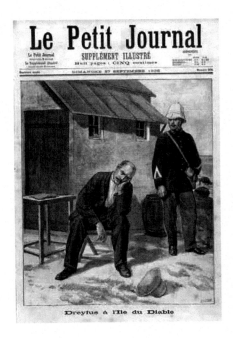

Figure 5. A drawing of Alfred Dreyfus in the Devil's Island penal colony, by F. Méaulle for *Le Petit Journal illustré*, number 306, September 27, 1896. (Bibliothèque Nationale de France.)

Figure 6. Photograph of the 1878 cohort of the École normale supérieure. Jean Jaurès is sitting second from the left in the first row and Henri Bergson is standing at the right end of the first row. (École normale supérieure bibliothèque Ulm-Jourdan, Fonds photographique, ENS01_PHOD_2_1878_4.)

Figure 7. Jean Jaurès at the trial of Alfred Dreyfus in Rennes, 1899. (Author unknown, Archives de Rennes.)

Figure 8. Caricatures of Jean Jaurès. Left: *Le Frelon*, number 8 (1903), by Bobb. Right: *Le Crayon*, number 67 (1906): "L'Hirondelle de Mr de Bulow" ("Mr. de Bulow's swallow"), by Molynk. (Both images from EIRIS, https://www.eiris.eu/articles/etudes/les-animalisations-de-jaurs/.)

145

Figure 9. Albert Thomas at the Cabinet of Armaments.
"Le dernier né d'Albert Thomas / L'Obus de 400." (The youngest child of
Albert Thomas / the 400 mm grenade). Photo collage of "Hermann." Published
on the title page of the French weekly *J'ai vu*, Paris, number 74, April 16, 1916.
©akg-images. (https://www.akg-images.fr/archive/-2UMEBMQEV7_A.html)

Figure 10. Lucien Lévy-Bruhl at the Great Wall in China, 1919.
(Lucien Lévy-Bruhl collection, Musée du quai Branly, RMN-Grand Palais,
photographer unknown, PA000071.)

Figure 11. Lucien Lévy-Bruhl with two men on the Island of Luzon, Philippines, 1920. (Lucien Lévy-Bruhl collection, Musée du quai Branly, RMN-Grand Palais, photograph by Henri Otley-Beyer, PP0101763.)

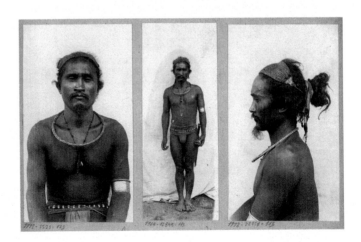

Figure 12. Photograph of an Igorot man following the anthropometric model, bought by Lucien Lévy-Bruhl before or after his travel to the Philippines. (Lucien Lévy-Bruhl collection, Musée du quai Branly, RMN-Grand Palais, photograph by Charles Martin, PP0025606.)

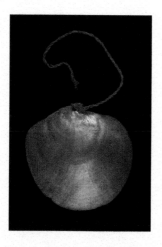

Figure 13. A shell used as knife and as ornament by Kanak women, offered to Lucien Lévy-Bruhl by Georges Baudoux. (Lucien Lévy-Bruhl collection, Musée du quai Branly, RMN-Grand Palais, 71.1931.40.2.)

Figure 14. An anthropomorphic figure from the Igorot society, probably bought by Lucien Lévy-Bruhl in the Philippines in 1920. In his preface to the *Carnets*, Maurice Leenhardt talks about Lucien Lévy-Bruhl's taste for "primitive art" and the objects surrounding his office in Paris. (Lucien Lévy-Bruhl collection, Musée du quai Branly, RMN-Grand Palais, 71.1939.78.35.)

Figure 15. Knives manufactured in the Barong society, probably bought by Lucien Lévy-Bruhl in the Philippines in 1920. (Lucien Lévy-Bruhl collection, Musée du quai Branly, RMN-Grand Palais, 71.1939.78.27.1-2.)

Figure 16. José Rizal in Barcelona, Spain. Public domain, Wikimedia Commons. (https://commons.wikimedia.org/wiki/File:Jose_Rizal_in_Spain.jpg.)

Figure 17. Photograph of Lucien Lévy-Bruhl and Cândido Rondon taken in a studio in Sao Paulo in 1922. (Lucien Lévy-Bruhl collection, Musée du quai Branly, RMN-Grand Palais, photograph by Albert Migot, PP0101758.)

Figure 18. Nguyễn Văn Huyên. (From *Souverains et notabilités d'Indochine*, by Editions du Gouvernement General de l'Indochine, 1943. https://archive.org/details/SouverainsEtNotabilitesDindochine/1522/.)

Figure 19. Paul Rivet, Maurice Leenhardt, and Lucien Lévy-Bruhl around 1936. (Lucien Lévy-Bruhl collection, Musée du quai Branly, RMN-Grand Palais, photographer unknown, PP0098579.)

Figure 20. Albert Einstein and Lucien Lévy-Bruhl at the Davos Forum in March 1928. (Lévy-Bruhl archive, Institut mémoires de l'édition contemporaine.)

Figure 21. Lucien and Alice Lévy-Bruhl with their sons Marcel, Henri and Jean after the First World War. (Lévy-Bruhl archive, Institut mémoires de l'édition contemporaine.)

Figure 22. Marcel Lévy-Bruhl, Lucien's first son. (Archives Institut Pasteur.)

Figure 23. Henri Lévy-Bruhl, Lucien's second son by Harcourt. (Courtesy of Emmanuelle Chevreau, Dept de Droit Romain et d'Histoire du Droit, Université Paris-Panthéon-Assas.)

Figure 24. Jean Lévy-Bruhl, Lucien's third son. (Family archives.)

Figure 25. Raymond Lévy-Bruhl, Jean's son. (Family archives.)

Figure 26. Portrait of Lucien Lévy-Bruhl around 1936. (Lévy-Bruhl archive, Institut mémoires de l'édition contemporaine.)

PART III: TRANSFORMATIONS (1939–2023)

CHAPTER 9

Defending a Threatened Heritage

Lucien Lévy-Bruhl's death, on March 13, 1939, was announced the next day by Léon Blum on the front page of the *Populaire*, a socialist newspaper.

> Lucien Lévy-Bruhl had been Jaurès's close friend, without doubt the closest to his heart apart from Lucien Herr. During the war, Lévy-Bruhl had worked alongside Albert Thomas and had collaborated with *l'Humanité*. ... I was linked to Lucien Lévy-Bruhl for more than forty years. His noble and tender face, not altered by age, is mixed with the dearest memories of my youth. I mourn with his family, a mourning that, at the same time, evokes other mournings. (Blum 1939)

Two days later, Marcel Mauss wrote a longer article in the same newspaper on Lévy-Bruhl's scientific career, specifying that "Jaurès was delighted" with the publication of *Les fonctions mentales dans les sociétés inférieures* in 1910 (Mauss 1939). For those who knew both of them, the death of Lévy-Bruhl on the eve of the Second World War could not fail to evoke the assassination of Jaurès a few days before the outbreak of the First World War, raising the same question: how could their work stemming from the Dreyfus Affair shed light on current threats?

The far-right newspaper *Candide* published an ambiguous text entitled "Tristesse philosophique" (Philosophical sadness) that paid tribute to the Sorbonne philosopher while invoking certain anti-Semitic stereotypes.

> Lévy-Bruhl, who recently passed away, was extremely sensitive and could not bear the anxieties of the present time. He was distressed by anti-Semitism and he had a passion for savages, not only out of curiosity as a sociologist and according to the method of his master Durkheim but out of tenderness of heart and personal sympathy. Already very ill these last months, he had suffered no less in his mind than in his body. One day, when someone exclaimed that his masterpiece, *La mentalité primitive*, was confirmed by many of our contemporaries, Lévy-Bruhl could not refrain from protesting: "What characterizes the civilized is to be lower than primitive mentality." (*Candide* 1939)

This portrait depicts Lévy-Bruhl as an anguished and plaintive thinker who recognized, finally, that "savages" are superior to civilization, a statement which was interpreted positively among extreme right circles. By contrast, *L'Univers israëlite* published a long eulogy of Lévy-Bruhl's work, which concluded as follows:

> Being French above all, he never stopped feeling himself as Jewish. He was a citizen of a world where these two qualities were not in conflict. If he is among those who, at the present time, do the most honor to French thought and to whom the human spirit owes new clarity ..., he is also the pride of Judaism, which his enemies like to present in hideous terms. (Gottlieb 1939)

The Trauma of the Occupation

On September 1, 1939, when Nazi Germany invaded Poland, Henri Lévy-Bruhl, then aged fifty-five, proposed a solemn protest to his colleagues at the Faculty of Law, but was met with silence: several of them had already supported the invasion of Ethiopia by Mussolini's army in 1935 and one of them, Louis Le Fur, had even defended Franco's army in Spain (Audren and Halpérin 2013: 197–99). Two days later, France declared war on Germany, which launched an offensive over their common border on May 10, 1940. After the armistice of June 22 of the same year, which established a German occupation zone in northern and western

France, the Lévy-Bruhl family was dispersed. Mobilized as an officer at the Bordeaux military tribunal, Henri Lévy-Bruhl could not cross the demarcation line between the free and occupied zones and had to give up his teaching post in Paris. He found refuge in Lyon, where a position as professor of Roman law was vacant, but his appointment to this position by an order of October 30, 1940, was threatened by a new law on the status of Jews in the French civil service. Henri declared to the Dean of the University of Lyon, Paul Garraud, that he was "of old French stock," that his father was a member of the Institute of Ethnology, that he and his brothers had fought and been wounded in the Great War, but nothing could be done: in December 1940, he had to stop teaching in Lyon, after being interrupted by violent anti-Semitic demonstrations.

Added to this humiliation was a concern for his son Jacques, born in 1918. Jacques was taken prisoner of war at Dunkirk in 1939 and then transferred to a camp at Eylau, East Prussia, from which he would return considerably weakened. Henri Lévy-Bruhl refused offers of a position in the US in order to remain in contact with his son. The second law on Jews, published on June 2, 1941, gave him hope of reintegration, because it granted exceptions for Jews whose family members were prisoners of war. Henri Lévy-Bruhl was reinstated in higher education by a decree of January 4, 1942, but the Secretary of State for National Education, the historian of ancient Rome Jérôme Carcopino, advised the Rector of the Academy of Lyon not to allow Lévy-Bruhl to resume his courses (Halpérin 2009; Chevreau, Audren, and Verdier 2018: 28–34). Henri found refuge in Decazeville, whose mayor, Paul Ramadier, was a socialist close to Blum, who, in turn, had voted against the granting of full powers for Marshal Philippe Pétain. Through his intermediary, Henri Lévy-Bruhl entered the Résistance networks and ended the war as an inspector of military justice for the French Forces of the Interior (Israel 2001). His daughter, Françoise, known as Fanchette, went to school in Figeac under the name Jacqueline Allier.

Jean Lévy-Bruhl, Lucien's youngest son, took refuge with his family in Arreau, in the south of France. He wrote a letter to the Veterans League (Légion des Combattants) to denounce his dismissal from the army, pointing to the lung injury he carried since suffering a gas attack on the front in 1917, an impairment that would lead to his death in 1960 at the age of seventy. His son, Raymond, born in 1922, was about to enter preparatory classes for high school when the conflict suspended his hesitation between literary and scientific studies. After attending courses in law, mathematics, and chemistry in Toulouse in 1942, he obtained false papers that allowed him to escape the Compulsory Labor Service (Service du travail obligatoire) required of all men of working age and to be recruited, in 1943, under a pseudonym by the chief engineer in charge of infrastructure (Ingénieur en chef des ponts et chaussées). Raymond Lévy-Bruhl took advantage of this position to provide information to the Résistance networks and to issue them with travel permits. He joined the French Forces of the Interior in September 1944 and fought in Alsace and in the Alps (Desrosières and Touchelay 2008).

Marcel Lévy-Bruhl, Lucien's eldest son, was dismissed from the Boucicaut Hospital where he worked as the head of a laboratory. He wrote to the director of the Pasteur Institute, Jacques Tréfouël, to request a full-time position there, but the latter did not accede to his appeal. Marcel Lévy-Bruhl's letter to Jacques Tréfouël, dated to January 23, 1941, is poignant, because it describes a terrible situation with dignity:

> Contrary to the conclusions of the Medical-Surgical Commission of the Administration of Public Assistance, the Ministry of the Interior has reaffirmed my revocation. Finally, my wife, by virtue of the law on Jews, lost her job in career guidance in Boulogne-sur-Seine. And we have three children aged 18, 15, and 12. This is the material situation to which I would like to draw your kind attention.[1]

Marcel Lévy-Bruhl died in Lyon in 1941, aged fifty-eight. His first son, Léon Lucien, who was studying philosophy at the Lycée Louis-Le-Grand before the armistice, joined the Résistance on September 1, 1943, under the name Paul Monpazier. He was arrested at the age of twenty-two on February 4, 1944, by the German army for "terrorist activity," after being denounced. Interned at Fort Montluc near Lyon, he was transferred to Drancy on March 7 as a Jew, then deported to the Monowitz camp at Auschwitz. There he performed various tasks, such as welding, until the camp was evacuated by the German army on April 18, 1945. Léon Lucien did not return from the death marches. Through the efforts of his mother, Berthe, the prefecture of the Seine department declared him "deceased for France" on April 12, 1948. On September 23, 1952, the Ministry of Veterans Affairs declared him a "deported resistant."[2]

---

1. Archives of the Institut Pasteur, Letter from Marcel Lévy-Bruhl to Jacques Tréfouël, January 23, 1941.
2. Division des archives des victimes des conflits contemporains of the Service historique de la Défense in Caen, File of Léon Lucien Lévy-Bruhl.

The period of occupation, thus, raised a strong feeling of distrust, and even anger, among the Lévy-Bruhl family toward the French state. This feeling contradicted the virtues of rigor and discipline that had been cultivated from generation to generation and justified a duty of resistance, even disobedience. The use of pseudonyms to act in the name of truth and justice followed what Lucien Lévy-Bruhl did when he mobilized his networks in the Dreyfus Affair or wrote in *L'Humanité* during the First World War. The tragic loss of members of the Lévy-Bruhl family who had all survived the First World War confirmed the warning signals of catastrophe that the family had been perceiving since the early 1930s. It was, thus, all the more important for Lucien Lévy-Bruhl's descendants to publicly defend their name and to resume their intellectual heritage after the Second World War, in the period known as "Libération."

The Humiliations of the Liberation

When Henri Lévy-Bruhl returned to his Paris apartment in October 1944, it had been devastated by the German army. He publicly described this episode in 1958: "While we were away, the Germans entered our apartment and systematically looted us: only the walls remained. One loss that was particularly sensitive to me was that of my library, my papers, and all the notes I had accumulated for the history of commercial law" (Chevreau, Audren, and Verdier 2018: 152).

In the way in which Henri Lévy-Bruhl told his history, this looting by the German army played as important a role as the humiliation by the Vichy government. His career was based on two pillars between which he built his thinking in the intellectual effervescence of the sociology of the young Durkheimians: commercial law and Roman law. From this point on, he would devote himself solely to Roman law, which he proposed to study as an ethnologist, taking up his father's method at a time when it seemed more and more outdated.

Jean Lévy-Bruhl's apartment at La Selle Saint-Cloud was also looted. It contained the box in which Lucien Lévy-Bruhl had stored all his documents dating from the Dreyfus Affair, which he wanted to pass onto his grandson Raymond. Before his death in 1939, however, Lévy-Bruhl had entrusted his collection of Filipino objects, photographs of Asia, and his correspondence with his wife Alice during his travels to Paul Rivet at the Musée de l'Homme. They were transferred to the Musée du quai Branly in 2005, where they are conserved under Alice Lévy-Bruhl's name as donor. This intriguing feminization of the name of the donor may have occurred at the request of Lucien Lévy-Bruhl, who wished to pay tribute to his wife, who had died before him, in 1935. Odette Dreyfus-Sée, wife of Jean Lévy-Bruhl, recovered the letters between Lucien and Alice from the museum in 1945 and they are still conserved in the family archive. The family collection also contains Kanak objects that the Caldoche prospector and writer Georges Baudoux had offered Lucien Lévy-Bruhl, no doubt to thank the latter for the preface he had written to Baudoux's *Légendes canaques*, through the mediation of Maurice Leenhardt.

It is likely that Henri Lévy-Bruhl found in these same boxes preserved at the Musée de l'Homme the notebooks his father had written shortly before his death in preparation for a future work. Dated from January 1938 to February 1939 and written during walks in the woods of Batagelle and Boulogne and during stays in Normandy and Brittany, they attest to the intellectual mobility of the octogenarian philosopher, recapitulating the difficulties encountered and the tasks to be accomplished by his next book. The last notebook concludes with these words: "I must now take up successively each of the aspects by showing the solidarity with the others—and, before passing to participation, distinguish the different kinds and also try to bring out what they have in common" (Lévy-Bruhl 1949: 252).

Henri Lévy-Bruhl proposed to Henri Bréhier, director of the *Revue philosophique*, that he publish a selection of these notebooks. Bréhier chose the third notebook, where Lucien Lévy-Bruhl affirmed his "definitive abandonment of the term prelogical" and mentioned a "reflection on Einstein" and an "agreement with Leenhardt." These notebooks bring to light the conceptual displacement at work, in contrast to the apparent continuity of his books on "primitive mentality": participation was no longer a logical principle opposed to contradiction but a set of facts that should be described in their internal variations. Henri Lévy-Bruhl wrote to Leenhardt, who had just spent a year in New Caledonia founding the French Institute of Oceania, to thank him for sending his autographed book *Do Kamo*—"one of the most beautiful books I have read in a long time"—and to ask Leenhardt to write the foreword for the publication of Lucien Lévy-Bruhl's complete notebooks by the Presses universitaires de France.[3]

---

3. Maurice and Raymond Leenhardt Archives, Letter from H. Lévy-Bruhl to M. Leenhardt, June 29, 1948.

But Henri Lévy-Bruhl did not agree with the way Leenhardt presented the notebooks. Leenhardt paid tribute to "the filial piety of his children (who) allowed his eldest son to find and save these last notebooks" (Leenhardt 1949: xxxix). However, he also read the notebooks as opening a double field of research on the threshold of which Lévy-Bruhl would have remained because of the Kantian epistemology in which he had been educated:

> There are, in fact, two fields that, at the end of the last century, were still closed, and that his work contributed to open: that of the aesthetics of the primitives and that of myth. Of the first he did not have to cross much more than the threshold. He liked to show the objects of indigenous art that he had in his vestibule or his office; I and his philosopher friends had difficulty following him in his enthusiasm. ... But in the second field, the myth, he has indeed crossed the threshold and traced an avenue where all the mythologists encounter him. (Leenhardt 1949: xlvii)

Leenhardt thus lay the ground for the two fields in which he was to engage in the afterwar years: mythology, which he was teaching at the Practical School of Advanced Studies where he had taken up Mauss's chair on "comparative religions of non-civilized peoples" in 1940, which would lead him to publish *Do Kamo* in 1947; and Pacific Studies, in line with his appointment as director of the Oceania department at the Musée de l'Homme in 1943, which would lead him to publish *Arts de l'Océanie* in 1947. This double engagement led Leenhardt to interpret Lévy-Bruhl's thought not as a metaphysics in the manner of Fondane but as an ontology of everyday life inspired by Heidegger. According to Leenhardt, participation was oriented "not at Being in itself, the abstract being, capable of evading and taking on the figure of God, but at the being of our daily encounter, which, on the other side of the world as here, lives on exchanges and whose spirit is variously shaped by the effects of their circulation" (Leenhardt 1949: lv).

In his own rereading of his father's work, Henri Lévy-Bruhl refused the existential phenomenology of the "lived myth" that Leenhardt proposed and he maintained the notion of mystical mentality in the sense of collective representations irreducible to individual rationality. He opposed Leenhardt's interpretation of the notebooks, first during a session chaired by Jean Wahl at the Collège de philosophie and then after reading a first version of the foreword.

Confident in my father's thinking and certain that I am not mistaken, I can assure you that he never, at any time in his life, disputed the ideas that he had proposed in his first volume and which, in several very diverse fields, have shown their efficiency and their fruitfulness. I deeply regret that one can draw a diametrically opposite conclusion from your lecture and that is why I could not hear it without feeling real sorrow. ... You insist that my father had expressed self-criticism in these writings intended for him only, which makes me almost regret having given these notebooks to the public. At least the attentive reader will be able to realize the effort of his inner thought. But it seems to me that the role of the writer who presents these pages to the public and who, by this very fact, whether he likes it or not, orients the reader's thoughts is not to give any interpretation, especially since these pages are by a dead man who is no longer there to defend himself.[4]

The tone of these letters says as much about the vigor of intellectual exchanges in the postwar period as it does about the wounds affecting Henri Lévy-Bruhl at the end of the war. His position as defender of the family heritage led him to adopt a fixed epistemological position, whereas his work before the war showed an ability to seize new objects in order to connect them to collective research in the making. This can be clearly seen in another polemic after the war that placed him in opposition to Henri-Irénée Marrou, a professor of the history of Christianity, who was close to the journal *Esprit* in which he signed articles under the pseudonym of Henri Davenson. Henri Lévy-Bruhl probably encountered Marrou at the Faculty of Lyon in 1940, where Marrou taught at the beginning of the war and encouraged his students to join the Résistance before succeeding his master Jérôme Carcopino at the Sorbonne in April 1941, when the latter became secretary of state for public instruction. The association between Marrou and Carcopino, who advised against Henri Lévy-Bruhl resuming his courses in 1942, may explain the note of resentment in Henri Lévy-Bruhl's criticism of a text that Marrou published in a volume of homage to Bergson, who died in 1941. Henri Bergson thus left a testament in which he famously declared: "My reflections have brought me closer and closer to Catholicism, where I see the definite completion of Judaism. I would have converted, had I

---

4.   Maurice and Raymond Leenhardt Archives, Letter from Henri Lévy-Bruhl to Maurice Leenhardt, June 6, 1949.

not seen over many years the preparation ... of a formidable wave of anti-Semitism that is going to sweep over the world. I wanted to remain among those who will be persecuted tomorrow" (Soulez and Worms 1997: 277). The polemics about Bergson's legacy, therefore, concerned his hesitation between Judaism and Catholicism in the context of the postwar debates on what "Libération" meant.

Under the title "Bergson and history," Marrou placed himself in line with Charles Péguy to affirm that the "Bergsonian revolution" liberated the historian from "determinism" and "sociologism" by valuing the unpredictability of the event (Marrou 1941). Lévy-Bruhl replied in an article entitled "History and Bergsonism," published by the *Revue de synthèse* in 1945, that criticized this call to a subjective conception of history. The determinist philosophers of the nineteenth century could appear reductive in the eyes of Bergsonians like Péguy and Marrou only because, Lévy-Bruhl argued, "they ignored the very considerable part that the mystical aspirations of sentimental life hold in human history. They have tended, from then on, to explain all social phenomena by causes of a material order and this has led them to certain errors" (H. Lévy-Bruhl 1945: 144). In the same way, the history of law "does not take into account the mystical environment in which primitive societies live, the tight network of prescriptions and prohibitions that hinders any activity of the individual there" (H. Lévy-Bruhl 1945: 144). In the eyes of Henri Lévy-Bruhl, Bergsonism played an important role in criticizing the privilege given to mechanical causalities in human history but threatened the rigor of the rationalist method by its appeal to intuition. Lévy-Bruhl, who followed his father's narrow path between Bergson and Durkheim, concluded his article combatively: "On the whole, history has resisted, and must continue to resist, the seductions of a doctrine that, if we are not careful, risks rendering futile its age-old efforts to become a scientific discipline" (H. Lévy-Bruhl 1945: 149). Marrou responded to this in 1946 in *Le Monde*: "When we speak of history, Mr. H. Lévy-Bruhl (and this is quite natural from the heir to this illustrious name) means sociology. ... But to assign, as he does, the search for causes as the essential task of the historian is to destroy, for the benefit of a hypothetical sociology, all the originality of historical knowledge" (Riché 2003: 179).

Marrou then cited Wilhelm Dilthey's conception according to which history is a comprehensive knowledge of singularities. Following Raymond Aron, he thus introduced in France the distinction between explaining and understanding that, in neo-Kantian philosophy, separated the sciences of nature from the sciences of culture (Aron 1961). Where

Lucien Lévy-Bruhl had prudently kept away from the polarity between Bergsonism and positivism, between understanding and explaining, his son Henri thus became associated with a conception of the human sciences that had been overtaken by the new impulse of the Liberation period. Henri Lévy-Bruhl reacted to this humiliating situation by participating in a collective effort to reconstruct the social sciences.

The Reorganization of the Social Sciences in the Postwar Period

In 1946, Henri Lévy-Bruhl allied himself with Gabriel Le Bras and Georges Gurvitch to found the Center for Sociological Studies (Centre d'études sociologiques), the first social science institution to receive support from the young National Center for Scientific Research (Centre national de la recherche scientifique), which had been created in 1939 by the physicist Jean Perrin. Le Bras, born in 1891 in Brittany, was a former member of the École française de Rome, a professor of the history of canon law at the University of Paris, a professor at the Institute of Political Studies (Institut d'études politiques) in Paris, president of the Society of the Religious History of France (Société d'histoire religieuse de la France), and director of studies at the Practical School of Advanced Studies. Gurvitch, born in 1894 in Russia, defended a thesis on Fichte at the University of Berlin in 1925, then a thesis on social law in Paris in 1932, before succeeding Maurice Halbwachs as the chair of sociology at the University of Strasbourg (Bosserman 1981; Heilbron 1991; Marcel 2001). During the war, he created and directed the French Institute of Sociology at the Free School of Advanced Studies in New York, where he had gone into exile to escape the laws on Jews introduced by the Vichy government. Henri Lévy-Bruhl thus added the prestige of his name to the academic legitimacy of the former and the scientific legitimacy of the latter. He also associated it with that of Halbwachs's widow and Victor Basch's daughter, Yvonne, who worked in the center's administration.

The center aimed to take up the torch of Durkheimian sociology, which was then kept by the two holders of the chairs of sociology at the Sorbonne, Albert Bayet and Georges Davy. In 1949, Gurvitch, Le Bras, and Lévy-Bruhl revived *L'Année sociologique*, the journal founded by Durkheim, and invited Bayet, Davy, Mauss, and Leenhardt to its new editorial board. With a rich library that Gurvitch brought back from the US and a new journal founded in 1946, the *Cahiers internationaux de sociologie,* the Center for Sociological Studies organized conferences that attracted young researchers who were eager to embark in studies in the social sciences and attempted to orient them toward empirical research. Georges Balandier, Michel Crozier, Henri Mendras, Edgar Morin, and Alain Touraine thus attended the center.

The alliance with Gurvitch allowed Henri Lévy-Bruhl to place himself at the core of French sociology to defend the heritage of his father, but it also risked neutralizing him in the powerful innovative currents that were recomposing the intellectual field. Gurvitch was in rivalry with Lévi-Strauss, whom he had met at the Free School of Advanced Studies in New York. Lévi-Strauss had benefited more than Gurvitch from scientific innovations in the US such as linguistics and cybernetics (Jeanpierre 2004). While Gurvitch placed the sociological theories of Parsons, Merton, and Sorokin in discussion with a philosophy of "levels of consciousness" with the intention of reconciling Durkheim, Bergson, and Lévy-Bruhl, Lévi-Strauss relied on the ethnological work of Boas, Sapir, and Lowie, as well as Jakobson's structural linguistics, to build a new anthropology based on the "structural unconscious." When Lévi-Strauss returned to Paris in 1945 in search of a position, Gurvitch, who enjoyed a more stable academic position, suggested that his rival write a chapter on French sociology in the volume on sociology that he was editing with two American colleagues. Lévi-Strauss was surprisingly complimentary about Lucien Lévy-Bruhl, no doubt to keep the favor of the founders of the Center for Sociological Studies. He underlined that the author of *La mentalité primitive* conceived of the individual as separate from society and that Lucien Lévy-Bruhl could henceforth be qualified as a "rebellious son" rather than a "docile pupil," since he refused the notions of collective consciousness and the sacred that held such a central place in Durkheimian sociology. "Thus Lévy-Bruhl, while disdaining what seems today the essential part of Durkheim's teaching, i.e. methodology, remained obsessed by the dangers introduced into it by philosophical survivals" (Lévi-Strauss 1945: 532).

In 1950, Gurvitch asked Lévi-Strauss to write the introduction to a collection of articles by Mauss that he had assembled under the title *Sociologie et anthropologie (Sociology and anthropology)* for the Presses universitaires de France. But Lévi-Strauss took advantage of this homage to Durkheim's nephew, who had just died, to emancipate himself from Durkheimian sociology, whose legacy Gurvitch and Lévy-Bruhl had preserved. Lévi-Strauss described Mauss as a new Moses who, on the ruins of Durkheimian sociology, discovered the structural unconscious as a new territory whose map remained to be drawn in order to occupy and exploit it (Lévi-Strauss 1950). Gurvitch presented this "Introduction to the Work of Marcel Mauss" as a "very personal interpretation" and criticized the concept of structural unconscious in the *Cahiers internationaux de sociologie* (Gurvitch 1955). He also refused to invite Lévi-Strauss to a commemoration of the centenary of Durkheim's birth at a colloquium that he organized at the Sorbonne in 1958 or to let him participate in the homage of the centenary of Lévy-Bruhl in a special issue of the *Revue philosophique* in 1957.

By taking up the heritage of sociology's founding father, Gurvitch and Henri Lévy-Bruhl defended a sociology that appeared conservative and defensive in relation to the intellectual innovations that were occurring in the social sciences after the Second World War. In 1950, Lévi-Strauss performed an operation with Mauss that was similar to what Leenhardt had done with Lévy-Bruhl a year earlier: he presented himself as the disciple accomplishing the scientific program that the master had only been able to sketch on the ruins of philosophy. But whereas Leenhardt was pulling Lévy-Bruhl towards a phenomenological ontology inspired by Heidegger, Lévi-Strauss was drawing Mauss towards a structural anthropology inspired by Jakobson. The opposition between "lived myth" and "mytho-logic," which can be brought back to Marrou's distinction between understanding and explaining, thus came to polarize the human sciences in France in a durable way. Lévi-Strauss won the battle as he replaced Leenhardt, after the latter's retirement in 1951, on the chair Leenhardt had held at the Practical School of Advanced Studies, which Lévi-Strauss renamed the chair of "Religions of Societies without Writing." Here Lévi-Strauss presented his own "structural" method for analyzing mythology. The severity with which Lévi-Strauss discussed Lévy-Bruhl's analyses of "a supposed 'principle of participation'" or "a mysticism impregnated with metaphysics" (Lévi-Strauss 2008: 599), when he himself turned to the classifications of "savage mind," was largely due to his attempt to distinguish himself from the phenomenological interpretation that Leenhardt gave, but also from Gurvitch's sociological method.

While Henri Lévi-Bruhl tried to maintain his father's method, the analysis of "primitive societies" attentive to a variety of facts, he found himself caught, at the end of the war and in the moment of the Liberation's intellectual ebullition, between two powerful intellectual currents,

German phenomenology and American structuralism, which both mar-
ginalized him. However, while he was in danger of appearing only as a
conservative heir of Durkheimian sociology, Henri Lévy-Bruhl managed to propose theoretical and methodological innovations based on
his use of statistics.

CHAPTER 10

Reconstructing the French Economy with Statistics

Henri Lévy-Bruhl's Investigations of Crime

In 1949, Georges Gurvitch, who had just been elected to the Sorbonne, entrusted the direction of the Center for Sociological Studies to Georges Friedmann, who worked on "the problems of the industrial world" by developing Marcel Mauss's ideas concerning the anthropology of techniques as connecting bodies and objects (Friedmann 1946). Gurvitch then turned towards philosophical questions by founding the Group of Sociology of Knowledge (Groupe de sociologie de la connaissance) at the Sorbonne, in which Roger Bastide, Jacques Berque, Jean Cazeneuve, Jean Duvignaud, and Lucien Goldman collaborated. This new orientation of the Center for Sociological Studies suited Henri Lévy-Bruhl, since it allowed him to launch a statistical survey in 1950 on what he called "smart crime" (what is today called "white-collar crime"), that is to say, crimes linked to commercial activities such as breach of trust or swindling. Lévy-Bruhl created a group of criminal sociology studies within the Center for Sociological Studies and, in 1956, entrusted its direction to André Davidovitch. This group carried out surveys among magistrates and police officers to establish statistics on this new form of criminality, using the methods of American sociology.

Such investigations allowed Henri Lévy-Bruhl to bring together again the two types of work he had carried out before the war and that the looting of his apartment had prevented him from carrying out: studies on archaic Roman law and analyses of modern commercial law.

His aim was to understand how archaic accusations of criminality were transformed in complex economic societies governed by the codification of trust through letters of credit. According to the definition given by André Davidovitch, "swindling is characterized as a disease of the trust essential to the functioning of economic institutions" (Chevreau, Audren, and Verdier 2018: 204). Lévy-Bruhl thus built on Émile Durkheim's reflections on anomie, revised through the interpretation of Robert Merton in the US. He showed how the development of society produced new forms of crime that escaped archaic moral categories, thus necessitating a new form of regulation. This is why he used statistics to reveal these crimes that passed under the legal radar but that affected what Durkheim had called the "collective consciousness" just as much as archaic crimes, because they occupied the daily life of the courts through their jurisprudence.

In 1958, Davidovitch and Henri Lévy-Bruhl published an article entitled "La statistique et le droit" (Statistics and law) in *L'Année sociologique* that, in many respects, constituted a real program for the social sciences by applying Durkheim's sociological method to industrial societies (H. Lévy-Bruhl and Davidovitch 1957–58). Henri Lévy-Bruhl opened the article with a "note on method" in which he recalled this principle of the sociology of law:

> There are a certain number of prescriptions that, without being written down anywhere, are commonly and, for some of them, unanimously observed. Because of their latent life, they generally escape the attention of jurists. They are, nonetheless, true rules of law, the manifestation of a customary law that constitutes what is most alive in even the most modern legal systems. (H. Lévy-Bruhl and Davidovitch 1957–58: 354)

To reach this living form of law, Lévy-Bruhl continued, the jurist should become a sociologist and practice investigation by multiplying the sources: jurisprudence, the acts of practice, the archives of notaries, the clerks of litigation, the civil status acts, the papers of large and small industrial and commercial enterprises, and many more. To these legal sources should be added statistics, that is, the documents that the state produces to know its population, such as the General Account of the Administration of Justice that France had published since 1927. This numerical information on judicial activity allowed sociologists to know the law not only in its principles but also in its application. Henri Lévy-Bruhl noted that the availability of statistics distinguished the study of Roman law from the study of modern law. "This absence of statistical information is, incidentally, one of the most regrettable gaps in our knowledge of Roman antiquity. This gap does not exist for modern law. We do not lack statistics, thank God! We would rather be overwhelmed by them" (H. Lévy-Bruhl and Davidovitch 1957–58: 354).

The difficulty for the sociologist was, therefore, to sort out among these abundant statistics the numerical data that would be relevant for his investigation, because these data had been produced with an administrative, not a sociological, aim. Rather than an epistemological reflection on the use of statistics for the sociology of law, Henri Lévy-Bruhl thus called for an extension of the use of statistics to cover all social activities. If legal statistics made it possible to "follow in time and space the modalities of criminality," it was necessary to widen criminology's field of study.

> Civil justice opens up perspectives on the family, inheritance, property, contracts, etc. Commercial justice sheds light on certain aspects of economic life, company law, bankruptcies, etc. … It would be interesting to know the matrimonial regimes practiced in France and their social and geographical distribution. In the same way, many questions arise concerning divorces and legal separations, inheritance, labor law, commercial companies, etc., to which surveys expressed in numerical data could provide a satisfactory answer. (H. Lévy-Bruhl and Davidovitch 1957–58: 356)

This 1958 text thus marked a real act of faith in statistics in a process of reorganization after the war. Since statistical data were much more abundant and precise than those available to Durkheim at the end of the nineteenth century and to his students between the two wars, the use of statistics was a real opportunity to relaunch Durkheimian sociology on a new basis.

Claude Lévi-Strauss expressed the same faith in a field of research parallel to that of Henri Lévy-Bruhl's: kinship, which he understood in the sense of rules of alliance rather than descendance. In his thesis, written in New York during the war and defended at the Sorbonne in 1947, Lévi-Strauss identified, from the archaic kinship systems governed by the prohibition of incest and observed by the ethnographic method, an elementary form consisting in a generalized exchange of women, goods, and words. For this he borrowed concepts from Mauss and Granet

(Lévi-Strauss 1949; Dumont 2006; Héran 2009). To study the transformations of this elementary form into complex systems of kinship, Lévi-Strauss proposed turning to statistics and relying on computers to sort out the data that would be relevant for sociological questioning. There was, in his eyes, only a difference in scale between the "mechanical" models that ethnology constructs and the "statistical models" used by history, its rival in the leadership of the human sciences, a difference that should be reduced by the progress of the structural method (Lévi-Strauss 1958: 337). Like Henri Lévy-Bruhl and in continuity with Durkheim and Mauss, Lévi-Strauss defined the social rules as modes of regulation of confidence and codification of credit, which led him to study the economic and the social as inseparable. The economy then appeared as a domain of regularities in which the sociologist could advise the state from an objective knowledge. "Structure," the buzzword of the human sciences in the postwar world, was a new way of thinking about how chance could be integrated into social rules, which was the problem that Lucien Lévy-Bruhl had raised in the interwar period. What, then, was the role of institutions in this integration and how could they play the role of sentinels, which Lévy-Bruhl as well as Lévi-Strauss considered them to be in their socialist engagement between the wars?

Raymond Lévy-Bruhl's Surveys in Labor Economics

Such a faith in statistics was rooted in the National Institute of Statistics and Economic Studies (Institut national de la statistique et des études économiques, INSEE) that was founded in 1946 by the provisional government to replace the National Statistics Service (Service national des statistiques) of the Vichy regime. Raymond Lévy-Bruhl, Henri's nephew, was one of the main actors at INSEE at the time of its foundation, so that the program launched by Davidovitch and Henri Lévy-Bruhl in 1958 can be seen as an echo of the discussions between uncle and nephew at the end of the war.

In 1946, Raymond Lévy-Bruhl resumed his studies in Paris and obtained three postgraduate diplomas, in law, political economy, and economics. On the advice of André Mayer, professor of physiology at the Collège de France, he sat for an external competitive examination at INSEE, where he was recruited as an administrator. His director, Francis-Louis Closon, authorized him to study in the US on a Rockefeller Foundation grant. He spent six months at Columbia University in New

York studying mathematical statistics, then one month at the Bureau of Labor Statistics, and two months at the Census Bureau in Washington. He brought back documents on the method of random sampling, which had been invented in the context of New Deal policies. The innovation of this statistical technique consisted of defining samples by calculating probabilities on a large enough population and combining them with precise sociological questions. It obtained better statistical results than the quota method, which was used in opinion polls by Gallup and imported to France by Jean Stoetzel, creator of the French Institute of Public Opinion in 1938 (R. Lévy-Bruhl 1951; Blondiaux 1998). It also differed from the aureole method used by Alfred Sauvy when he created and directed the National Institute of Demographic Studies (Institut national d'études démographiques) between 1945 and 1962. The aureole method involved interviewing households using focus groups, whereas the random method defined representative samples by random drawing and stratified sampling. In 1948–49, Raymond Lévy-Bruhl, in collaboration with Pierre Thionnet, designed a set of random sample surveys on the partial abolition of textile rationing and on the consumption of nonquota food products. Thionnet, more of a mathematician, defined the samples, while Lévy-Bruhl, more of a sociologist, developed the questionnaires.

The significance of this method can be measured by comparing it to the work that Lucien Lévy-Bruhl carried out at the Ministry of Armaments with Albert Thomas—who later, at the International Labour Office in Geneva, trained the very statisticians who were to found INSEE. To assess the capacities of wartime factories, Lucien Lévy-Bruhl had to rely on workers' representatives, especially the unions, and aggregate their data in tables. The "industrial effort" during the war thus rested on the intensive participation of the workers in the knowledge of government, realizing the Jaurésian ideal of a "new army" endowed with social rights. But while this method constituted political progress compared to the military statistics at the time of the Dreyfus Affair, it also presented new risks, such as those that appeared in the scandals concerning industrial accidents. This led Lucien Lévy-Bruhl to pose the following question at the end of the war: how can "primitive mentality," understood as a spontaneous collective thought that animates the greater part of human activity, give meaning to chance, this recent construction resulting from the calculation of probabilities and integrated into statistics? Such a question, which became increasingly urgent as new economic and political crises emerged in the interwar period, led Lucien Lévy-Bruhl to outline a policy of vigilance based on the analysis of participation in "primitive mentality."

However, such an experiment in participation, which had echoes in American pragmatism, came to an end after the Second World War, notably through the statistical work of Raymond Lévy-Bruhl. By defining samples randomly and relying on the law of large numbers to produce an entity that modelized the social, New Deal statistics departed from the fragile compromise between representation and participation that had prevailed in the interwar period, when farmers and the unemployed reported their own numbers of activity. The samples defined by Thionnet and the questionnaires built by Raymond Lévy-Bruhl integrated chance no longer as an entity external to the social but as a necessary tool for the design of sociological models (Didier 2020).

Random surveys can, then, be described as preparedness techniques, in contrast to the statistics employed since the end of the nineteenth century that were based on probability calculations and prevention techniques. While prevention is based on laws of probability allowing statisticians to calculate risks, preparedness anticipates future events whose probability cannot be calculated and whose consequences can be catastrophic. If random surveys seemed at first to reduce social diversity to randomly defined samples, they recomposed this diversity from the sample itself, thanks to questionnaires that give access to its internal composition. It was then possible, through simulation and variation, to compare each sample with other similar samples to anticipate the effects of an economic shock. In contrast, the statistics consulted by insurance companies were based on the data of actuaries, who calculated premiums and levies, so that they provided only a very imperfect picture of the social groups they were supposed to represent but were sufficiently accurate to calculate risks from the vulnerabilities for each social group. Hence Ernest Seboul's famous definition of insurance in 1863 as "the compensation of the effects of chance by mutuality organized according to the laws of statistics" (Ewald 2020: 165). By integrating chance into the definition of samples, random surveys made it possible to compensate for economic shocks, events with a low probability and catastrophic consequences, by using simulation methods.

In 1950, Raymond Lévy-Bruhl was assigned to the social statistics division of INSEE, which included about sixty agents from the Ministry of Labor and was thus autonomous from both INSEE and the Ministry. This gave Lévy-Bruhl the opportunity to launch a series of surveys based on questionnaires he had written and simplified himself. These surveys provided the government with information on wage and price levels, the number of employees and weekly working hours, allowing them to simulate the effect of an economic shock on the social infrastructure. An article in the April 8, 1955, issue of *Informations industrielles et commerciales* described Raymond Lévy-Bruhl as follows after he announced that employees had an additional Fr 300 billion of purchasing power as a result of government reforms of wages and family benefits: "He is the perfect example of an intellectual. Shy, self-effacing, he would seem insignificant if not for his extraordinary intelligence. It is perfectly useless to ask him about himself and his tastes; he is entirely captured by his passion for statistics. My personality, he confides, is simply the point of intersection of a certain number of statistical facts." The article noticed that Raymond Lévy-Bruhl belongs to "an old family of men of thought," mentioning in particular his grandfather Lucien and his uncle Henri, described as "sociologists," but also his father Jean, "a renowned chemical engineer." It concluded with a description of the division of social statistics under Raymond Lévy-Bruhl's leadership: "In the cellars of the ministry, a workshop of statistical machines permanently grinds millions of perforated cards whose codes make it possible to follow the evolution of the payroll of 20,000 companies hiring more than fifty people with the most extreme rigor" (*Informations* 1955).

The decade during which Raymond Lévy-Bruhl developed labor statistics at the Ministry enabled him to make a reputation for himself and to rise in the hierarchy, even though he was not a polytechnician like most of the INSEE managers. In 1962, Claude Gruson, INSEE's new director general, brought Raymond Lévy-Bruhl back to the main site at quai Branly to coordinate the reorganization of the institute. In particular, he integrated the Economic and Financial Studies Department and transformed the Colonial Statistics Department to train French-speaking statisticians in the former colonies, an approach then called "cooperation." In 1966, INSEE's then new director general, Jean Ripert, made Raymond Lévy-Bruhl his chief of staff. In 1968, this led Lévy-Bruhl to negotiate with the unions, who questioned the administrative hierarchy but respected Lévy-Bruhl for his socialist pedigree. In 1972, when he was appointed secretary general of INSEE, his first task was to supervise the transfer of the institute from the quai Branly to the Porte de Vanves. In 1974, he had to deal with a controversy over the price index with the main Communist trade union, the Confédération générale du travail, which accused INSEE of manipulating its index to allow President Giscard d'Estaing to set lower wages. Following this crisis, Edmond Malinvaud, a Keynesian economist known for his work on unemployment, was appointed director general and worked with Raymond Lévy-Bruhl between 1974 and 1987. Malinvaud paid tribute to him after his death in 2008: "Throughout his career, Lévy-Bruhl was recognized as a statistician with strong moral values and technical skills, who contributed greatly to the consolidation and independence of INSEE and thus to the quality of public service in his country."[1]

Raymond Lévy-Bruhl's career thus seemed to realize the dream of reconstructing the French economy through statistics, for which his uncle Henri Lévy-Bruhl brought the support of Durkheimian sociology. An agency producing knowledge of social activity as close to the state as INSEE, while claiming scientific autonomy by importing innovations from abroad, could realize the socialist program of establishing a knowledge of society that would orient social development. With the method of random surveys, chance was no longer considered to arrive from outside the social sphere as a threat but was integrated into statistical knowledge in order to come as close as possible to social reality. One can say that Lucien Lévy-Bruhl's socialist project to integrate the "primitive mentality" into the "civilized mentality" was thus accomplished by his son and grandson through statistics. However, the last part of Raymond Lévy-Bruhl's life revealed a personal concern, which shed new light on his career as a statistician.

1.   Daniel Lévy-Bruhl private collection, Edmond Malinvaud, "In Memoriam Raymond Lévy-Bruhl (1922–2008)."

CHAPTER II

The Return of the Dreyfus Affair in Decolonization

Raymond Lévy-Bruhl's Research on Statistics under Vichy

In a course on statistics he gave at INSEE, Raymond Lévy-Bruhl contrasted the confidence of Americans in statistics as a "science of government" with the skepticism of the French, who viewed statistics as "only a refined form of lying."[1] This ironic note indicated that Raymond Lévy-Bruhl's career was an effort to save French statistics from its compromise with the lies the state had made during the Dreyfus Affair and the Vichy regime, by relying on the development of American statistics. In 1992, INSEE Director General Jean-Claude Milleron entrusted Raymond Lévy-Bruhl, who had retired four years earlier, with a research project on the role of the National Statistics Service (Service National des Statistique, SNS) under the Vichy regime. Raymond Lévy-Bruhl joined forces with historians Jean-Pierre Azéma and Béatrice Touchelay to undertake this investigation, which resulted in a report published by INSEE in 1998. This report definitively established that the SNS had not been used for the police registration of Jews as a first step toward deportation nor for sending young men to the Compulsory Labor Service.

The SNS was founded in November 1941 by the polytechnician René Carmille, who had previously worked as a general controller in the army. It merged the General Statistics of France, an institution

---

1. Daniel Lévy-Bruhl private collection, documents on course given by Raymond Lévy-Bruhl at INSEE in 1960.

founded in 1833 by Adolphe Thiers at the Ministry of Commerce, with the Economic Observation Service (created in 1937), the Institute of Business Conditions (created in 1938) and the Demographic Service, which Carmille had created in December 1940 to transfer the records of the military recruitment offices to the Ministry of Finance. Carmille was an advocate of mechanographic methods in the administration, that is, the use of punch cards. He introduced the identification number, which made it possible to assign a thirteen-digit number to each individual from birth to death. He standardized all the files centralized by the SNS to integrate the information available on the identity card instituted by the Vichy regime. The SNS was set up in the free zone in Lyon, with a large budget that enabled it to recruit nearly a thousand people and to buy mechanographic equipment. It relied on eighteen regional offices in the free zone and in Algeria to provide the Vichy regime with information on its population. The question that Raymond Lévy-Bruhl posed was to know whether this mass of statistical data may have allowed the French administration to collaborate with the occupying army in massive transfers of populations, such as the deportation of Jews and the Compulsory Labor Service. The war was a threshold in the history of statistics in France: services that, though poorly equipped, had allowed the state to adapt quickly to new circumstances following the liberal principles of the Third Republic suddenly became administrations massively equipped to justify the interventions of an authoritarian regime, a trend that was later accentuated in the Fifth Republic. Raymond Lévy-Bruhl wrote in his report:

> The desire of the SNS to have as much information as possible in order to update the files, to use mechanographic equipment, and to show the effectiveness of the information apparently outweighed the awareness of the risks that this information poses to certain categories of the population. Some may point to the oral instructions to slow down the work, but others may see, behind the blindness of the service's managers, a deliberate desire to compile files with a racist or political objective. (Azéma, R. Lévy-Bruhl, and Touchelay 1998: 28)

The confidential report signed by Azéma, Raymond Lévy-Bruhl, and Touchelay in July 1998 and sent to INSEE's director general validated Carmille's statements that the SNS was doing statistics and not policing. The report concluded that "the SNS as a whole was not collaborationist" (Azéma, R. Lévy-Bruhl, and Touchelay 1998: 29–30). It also reminded the reader that Carmille had "a heroic destiny": after "deploying a praise-worthy energy to implement a clandestine mobilization" (Azéma, R. Lévy-Bruhl, and Touchelay 1998: 40), he was arrested by the Gestapo on February 3, 1944, tortured by Klaus Barbie, and deported to Dachau on January 25, 1945, where he died of typhus on July 2, 1945.

The behavior of Carmille and his employees during the war led Lévy-Bruhl to ask the following question: "How far can a civil servant serve a state that ceases to be a state of law and openly practices repression and exclusion?" (Azéma, R. Lévy-Bruhl, and Touchelay 1998: 58; Baruch 1997). Consulting the SNS's incomplete archives revealed to him a shift in 1943 from a reformist zeal in a climate of moral crisis to a loss of confidence in the legitimacy of the regime. The report continued:

> René Carmille seems to belong to this ambivalent category of people, more numerous and more important than is generally believed, which historians classify as "vichysto-resistant." Like them, Carmille was unquestionably anti-German but served Vichy loyally, believing at first that the national revolution would effectively prepare for revenge. When he understood that Philippe Pétain was not playing a double game and that the regime had lost, after November 1942, all legitimacy, he entered the Résistance as a conscious and organized volunteer. (Azéma, R. Lévy-Bruhl, and Touchelay 1998: 46)

By taking up the term "vichysto-resistant" as proposed by Jean-Pierre Azéma and Olivier Wieviorka (1997), Raymond Lévy-Bruhl opposed those he called "the unconditional supporters of the SNS or of the memory of René Carmille" who wanted the latter to be considered a full-fledged "resistant" (Azéma, R. Lévy-Bruhl, and Touchelay 1998: 52). He pointed to a letter dated June 18, 1941, in which Carmille had offered his help to Xavier Vallat, the Vichy government's general commissioner for Jewish questions, to develop a form that would make it possible "to gather all useful information on the Jews, to discover those among them who have not made their declaration, to organize a control of the state of their property and their possible transfers, and, in the end, to be enlightened exactly on the Jewish problem" (Azéma, R. Lévy-Bruhl, and Touchelay 1998: 53). It seemed, however, that, after Xavier Vallat's first negative and then positive response, Carmille dragged his feet in sending him the necessary information, so that the arrests of the Jews were finally not based on SNS files. Taking up the distinction made by the German historian Martin Broszat (1981) between *Resistenz* (voluntary inertia) and *Widerstand* (active resistance), Lévy-Bruhl and his fellow historians wrote:

> The administrators of the SNS—like those in charge of almost all French administrations—initially treated the Jewish question as one among others, admittedly in a non-police manner but certainly administratively, especially since most of them were not *a priori* opposed to the Vichy ideology. At the end of 1942 or in the spring of 1943, their attitude changed and they gradually adopted *Resistenz*. (Azéma, R. Lévy-Bruhl, and Touchelay 1998: 52)

Raymond Lévy-Bruhl's assessment of Carmille's role in the Vichy government is comparable to that of his grandfather on the role of Commandant Picquart in the Dreyfus Affair. Like Picquart, Carmille was a loyal French officer who shared the anti-Semitism of his contemporaries and who only stopped supporting his hierarchy when the course of events had profoundly affected its legitimacy (Duclert 2006). According to Raymond Lévy-Bruhl, Carmille was one of those "technocrats" who took advantage of the Vichy regime to pass reform projects that they had seen blocked by the parliamentary regime. This is evidenced by Carmille's own testimony at the trial in Riom on January 4, 1941, where he accused the secretary general of national defense in the Blum government, Robert Jacomet, of not implementing the reforms he advocated (Azéma, R. Lévy-Bruhl, and Touchelay 1998: 48). At the same trial, Léon Blum defended the Popular Front policy with the same passion of argument that Jean Jaurès had shown at the Rennes trial.

The report signed by Raymond Lévy-Bruhl had little resonance outside INSEE, which had just celebrated its fiftieth anniversary. Internally, his factual and moderate approach provoked criticism from both sides: those who wanted a stronger reprobation of the SNS activities and those who would have liked to see a rehabilitation of its director. Raymond Lévy-Bruhl simply noted that INSEE sent the SNS files and identification procedures to the National Commission on Information Technology and Civil Liberties (Commission nationale de l'informatique et des libertés), created in 1978, and he wondered about the use that an authoritarian regime could make of them. His detached consideration of the transformation of the SNS into INSEE in 1946 was facilitated by the fact that he was one of the only people to enter INSEE at its creation without having first attended the SNS school, thanks to an exemption for those who had been excluded from higher education by the anti-Jewish laws. No wonder then if he was reproached by his colleagues for his critical gaze on the institution he had worked for during all his professional life.

Henri Lévy-Bruhl's Teaching in the Ethnology of Law

Raymond Lévy-Bruhl's belated concern about the role of the French state during the war, at the end of a career during which he had served it loyally, echoes the last work of his uncle Henri before his death in 1964. If Henri Lévy-Bruhl's most innovative research was carried out at the Center for Sociological Studies on the sociology of crime based on statistics, it should be remembered that most of his career was spent at the Faculty of Paris, where he was reinstated by a decree of September 29, 1944, and where he created the Institute of Roman Law in 1948, and at the Practical School of Advanced Studies, where he taught history of law (Soula 2015). This contrast between apparently conservative academic positions and truly innovative statistical research constitutes the singularity of Henri Lévy-Bruhl's position in the postwar social science landscape. However, the 1960s marked a turning point in his thinking, since he responded to public demands by putting forward the ideals of truth and justice that were at the heart of the Dreyfus Affair.

Two speeches and three publications allow us to grasp Henri Lévy-Bruhl's thinking in the second part of his life. At the establishment of the Institute of Roman Law in 1948, Lévy-Bruhl underlined the institute's function by recalling what the history of Roman law and the most recent events had shown: a rational monument such as a system of law could be invaded by obscure forces; one should know the former in order to better control the latter.

> The feeling of justice is equally shared among all the peoples of the earth, but the rules of substance and form according to which it is dispensed are not all so happily conceived. It is the greatest glory of Rome to have created a legal system that, after so many centuries, can still be considered a masterpiece and whose beneficent effect has not yet been exhausted. Hailed in the Middle Ages as the very expression of reason, it has found new prestige since, after a long battle and at great sacrifice, the forces of reason have prevailed over a dark mysticism. This is why the University of Paris wanted to build a monument to honor it, in the form of an institute, which, unfortunately, has no

material existence but which will nevertheless render the greatest services to all those, and they are numerous, who worship Roman Law. (Chevreau, Audren, and Verdier 2018: 124)

Ten years later, when he was presented with a collection of papers in his honor on his retirement, Lévy-Bruhl recalled his career as a professor of history of law in apparently similar terms:

There is, in my opinion, no more beautiful profession, and if I were given a second life, I believe I would make the same choice. In any case, in the life that is ending on this beautiful day, I am aware that I have practiced it to the best of my ability for forty years. I would consider my efforts amply recompensed if I had been able to inculcate in a few young people—even in just one of them—these two religions, all of which are earthly but whose worship requires a great deal of effort and sacrifice: Truth and Justice. (Chevreau, Audren, and Verdier 2018: 102)

These two speeches are personal and conventional in the same rhetorical movement; yet, if examined closely, they seem to contradict each other. The first asserted that Roman law was the form through which justice had been realized in humanity, even if it had, since its origin, always been in danger of being contaminated by mystical forces. The second suggested, on the contrary, that truth and justice were two divinities that remained external to their earthly realization, so that only at the end of a life of study could they be contemplated. The "sacrifice" that Henri Lévy-Bruhl mentioned took different meanings: in the 1948 speech, it was the struggle against the Nazi enemy at the risk of one's life; in the 1958 speech, it was the pain of the student of law. In both cases, the sacrifice made it possible to realize on earth what should remain transcendent. One may then ask whether Henri Lévy-Bruhl did not betray the teaching of his father Lucien by claiming to have realized this value that the latter always maintained to be located on the horizon. For Lucien Lévy-Bruhl, since no society has achieved the ideal of justice, it is necessary to compare the various ways in which this ideal is expressed without relating them to a particular society considered as a model. This may be consistent with the shift Lucien Lévy-Bruhl made from the sentinel, who perceives changes in the invisible tissue of social life oriented by the ideal of justice, to the whistleblower, who denounces publicly the encroachments on this ideal of justice.

It is, thus, surprising to read in a small book on the sociology of law that Henri Lévy-Bruhl published in 1961 pages on "primitive societies" that seem to justify the colonial enterprise by an evolutionary framework. When he examined ethnology among the various sources of the sociology of law, Henri Lévy-Bruhl wrote:

> Ethnology can serve as a hinge between the present and the past. These primitives, who are our contemporaries in the chronological sense of the word, are, from the sociological point of view, our distant ancestors. It follows that, if the comparison of their institutions with ours can be useful, it is at least as true of the societies that preceded us in more recent times and that are undoubtedly closer to us. (H. Lévy-Bruhl 1961: 115)

According to this text, which was addressed to a large audience, members of non-European societies offered European societies a reflection of their own evolution. In this reflexive turn of Europe on itself, Roman law constituted a point of reference, since it presented a universal character even if it was always contaminated by archaic mystical forces. In sum, the singular situation of Roman law in human history justified exporting it to other societies where it should achieve universal justice. "As it has been constructed, it is stripped, to the greatest extent possible, of any special character, whether religious, moral, political, or otherwise. Whether by design or by happy accident, it is not ethnic but human and it is, therefore, broadly applicable to any society based on the principle of equal rights" (H. Lévy-Bruhl 1961: 120).

Another text that Henri Lévy-Bruhl published in the 1960s confirms this analysis, which cannot fail to arouse a feeling of unease today. It is an introduction to the articles on the anthropology of law in the encyclopedia published by the prestigious "Pléiade" editorial collection. These articles, assembled by Jean Poirier in 1968, announced the publication of further Pléiade volumes on regional ethnology, which appeared in 1972 and 1978. Henri Lévy-Bruhl's introduction thus brings the legitimacy of the family name to an ambitious scientific enterprise, but it also associated it with a dated stage of the ethnological discipline. It used the term "primitive mentality" uncritically and borrowed empirical cases from Lucien Lévy-Bruhl, who himself had borrowed them from sometimes dubious observers. Thus, a "fact" that Lucien Lévy-Bruhl mentioned in *La mentalité primitive* in 1922 and in his notebooks—a misunderstanding between a missionary and natives in

Paraguay in the 1890s—was summarized by Henri Lévy-Bruhl in 1961 as follows:

> The specific character of the primitive mentality can confuse even the notion of the obvious. An American missionary, Dr. Grubb, reports that, while residing among the Lingua of Paraguay, he was once accused by a neighbor of stealing pumpkins from his garden. The missionary was very surprised because on the day the alleged theft took place, he was several dozen miles away from that place. The neighbor did not deny this, but he persisted in his accusation. He was deeply convinced that he was telling the truth because he had seen Dr. Grubb steal his pumpkins in a dream. A method of proof that we rightly consider irrefutable, the alibi, was made useless by supernatural preconceptions. (H. Lévy-Bruhl 1968: 1164)

This "disagreement" between customary law and "modern law" revealed, according to Lucien and Henri Lévy-Bruhl, that "primitive mentality" ignored the logical impossibility of being in two places at the same time. Returning to the reformist policy of his father, Henri Lévy-Bruhl remarked that these logical incompatibilities "gave rise to unfortunate misunderstandings. Thus, the French administration has, unintentionally, deeply wounded the spirit of certain African tribes by considering fallow lands as *res nullius* belonging to the state" (H. Lévy-Bruhl 1968: 1160). This moderate criticism of French colonialism as ignoring the uses of the land based on "mystical" rights repeated an analysis that Lucien Lévy-Bruhl had made thirty-five years earlier:

> Black people do not conceive that land can really be sold. But neither do White people understand that such a simple transaction is unintelligible for the natives. From there occur misunderstandings, quarrels, violence on both sides, reprisals, eviction, and, finally, extermination of the former masters of the land. When a conflict breaks out, White people, in general, are unaware of the mystical obligations that the natives cannot refuse to obey and that the latter believe themselves to be truly wronged. Soon this ignorance of the primitive mentality is joined by bad faith and the abuse of force. This chapter in the history of the relations of the White people with the natives offers a spectacle as monotonous as it is revolting. (L. Lévy-Bruhl 1927: 124)

Henri Lévy-Bruhl did, however, bring to ethnology an element that his father lacked: his knowledge of Roman law. But rather than this being an asset in developing new ethnological knowledge, it seemed to be a handicap, for his legal conception made him return to ethnological theses that his father had himself criticized. Thus, in an astonishing analysis published in 1968, Henri Lévy-Bruhl uncritically took up the term "degeneration" to explain why some societies remained "primitive." He thus revived a conception that anthropology used a century earlier in the heyday of criminology and that Michel Foucault set out to criticize at the same time in his work on the norms of the disciplinary system (Foucault 2016).

> More and more one realizes, now, that even the most rudimentary societies, which consequently one could view as the most archaic, can have a history going through numerous vicissitudes. It is possible that their "primitiveness" is not natural but acquired and that, far from being original, it is the fruit of a degeneration due to various conjunctures: that which is sometimes called "pseudo-primitivism." In a certain number of cases, this observation is likely to explain the analogy, even the similarity, between the customs of social groups that are neighbors but currently distinct from one another. But it would be wrong to believe that this has always been the case. In many cases it is if not impossible, then at least very difficult to admit that neighboring regions have been subject to the same political power. For them it is thus advisable to modify this explanation by appealing, for example, to the influence that such or such system of customs could have on neighboring populations (or even distant ones) that borrowed it. (H. Lévy-Bruhl 1968: 1124–25)

This analysis made sense in the context of the great debates at the end of the nineteenth century on the origins of primitive customs. The evolutionary conception claimed that customs originated in a mentality common to all humans, from which they would have progressively distanced themselves by observations recorded in laws. By contrast, diffusionist anthropology argued that the sources of primitive culture may have been multiple, so that customs could be borrowed, imported, and transformed. The extreme case, in that conception, was when a society was brought back by another society to an apparently "primitive" stage where it would no longer have any custom. "Degeneration" was defined as that extreme situation when contact between a society and other cultures prevented it from expressing its own dispositions (Stocking 1974).

However, if we carefully read the rest of Henri Lévy-Bruhl's text, we see that the solution he proposed to this classical debate was similar to that proposed at the same time by Claude Lévi-Strauss with quite different means. In a clear and precise way, Lévy-Bruhl summarized Lévi-Strauss's analyses in the *Elementary Structures of Kinship* on the prohibition of incest as a negative rule that conditions all the other social rules by compelling one to look for a spouse outside one's group. For Lévi-Strauss (1949), psychoanalysis and linguistics revealed a "structural unconscious," constituted by rules of symbolic exchange common to all the societies, from which they combine social organizations and ideological forms. In the eyes of Lévi-Strauss, one cannot, therefore, speak of "degeneration," since even a society reduced by the violence of colonization to the most extreme misery, like the Nambikwara whom he met in 1938, maintains the minimal structures necessary for social life. Just as the structural unconscious allowed Lévi-Strauss to compare very different societies, so Roman law, according to Henri Lévy-Bruhl, could serve as a reference space for the comparison of different legal forms, since it still bears traces of primitive customs, such as ordination or the oath, while announcing modern law by its rigor and clarity. Henri Lévy-Bruhl's text in 1968 concluded as follows:

> Numerous are the cases where legal realities from a distant past have been perpetuated in a quite different context after undergoing sometimes surprising metamorphoses. Here, ethnology again provides the key to their origin. Thus, one of the most positive and least mystical legal systems known to mankind, Roman law, contains rules that can only be explained by reference to manifestly primitive ways of thinking. (H. Lévy-Bruhl 1968: 1175)
> One cannot explain many of our present legal institutions without going back not only, as is generally done, to Roman law or to customary law of Germanic origin but, beyond these legal systems, to primitive law—or prelaw—which brings us face to face with the earliest conceptions that humanity has elaborated of the compulsory relations between its members. (H. Lévy-Bruhl 1968: 1177)

Roman law, being situated halfway between primitive law and modern law, offered the ethnologist a common language between these two apparently incompatible legal forms whose "disagreements" produced "misunderstandings." Such was the conclusion of the work that Henri Lévy-Bruhl transmitted to young ethnologists, citing in particular the research of Georges Balandier and Roger Bastide on the "acculturation" of "primitive people," which he defined as the set of "problems, generally but not exclusively of a practical nature, that their contact with more evolved civilizations poses" (H. Lévy-Bruhl 1968: 1178). We may today question such confidence in Roman law or in what Lévi-Strauss described as the "structural unconscious," which today appears as a modernist dream of equipping "primitive mentality" with computer machines as sophisticated as those Raymond Lévy-Bruhl had at his disposal at INSEE. This is not only because it manifested a positivist hope that our "postmodern" societies have renounced or because it resorted to an evolutionist vocabulary that the human sciences have learned to criticize but, more profoundly, because it indicated a relationship between the Lévy-Bruhl family and the state that the Dreyfus Affair should have disturbed. To claim that Roman law or the structural unconscious were invariants allowing social scientists to compare apparently primitive and modern forms involved a belief in the stability of the French state and in its capacity to embrace all human societies through a universalist knowledge. It was, in a sense, a way to jump from the position of the sentinel, perceiving invisible causes in a "mystical" way, to that of the whistleblower, who publicizes these causes in stable representations.

The last text by Henri Lévy-Bruhl that we consider here, *La preuve judiciaire* (*The legal proof*) published in 1964, reveals the frailties of this republican leap of faith. In this small book, undoubtedly Henri Lévy-Bruhl's most personal work, the memory of the Dreyfus Affair plays a structuring role, as attested by the allusion to Jaurès's book *Les preuves* in the choice of the title. While the book as a whole is organized around the distinction between primitive law and modern law, the memory of the Dreyfus Affair led Lévy-Bruhl to shape it along the opposition between irrational and rational proof, or unwritten and written proof (H. Lévy-Bruhl 1964: 56). While written law is one of the criteria that allows ethnology to qualify a society as civilized or primitive—as in the title of Lévi-Strauss's chair at the Practical School of Advanced Studies, "Religions of Societies without Writing"—the Dreyfus Affair showed the return of archaic forms of accusation in modern societies, thus disturbing any evolutionary schema of the emergence of writing and revealing an original violence internal to writing itself (Derrida 1976). Henri Lévy-Bruhl thus noted: "During the Dreyfus Affair, experts in writing, charged to examine the essential piece of the file, called the 'bordereau,' were heavily mistaken and their ignorance greatly contributed to a serious legal mistake" (H. Lévy-Bruhl 1964: 118).

According to this analysis, the reestablishment of the law in its extra-historical purity allowed the French state to correct this "legal mistake" caused by the "ignorance" of its representatives. Another passage in this clear and rigorous book brought out once again the political sensitivity of Henri Lévy-Bruhl:

> Ordeal should not be understood as a kind of torture intended to provoke a confession. Torture does not exist among the primitives, unless one calls the cruel practices that often accompany the killings by this name. In any case, it is not used in the mechanism employed to discover the truth: it is not a means of proof. ... In this respect, the criminal law of modern times has marked a clear regression for a long time. (H. Lévy-Bruhl 1964: 130, 131)

Surprisingly, this analysis claimed that modern law has regressed in relation to primitive law, because it had moved further away from the ideal of Roman law, where the truth was guaranteed by procedures of testimony and not, as in Christian law, by the confession that the subject makes of his crime. Dreyfus resisted a perversion proper to modern law, namely the request of an adequacy between the subject and his crime, when he refused to submit to the simulacrum of sacrifice that the French army proposed to save his honor and when he multiplied the testimonies through the sheer fact of his survival. Following Henri Lévy-Bruhl's interpretation, Dreyfus played on the margins of freedom granted to him by "primitive law."

Such an interpretation of the Dreyfus Affair resonated with Henri Lévy-Bruhl's socialist commitment, which went beyond the apparently conservative character of his writings and attenuated their most embarrassing formulations. Lévy-Bruhl was a member of the editorial board of the *Revue socialiste*, which was relaunched in 1945 by the Socialist Party (Section française de l'Internationale ouvrière, SFIO) and which was intended to promote socialism in the university. It was directed by Ernest Labrousse, professor of economic history at the Sorbonne, who launched many students into archival research with new statistical techniques. Together with Henri Lévy-Bruhl, he was also founder of the Society for the Study of Jaurès (Société d'études jaurésiennes) in 1959, to which he associated his students Maurice Agulhon and Madeleine Rebérioux. Labrousse advocated a conception of social progress based on the Marxist distinction between the movement of contradictions in the infrastructure and the resistance of mentalities in the superstructure (Braudel and

Labrousse 1979). Henri Lévy-Bruhl published about fifteen articles between 1946 and 1953 in the *Revue socialiste* on the sociology of law as a realization of the Jaurésian project and on the place of France in the Cold War between the US and the Soviet Union. He resigned in 1959, following Labrousse, to protest against the SFIO's European defense policy, which was moving further and further away from the communist bloc, and against its support for the colonial wars in Indochina and Algeria (Chevreau, Audren, and Verdier 2018: 47).

One can then assume that the pages of *The legal proof* on torture allude to the Audin Affair, launched after the arrest and disappearance, in June 1957, of the mathematician Maurice Audin, who supported the liberation front in Algiers. Pierre Vidal-Naquet, who had written a thesis on Plato with Henri-Irénée Marrou and a thesis on Jaurès with Ernest Labrousse, was teaching history at the University of Caen when he heard of this case. He reconstructed Maurice Audin's administrative file with the help of his widow, Josette Audin, the mathematician Laurent Schwartz (who organized a thesis committee in absentia for the young communist activist), and the publisher Jérôme Lindon. Vidal-Naquet, whose parents belonged to a family of lawyers who had participated in the Dreyfus Affair and were deported to Auschwitz, compared the lies of the French army after Audin's death under torture and after Dreyfus's conviction. The comparison was all the more striking as a military tribunal judging the Audin Affair was organized in 1959 in Rennes, as for Dreyfus half a century before (Vidal-Naquet 1989).

If Henri Lévy-Bruhl's critical positions on the violence of the colonial system echoed those of Labrousse and Vidal-Naquet, they were still expressed in a reformist vocabulary that he borrowed from his father in a way that seems outdated today, and may even have been outdated at his time in the light of the decolonizing movement. In his introduction to Victor Kanga's thesis on African customary law,[2] Lévy-Bruhl noted his awareness of the "inescapable, and on the whole beneficial, character of a modernization of the law" and his desire to see African customs "evolve and adapt to the conditions of modern life by a process of acculturation that would involve only a minimum of traumatization" (Chevreau,

---

2.   Victor Kanga, born in 1931 in the West Region of Cameroon, defended his thesis at the Faculty of Law in Paris in 1957. He became a customs inspector and served several times as a minister in Cameroon. Henri Lévy-Bruhl also directed the thesis of Enoch Wkaté Kayeb, defended in 1958 on "the institutions of public law of the Bamiléké country."

Audren, and Verdier 2018: 205). In 1946, he rejected the right of peoples to self-determination in order to justify a policy of the protectorate that, in his eyes, would correct the excesses of colonialism:

> There are states, especially in Africa, Asia, and Oceania, which, although sovereign, do not have a sufficient degree of culture to be able to govern themselves. They can be likened to children and it is precisely to make up for this deficiency that the system of mandate or trusteeship was invented, far superior to the old colonialism. (H. Lévy-Bruhl 1946: 462)

In the memory of the Lévy-Bruhl family, these public positions of Henri Lévy-Bruhl on colonization were the subject of lively discussions with his son Jacques. The latter passed the *agrégation* in mathematics in 1945 and, after a thesis in algebra, joined the National Center for Scientific Research where he participated in the emergence of computer science. While Henri Lévy-Bruhl remained a member of the old SFIO all his life, Jacques joined the new Unified Socialist Party (Parti socialiste unifié), founded in 1960 to contest the SFIO's support for the Algerian war and the Gaullist regime. His experience of the prison camps during the Second World War made Jacques Lévy-Bruhl distrustful of the army, so much so that he refused to participate in military exercises in 1954 in order not to fight in Algeria. It should also be noted that their traumatic experience of the war limited the number of trips Henri and Jacques Lévy-Bruhl took abroad to a few conferences on the European continent. Henri Lévy-Bruhl, too, received several invitations by his Cameroonian students to visit Africa but, according to Jacques's son Pierre, "his wife was afraid that his brain would be eaten."[3] One can explain Henri Lévy-Bruhl's reluctance to fully realize an anthropology of law, which his students asked him to oversee, by his reluctance to enter the colonial space still marked by the memory of the Dreyfus Affair, with its traumatic experience of the colonial prison in Guiana. Thus, after Henri Lévy-Bruhl's death in 1964, his intellectual legacy was divided into two separate schools, which revealed the two almost incompatible facets of his personality: a sociology of law, directed by Jean Carbonnier, and an ethnology of law, led by Jean Poirier and Raymond Verdier (Chevreau, Audren, and Verdier 2018: 207–47).

---

3.   Interview with Pierre Lévy-Bruhl, Paris, June 14, 2017.

It seems, then, that the Second World War led Henri Lévy-Bruhl and Raymond Lévy-Bruhl to implement the "politics of vigilance" launched by Lucien Lévy-Bruhl after the First World War in the wake of the Jaurésian formulation of the Dreyfus Affair, but in a way that betrayed the cautious attitude adopted by their father and grandfather after the trauma of Dreyfus's colonial experience. It is as if Henri Lévy-Bruhl had remained with the Lévy-Bruhl of 1910—who was close to the Durkheimian sociology of law but also to a form of evolutionism—while Raymond Lévy-Bruhl went as far as the Lévy-Bruhl of 1920—who reorganized the war economy on the basis of statistics and traveled to the US. It is, then, necessary to pass to the fourth generation, that of Daniel and Viviane Lévy-Bruhl, for this policy of vigilance to be developed on a global level and at a planetary scale. Indeed, Daniel and Viviane Lévy-Bruhl established new sentinel figures with knowledges coming once again from the US: epidemiology and environmental law.

CHAPTER 12

Monitoring and Regulating Public Health and the Environment

Daniel Lévy-Bruhl and Field Epidemiology

When he studied at the Faculty of Jussieu in the 1970s, Daniel Lévy-Bruhl hesitated between mathematics, the field of his father Raymond and his uncle Jacques, and medicine, the field of his brother Alain and his great-uncle Marcel. He finally turned to medicine, but with an orientation toward research. He discovered epidemiology on the Caribbean island of Dominica while on a contract with the Pan American Health Organization, which extended his position as a district medical officer for a year during his military service. He was in charge of implementing a health information system throughout the island. In 1984, Daniel Lévy-Bruhl traveled in the Amazon for several months to vaccinate the Yanomami against several infectious diseases, after a measles epidemic had decimated several villages. This action was co-organized by Médecins du Monde and the Commission for the Creation of the Yanomami Park. One of its founders was the French anthropologist Bruce Albert, whom Daniel Lévy-Bruhl had met in Paris before leaving for Brazil. This vaccination campaign raised a controversy in the years 2000, after accusations that another vaccination campaign had worsened or even caused a measles epidemic among the Yanomami in 1968, but Bruce Albert showed, based on his regular exchanges with medical and public health specialists, that these accusations were erroneous and unfounded (Albert 2003). At the time of Daniel Lévy-Bruhl's engagement in Brazil, UNICEF had just declared the goal of vaccinating all children around the world by 1990 and resources were pouring in to achieve this objective. In 1985, Daniel Lévy-Bruhl became a consultant for the World Health Organization (WHO), which sent him to Benin to evaluate its Expanded Programme on Immunization. By contrast with South America, West Africa was marked by a lack of medical infrastructure and vaccine resources (D. Lévy-Bruhl et al. 1993; D. Lévy-Bruhl et al. 1997). He then conducted several missions for both the WHO and UNICEF, just after the latter had declared its objective of universal vaccination of children.

During these missions, Daniel Lévy-Bruhl was able to witness the tensions between the WHO and UNICEF on public support to vaccination strategies. Initially, the WHO advocated for primary health care while UNICEF set ambitious targets for immunization alone. In a second phase, the positions tended to be reversed. The WHO defended more vertical interventions, aiming at efficiency on precise disease elimination or eradication objectives, while UNICEF supported a more "horizontal" policy involving local communities, where vaccination was part of a package of minimal preventive and curative interventions. By taking the success of the Salk vaccine against poliomyelitis in the US after 1955 as a model and by systematizing the vaccination methods of Edward Jenner in England and Louis Pasteur in France, the WHO succeeded in eradicating the smallpox virus from the human population in 1977. Daniel Lévy-Bruhl was interested in how vaccination, so effective on a global scale for specific diseases such as smallpox, could be integrated in local communities, for instance in Africa or South America, to tackle more diverse and complex diseases. To follow on this public health concern, he joined the International Center for Childhood (Centre international de l'enfance) in 1986.

This center was founded by Robert Debré in 1949 within the framework of UNICEF. It was directed by the Polish bacteriologist Ludwick Rajcham with the objective "to promote in the different countries of the world the study of problems affecting children, the dissemination of hygiene and child care rules, and the technical training of specialized personnel" (Debré 2018: 283). After the Dreyfus Affair, Debré had been involved in the socialist movement, particularly in popular education, and defended its values in the context of European reconstruction after the Second World War and at the international level.[1] The center organized courses, seminars, and colloquiums at the Château de Longchamp, located in the Bois de Boulogne near Paris, to which speakers and listeners from around the world were invited. It also launched fact-finding, training, and evaluation missions, mainly in French-speaking Africa and Latin America. Financed by the Ministry of Foreign Affairs and, to a lesser extent over time, by UNICEF, situated in a space in between the national and the international levels, the International Center for Childhood took advantage of the bilateral relations between France and its former colonies to develop an alternative cooperation network within the framework of the multilateralism set up by the US after 1945. Daniel Lévy-Bruhl looked back at this experience in 2014 in an interview with Gaëtan Thomas: "Through the International Center for Childhood, France had an extraordinary opportunity in this small field of epidemiology and support for the health policies of the countries with which we worked. There was an opportunity to build a strategy together, but it was not taken up by politicians" (Thomas 2018: 174).

When the socialist government headed by Lionel Jospin closed the International Center for Childhood in 1997, Daniel Lévy-Bruhl joined the National Institute of Health Vigilance (Institut national de veille sanitaire, INVS) at the invitation of Jacques Drucker, whom he had met while attending courses at the Institute for the Development of Applied Epidemiology (Institut pour le développement de l'épidémiologie appliquée, IDEA). The IDEA was created in 1984 with the support of Louis Massé, professor of epidemiology at the National School of Public Health (École nationale de santé publique), and the industrialist Charles Mérieux, who welcomed him to his family property in Veyrier-du-Lac in Haute-Savoie (Drucker 1997). It was modeled on the Epidemic Intelligence Service created by Alexander Langmuir at the Center for Disease

---

1. Robert Debré was born in 1882 into a family of rabbis from the Jewish communities of Metz and Sedan. His family moved to Neuilly in 1886. His father Simon (1854–1939) was a contemporary of Lucien Lévy-Bruhl and his uncle was the mathematician Jacques Hadamard (1865–1963), who had family ties to Alice Bruhl and Alfred Dreyfus. After being engaged in the movement of "popular universities," he studied philosophy at the Sorbonne and then medicine at the Faculty of Paris and immunology at the Pasteur Institute. He was a pediatrician at the Necker Hospital. He died in 1976, leaving behind a dynasty of politicians, doctors, artists, and writers who played a founding role in the Fifth Republic (Debré 2018).

Control in Atlanta, US, in 1951 (Fearnley 2010), some of whose members came to give courses at the IDEA in the early years. In 1992, several IDEA students joined the newly created National Public Health Network (Réseau national de santé publique). The mission of this organization was to inform and alert the Department of Health about the spread of epidemics or the appearance of environmental hazards. This network was the basis on which the director general of health, Jean-François Girard, built the INVS. The Kouchner Law of 1999 created three agencies to evaluate health products in a transparent and independent manner after the major crises of the 1990s (Tabuteau 2002; Benamouzig and Besançon 2005; Alam 2010). The French Agency for Food Safety was created in response to the "mad cow crisis," the Health Products Agency was founded in response to the AIDS-tainted blood transfusion crisis, and the INVS was a response to accusations that the hepatitis B vaccine was causing multiple sclerosis. Daniel Lévy-Bruhl, who was in charge of the vaccine-preventable diseases unit at the INVS, confided in the same interview in 2014 that

> I have always found that vaccination is fabulous and I cannot understand how there are so few people who are passionate about it. I'm passionate about the interface between immunology, economics, politics, sociology. Everything is there in the vaccination program. It is really at the interface between many approaches and many sciences, aspects of society, and purely scientific aspects of antibody levels. (Thomas 2018: 45)

In Daniel Lévy-Bruhl's view, vaccination against an infectious disease, in contrast to the treatment of diseases such as cancer, allowed for public health intervention in a relatively short time: from the development of a vaccine to the clinical trials, to the collective decision if and how to administer it, to its implementation in a large-scale population, and, finally, to the risk–benefit evaluation of its effects. Such rapid action in public health relied on a central element of the French health care system: the population's trust in vaccines. This trust was built up between the wars around the bacillus Calmette-Guérin (BCG) vaccine against tuberculosis, manufactured by the Pasteur Institute, and reinforced after the Second World War by the vaccines against diphtheria and poliomyelitis (DTP), within the framework of a paternalistic model linking the state, doctors, families, and patients in a vertical manner, marginalizing the first anti-vaccination groups organized throughout the nineteenth century. This trust has been eroded and new forms of anti-vaccination movements have appeared since the arrival on the market of new vaccines against measles, mumps, rubella, and hepatitis, often manufactured in the US with the capital and according to the procedures of the pharmaceutical industry, and with the implementation of personalized medicine relying more on social networks than on the family doctor. Since some experts announced the end of infectious diseases in 1978 after the eradication of smallpox through the global vaccination campaign, which was based on both the availability of the vaccine and the fact that smallpox is only transmitted between humans, new epidemics have appeared, either because pathogens have been transmitted from animals to humans, such as Ebola, HIV/AIDS, SARS, or avian/swine influenza, or because vaccination coverage has plateaued or even broken down, as in the case of measles and rubella.

In this new context of uncertainty about vaccines, Daniel Lévy-Bruhl mobilized epidemiology as it was formed in the US after the Second World War to model and predict the effectiveness of vaccine policies. The French term *épidemiologie* was coined by Pierre-Hubert Nysten in 1814 to designate the study of infectious diseases that may suddenly strike a population, but it has been progressively broadened to include other communicable diseases. At first it was based on the classical techniques of public hygiene, such as the statistics of notifiable cases, but then it was transformed by Pasteurian medicine, which introduced screening of patients and tracking of pathogens. In contrast to these two forms, American epidemiology is more defined by field research in the sense that it actively seeks data in order to anticipate epidemics as they emerge, instead of passively recording them once an epidemic has begun (Gregg 1996; Buton and Pierru 2012).

This new form of field epidemiology is also based on new techniques for calculating probabilities, called biostatistics, which allow statistical data to be traced back to biological models of disease transmission. In France, such methods were developed at the Teaching Center for Statistics Applied to Medicine and Medical Biology (Centre d'enseignement de la statistique appliquée à la médecine et à la biologie médicale), founded in 1963 by Daniel Schwartz. It was part of the National Institute of Hygiene, which was created under the Vichy regime in 1941 and merged into the National Institute of Health and Medical Research (Institut national de santé et recherche médicale) in 1964. Born in 1917, Daniel Schwartz was an engineer trained at the Polytechnic School who first worked for the tobacco company Seita before becoming a professor of medicine in 1968; he was also the nephew of Robert Debré. His arrival at the National Institute of Health and Medical Research coincided with the separation between fundamental epidemiology, which researched the causes of diseases, and applied epidemiology, which established statistical data. The "field" epidemiology practiced by Daniel Lévy-Bruhl and his colleagues challenged this division. They defined it as a technique of describing and investigating acute threats such as epidemic outbreaks in order to identify their cause and, therefore, control them, but it also included modeling the epidemic curve to rapidly identify thresholds or critical points in the transmission of a disease. In his interview with Gaëtan Thomas, Daniel Lévy-Bruhl described it as follows:

> Modeling consists of reproducing the epidemiology of a disease in silico [on a computer], taking into account the social environment in which it occurs, with discussions of the determinants of transmission, and grafting on an intervention, in this case a vaccination, to see what happens to the disease. When it comes to specific diseases with simple transmission, such as measles, it is not very complicated to reproduce the way a disease is transmitted with a few equations; what is complicated is to reproduce the social environment. (Thomas 2018: 235)

Investigating and modeling epidemics formed the basis of a new form of public health policy called "vigilance" rather than "surveillance." The change in terminology was significant: vigilance meant not only mobilizing medical forces to anticipate a disease but also involving public health actors who are concerned by its social impact. While surveillance in the US was based on early warning systems set up to detect the first signs of an epidemic (Etheridge 1992; Farmer 1999), surveillance in France relied, among other sources, on a "sentinel network" of physicians who produced both quantitative and qualitative data in contact with patients and who could therefore identify as-yet-unknown symptoms of a new disease (Guerrisi et al. 2018). After the studies of John Snow and Louis Villermé on cholera and the works of Edward Jenner and Louis Pasteur on vaccination, epidemiology had been built around diseases affecting social groups according to a distribution of risk by social classes, such as cholera, tuberculosis, or smallpox, and, therefore, on techniques of prevention by calculation of probabilities. By contrast, the new "field epidemiology" targeted diseases whose collective transmission occurred in a more unpredictable way, thus mobilizing techniques of inquiry or survey to complement statistical modeling, techniques that can be encompassed under the term "preparedness." It can be argued, therefore, that Daniel Lévy-Bruhl's contribution to the shift from Pasteurian medicine to field epidemiology was based on Lucien's and Henri's sociological method, on Marcel's conception of new infectious diseases and on Raymond's statistical modeling. To operate this shift, he used biostatistical models of epidemic development, based on hypotheses about the speed of transmission and population behavior, but he also implemented collaborations between biostatisticians, epidemiologists, and social scientists to define critical thresholds for disease transmission. The new field epidemiology would equip a network of physicians as sentinels of new infectious diseases, to raise alert and trigger quick intervention at the center of the French state.

Daniel Lévy-Bruhl conducted research at the INVS on many vaccine-preventable diseases such as measles, rubella, pneumococcal and meningococcal diseases, as well as pandemic influenza (D. Lévy-Bruhl, Six, and Parent 2004; Doyle et al. 2006; Bonmarin and D. Lévy-Bruhl 2007; D. Lévy-Bruhl 2010 and 2011). He also participated in the Technical Committee on Vaccination of the French High Council for Public Health, which evaluates the relevance of integrating a new vaccine into the vaccination schedule by weighing the risks of vaccination against its benefits. For instance, Daniel Lévy-Bruhl used mathematical modeling to show that, in the French context of a suboptimal coverage, the integration of the varicella (chicken pox) vaccine with the measles, mumps, and rubella vaccine in the vaccination schedule could cause negative epidemiological effects, which led the committee to issue an unfavorable opinion on infant vaccination against varicella. Daniel Lévy-Bruhl also used epidemiological studies including mathematical modeling to assess the relationship between vaccine intervention and occurrence of diseases considered as "side effects," allowing the Technical Committee on Vaccination to make recommendations taking into account the risk–benefit balance. Daniel Lévy-Bruhl stressed that those recommendations were made completely independently from the pharmaceutical industry and that the committee members should be free from any conflict of interest. "I have always defended the idea that rules should be followed in a transparent way in the evaluation process. This is the limit of the Anglo-Saxon model, which considers that declaring one's interest is sufficient. It works for minor conflicts of interest, but there are things that are unacceptable" (Thomas 2018: 175)

For Daniel Lévy-Bruhl, vaccination thus played a role analogous to that of Roman law for Henri Lévy-Bruhl and wage policy for Raymond Lévy-Bruhl: it should be oriented toward the ideal of public service realized by the French state, even if it takes various forms in social life. In these three cases, a model is used to understand how the state organizes spontaneous affective reactions to attenuate their uncertainties and foresee their consequences. This statistical logic of emotions follows Lucien Lévy-Bruhl's effort to understand "primitive mentality" in order to prepare French society for catastrophes within the colonial framework of the Third Republic. But Daniel Lévy-Bruhl's trajectory led him to work on a more global level than Henri and Raymond Lévy-Bruhl, who remained within the national framework. Preparing for pandemics, a contemporary form of surveillance of contagions, thus took over from the preparation for a global war that had oriented the ethnological work of Lucien Lévy-Bruhl, as wars against invisible viruses took over from wars against visible enemies.

It can be hypothesized, therefore, that, when he passed through South America and Africa, Daniel Lévy-Bruhl repeated the trajectory that the French state had imposed on Alfred Dreyfus. Lucien Lévy-Bruhl only partially followed this trajectory during his travels in America and Asia, since he never went to sub-Saharan Africa, but he quoted many travelers who went there. The memory of Dreyfus as a sentinel, which Daniel Lévy-Bruhl received both from his own family memory and from that of Debré and Schwartz, was inscribed in the postcolonial figure of the vaccinal subject, in the sense of the experimentation carried out by the French state on the immunity of its population, raising irrational accusations, false claims, and expert proofs. We can, then, trace vaccination as one of the running lines in this genealogy of French debates about "primitive mentality" up to the present, as a modern policy revealing new forms of the logic of emotions through figures of the sentinels and their discontents.

In late 2019, a new virus appeared in China and caused a disease named COVID-19. When, a few months later, the WHO declared that the virus had achieved pandemic dimensions, Daniel Lévy-Bruhl was one of the first experts at the INVS, which had merged with the French Agency for Public Health in 2016, whom the government and the media consulted.[2] For the previous ten years, epidemiologists had built the

---

2.   The following account of the COVID-19 pandemic is based on an interview I had with Daniel Lévy-Bruhl on December 30, 2020.

scenario of a pandemic that would emerge from afar and stop normal life, but it had been difficult for them to imagine how it would take place. In January 2020, they envisaged three scenarios: an outbreak controlled in its focus (as the SARS crisis in 2003); a pandemic with significant health and social effects (as was actually the case in early 2020); and a worsening of the pandemic because of a mutation of the virus (as was still dreaded in 2023 at the time of writing this book). If it soon became clear that controlling the initial outbreak was improbable, the exact moment when the virus entered France and the dynamics of its diffusion within the country depended largely on random events that were difficult to predict. This was because of what the French Agency for Public Health experts called "super-contamination circumstances," such as a mass religious gathering in Mulhouse or the intense, silent, and unidentified transmissions that occurred at Crépy-en-Valois. During the first weeks of the introduction of the virus in France, the objective was to slow down the spread of the pandemic. For this, epidemiologists investigated the transmission chains by retrospective and prospective tracing from each case. But once the pandemic had spread widely, this changed the working conditions for the epidemiologists at the national and regional health agencies: they moved from tracing individual cases to monitoring the population by indicators, such as the reproduction rate of the epidemic or the incidence rate of the disease. While the beginning of the epidemic was organized by a politics of vigilance, involving local actors in the management of the first cases, it was later monitored by a politics of surveillance, which gave power to experts and politicians in the media, opening them to accusations of authoritarianism and to all kinds of conspiracy theories.

In Daniel Lévy-Bruhl's view, the COVID-19 pandemic differed from both the SARS and the influenza pandemics by its high transmissibility, its contagiousness before the onset of symptoms, and the frequency of asymptomatic forms. This made it especially difficult to control the viral circulation and was the basis for the decision by the state to impose a national lockdown under the term "confinement." In a measure to "freeze" the epidemic, it imposed rigid rules to limit the movement of people and imposed authoritarian measures of punishment on those who disregarded these rules. In Daniel Lévy-Bruhl's view, the lockdown not only limited mortality and protected the hospital system but also gave epidemiologists additional time to collect data at a moment when exchange between international experts was rare and when information from China as the source of the virus remained dubious. According to him, the lockdown in the province of Wuhan gave French epidemiologists an opportunity to go beyond mathematical simulations as it provided them with an experimental model of its effects on the epidemic. It allowed them to build scenarios for the control of an epidemic by integrating a lockdown as a possible modality, a measure that was inconceivable until then. The Chinese government had achieved what French experts might not have dared to advise their health authorities, albeit at a huge social cost for the Chinese population.

An important aspect of the first lockdown in France was that it was imposed on the whole country, even if the epidemiological data were still very heterogeneous. This uniform approach, according to Daniel Lévy-Bruhl, made it possible to transfer patients from highly infected regions to others where hospitals were less strained; but it also blurred the epidemiological data. The serological test results available from March 2020 onwards allowed epidemiologists to study viral circulation and monitor the dynamics of transmission by identifying people who had been infected by the antibodies they had developed. Although these data were less covered by the media, which was more attentive to PCR tests, and although they raised problems of interpretation when seropositive people became seronegative again, they fed epidemiological models in a way that sustained scientific research and enlightened medical intervention.

The French Agency for Public Health was then largely involved in developing a vaccination strategy against COVID-19. The first announcements of the Pfizer and Moderna vaccines in December 2020 claimed unexpectedly high efficacy rates. But surveys conducted among the French population indicated a significant level of mistrust of vaccination, one that had been rising since the government had issued large orders for vaccines against the H1N1 pandemic in 2009. The French health authorities thus instituted careful precautions to supervise the consent of candidates for the vaccination. The Technical Commission on Vaccinations proposed a vaccination strategy that consisted of recommending vaccination to the elderly, who were considered more vulnerable, as a priority, in order to relieve hospitals, while retaining all distancing measures to control the spread of the epidemic among the rest of the population. The epidemiological models on which this vaccination strategy was based had to be constantly revised according to new infection and vaccination data, since people's willingness to get vaccinated was influenced by how likely they thought they were to become infected. By generating these two types of data—epidemic status and vaccination monitoring—the French Agency for Public Health fed the mathematical models that generated scenarios rendering the next phase of the pandemic predictable; these, in turn, were used by the health crisis managers to prepare the population for future waves of the pandemic. Located at this interface, Daniel Lévy-Bruhl also mobilized a sociological and a mathematical sense to follow the day-by-day developments of the pandemic, whose outcome remained unpredictable. For the three years of the COVID-19 pandemic, he had to remain on high alert, drawing on his experience of previous health crises and his sense of solidarity, both with experts and with the population.

When Daniel Lévy-Bruhl and I discussed his great-grandfather, he told me that he did not like to look back and that he preferred to look forward. But he was legally responsible for the family archives lodged at various public institutions and he had kept more intimate documents at home, such as letters from Lucien Lévy-Bruhl to his wife during the Dreyfus Affair and during his travels to South America. He was interested in a point of commonality between his father and his great-grandfather: the conduct of humans in situations of uncertainty, and the use of sentinel techniques to reduce this uncertainty.

Viviane Lévy-Bruhl and Environmental Protection

By discussing the most recent activity of Lucien Lévy-Bruhl's great-grandson, I do not want to give the impression that I have only narrated the genealogy of French experts in the face of political and health crises. Tracing the way in which these experts confronted the failures of the French state and the transformations of its colonial space has also led me to show how the Lévy-Bruhl family rationally thought about their own exposure to global threats after their experience of the Dreyfus Affair. I would like to end this genealogy with another family member who accompanied me in revisiting these archives: Viviane Lévy-Bruhl, Daniel's sister.

Perhaps the affinity between Viviane Lévy-Bruhl and me came from her training in environmental law, a field that was launched in France in the 1970s by Jean Untermaier and Michel Prieur, with whom she did a thesis on the legal status of wildlife and engaged in several associations. As I was studying the use of birds as sentinels of pandemics in China, I discovered how our perception of animals in the environment was changed by research in virology and epidemiology and how their status as sentinels of pandemics was still lacking legal consistency

(Keck 2020). Following the completion of her thesis, Viviane Lévy-Bruhl taught law and economics in the southwest of France and then worked as an assistant to the socialist senator of Tarn in Mazamet, an industrial town where Jean Jaurès had supported strikers in 1909. In our discussions, she recalled how she brought the people of Mazamet together to commemorate the centenary of this event, in a social environment where the labor movement perceived Catholic workers as "yellow," meaning that they were supporting company managers rather than their fellow workers. On her return to Paris, Viviane Lévy-Bruhl kept her job as a parliamentary assistant in the Senate and then joined the French Institute (Institut de France) as head of legal affairs. She is attentive to how this institution, created in 1795 to supervise five academies in science, literature, and art, orients the public debate on environmental issues. Lucien Lévy-Bruhl was a member of the Academy of the Moral and Political Sciences (Académie des sciences morales et politiques), where he regularly presented reports on ethnological research across the world.

Viviane Lévy-Bruhl mentioned how ornithologist Jean Dorst had inspired her engagement in environmental law and his role as a precursor of environmental protection in France. Born in 1924 and, like Alfred Dreyfus, in Mulhouse, he fled Alsace under German occupation in 1940 to study zoology in Paris at the National Museum of Natural History (Muséum national d'histoire naturelle). Much later, between 1965 and 1975, he headed this institution, now a global expert on bird migrations. His book *Before Nature Dies* (*Avant que nature meure*) was published in 1965, two years after the French translation of Rachel Carson's *Silent Spring* in 1963. Both were prefaced by another Alsatian, Roger Heim, born in Paris in 1900, who was trained in botany at the National Museum of Natural History but also in military chemistry at the Pasteur Institute—where he may have crossed the paths of Marcel and Jean Lévy-Bruhl. Heim entered the French Résistance in 1942 and was arrested a year later and sent to Mauthausen concentration camp, which he survived and from which he returned in 1945. When he was director of the National Museum of Natural History between 1951 and 1965, Heim created a Service for the Protection of Nature in this two-century-old institution, which sponsored the setting up of an inventory of fauna and flora in the surroundings of Paris (Charvolin and Bonneuil 2007). His 1952 treatise *Destruction and Protection of Nature* was one of the first public warning signals on the global environmental crisis. He claimed in its foreword that no problems are posed, with respect to the world as a whole, with as much acuity as those of which this book is the incomplete translator. The Danger that they awaken is as serious for the future of humanity as the possibility of new wars or the emergence of some exceptional epidemic. It is also, and especially, immediate. Man today stands on a precipice, facing the abyss he has dug. (Heim [1952] 2020: 26–27)

This precocious diagnosis is the reason why Heim wrote prefaces for Carson's and Dorst's books, as both confirmed his warnings on the effects of species destruction. With the same passion as Carson but in a less literary style, Dorst discussed the effects of pesticides on birds and warned about the impact of the human demographic explosion on the extinction of other animal species, for which he twice used the term "genocide" (Dorst 1965: 292, 460). While Carson played a central role in the creation of the Environmental Protection Agency in the US, Heim and Dorst contributed to the foundation of the International Union for the Protection of Nature in Paris in 1945 (which later became the International Union for the Conservation of Nature). Through this institution, they supported the creation of nature reserves as "sanctuaries" in the conservation of "reliques" (relics), using a religious vocabulary to foster public education and prepare citizens for the environmental crises to come. But while Heim has been criticized for colonial statements such as those accusing local inhabitants of destroying "our land" by fire, Dorst played a central role in the promotion of ethnosciences—the knowledge of local inhabitants in the management of their environment—and environmental law—the elaboration of different rules to protect "nature" at local, national, and global levels. Dorst thus concluded his book:

As Prof. Roger Heim once noticed: "Man cuts the bridges with his own history, attempts to choke the sources of life, and, from the immense tower he has built, dives into what he calls the future." But what if man had made a mistake? What if the trust he placed in his new toys was misplaced? The civilization we are creating destroys everything that made up the context of our life up to now and it may be a dead end: it may lead nowhere but to the ruin of humankind. Even if man decides to follow the modern shepherds blindly, he should not break all ties with the milieu in which he was born. If the modern technical civilization proved to be a mistake, a new civilization could arise from what remains of primitive nature. Future historians will then describe the technical civilization of the twentieth-century as a monstruous cancer which almost brought humankind to its total loss, but which was discarded by the remains of the former, often more brilliant, remains of civilizations and the scraps of wild nature with which they were in balance, rejected by the stock to give a new sprout. (Dorst 1965: 521)

Viviane Lévy-Bruhl attentively followed the genesis of this book on the Lévy-Bruhl family. She had some doubts on Lucien Lévy-Bruhl's commitment to the socialism of Jaurès and on his capacity to foresee the rise of anti-Semitism in the interwar period. For her, Lucien Lévy-Bruhl was representative of Jews assimilated in the republic who distanced themselves from Judaism for the sake of humanism. Because Lucien was close to Dreyfus by family links, the Dreyfus Affair strengthened his demand for justice. Viviane Lévy-Bruhl emphasized the role of women in the constitution of a family genealogy in which this demand was transmitted. Lucien's mother, Arlestine, was attracted to literature and educated her son in a way that led him to enter the great schools of the republic. His wife, Alice, brought him a large dowry from which he drew to support the creation of *L'Humanité* by his friend Jaurès. Perhaps in recognition of Alice's strong presence at his side, Lucien Lévy-Bruhl gave his collection of ethnographic objects and photographs to the Musée de l'Homme in the name of his wife, who had died several years earlier. His daughter-in-law, Odette, who had married his son Jean following the Jewish ritual, preserved and transmitted the memory of her father-in-law, returning the correspondence between Lucien and Alice from the museum to the family. Viviane Lévy-Bruhl remembered that Odette took each of her grandchildren on a trip to Israel and that she, in turn, accompanied Odette to Israel. She did not know about Lucien Lévy-Bruhl's trip to Israel, as mentioned in his correspondence with Meyerson. My exchanges with Viviane Lévy-Bruhl brought to this genealogical investigation a dimension that would have been missing had I kept only to the official archives and expert knowledge: the dimension of care, in the sense of the attention given to people and the concern for the environment.

In her flat in Paris, Viviane keeps a photograph that Lucien Lévy-Bruhl owned and that he loved looking at. Reproduced on the cover of this book, it shows a wide-eyed boy clinging to a tree. The legend at the back of the picture says: "Dyak boy watching a cockfight at the Dyak Long House of Chief Lanting near Barau Front on the Barau River. Sarawak, July 1912." Even if it is unsigned, we can imagine it as a gift he received from Otley Beyer during his travels in the Philippines or a memento he bought during his stop-over in Djakarta in 1920. While anthropologists consider the cockfight as exemplary for how the symbolic order sheds lights on apparently irrational human behavior (Geertz 1973), it is interesting to think of this boy watching a cockfight with fascination and awe as a sentinel of global environmental changes. We can place this photograph in relation to contemporary caricatures of Jaurès fighting as a rooster with Clemenceau or mating with Dreyfus as a parrot, which I suggested illuminates Lévy-Bruhl's interest in relations between Bororo tribes and Ara parrots. Alfred Dreyfus reversing the gaze of his guard on Devil's Island and becoming a sentinel of justice can be seen as a counterimage to the ethnological analyses of symbolic rituals. When the sacrificial victim refuses to be destroyed so that the symbolic order can be reasserted, it opens a new game of light and darkness on the threats to come, characterized by Levinas as "impersonal vigilance." Much as Paul Klee's "Angelus Novus," who faces the future while looking back at the disasters of the past, or similarly to the image of the Bororo "bird spotter" that Claude Lévi-Strauss chose for the cover of the last volume of his *Mythologiques, L'homme nu*, because he holds an intermediary position between earth and sky, Lévy-Bruhl's Dayak boy is a reversal of the image of the enlightened thinker who looks ahead toward the promise of progress and *émancipation*. Taking the perspective of children was important to Lucien Lévy-Bruhl, Viviane said to me: it opened a path for future generations in a world under threat.

Conclusion

As an intellectual history of a French Jewish family, this book has engaged with the following question: how can we restore the modern promise of *émancipation* when it has been betrayed by the state? Following Rabinow (1989), this book has showed how "French moderns" invent "norms and forms of the social environment" when they attempt to reform the state using its colonies as resources for innovation, across the three main political crises that struck France after 1870: the Dreyfus Affair, the Vichy regime, and the Algerian War. The members of the Lévy-Bruhl family were engaged in the socialism of Jaurès as a promise of education by universal knowledge and participation by the workers in the government of the republic. Durkheim instituted the social sciences in France as an answer to this promise, but they had to account for a strange social fact, which was also a moral scandal and a legal problem: an individual promoted to the elite by meritocracy can suddenly be degraded by false accusations and racist classifications. For Lucien Lévy-Bruhl, who began his academic career with a thesis on moral responsibility and mental alienation, as a criticism of the advent of criminology after the Commune, this question took a very precise epistemological form: how can the social sciences integrate chance, such as the accidental encounter between an individual body and a proof of betrayal, as happened to Dreyfus, in their analysis of the social as a space of solidarity? This book has showed that Lévy-Bruhl's analysis of "primitive mentality" was an answer to this question, in the context of the reformation of France's colonial empire and growing tension with Germany. "Primitive mentality ignores chance," one of Lévy-Bruhl's most discussed statements, meant that accidents are stabilized by collective representations,

211

which replace mechanical or individual causalities by social or holistic causalities. Participation, which was a political ideal for Jaurès—all individuals participate in a government oriented by truth and justice—became a logical principle and a social fact for Lévy-Bruhl: individuals ignore contradictions when they experience participation through the "mystical" perception of invisible entities.

However, this book goes beyond the history of a Jewish family in its relation to the French state and to Jaurès's socialism. It also speaks to the contemporary debate on the anthropology of preparedness, as a technique of anticipation whose variants have been explored in France and in its colonial empire. I have endeavored to show the actuality of Lévy-Bruhl's thinking on participation in our current debates on preparing for global health crises, while taking into account the differences between these historical contexts. Without doubt, the events anticipated have changed form and meaning between his time and ours. We are preparing for terrorist attacks, natural disasters, pandemics, species extinction, and climate change, whereas Lucien Lévy-Bruhl was preparing for a new outbreak of anti-Semitism in Europe, a world war with Germany, and a general strike that threatened the colonial system, as became clear in his interwar public statements. But the knowledge mobilized in these various forms of preparedness led Lévy-Bruhl to think, in his formula in 1917, that it was necessary to "expect the unexpected" in order to mitigate its consequences. Preparedness is not a return to archaic techniques of divination but a transformation of modern prevention that takes into account the unpredictability of future events, as it changes statistics by the use of modeling, simulation, and sentinels. I have showed that Lucien Lévy-Bruhl was critical of nineteenth-century techniques of prevention such as criminology, insurance, and vaccination because of the new accidents that happened during the First World War. He used his knowledge of ethnographic data to think about alternative modes of anticipation of the future, which I have gathered around the term "preparedness" and which I compared to Jaurès's thinking on *préparation*. Read in this light, the transmission of the socialist ideals across four generations of Lévy-Bruhls allowed me to study them as a family of statisticians who wanted to restore the state and prepare it for future catastrophes through instituted knowledges such as ethnology, law, economics, and epidemiology. While preparedness is often criticized as a neoliberal rationality that has broken with the infrastructures of the welfare state and while public health has been criticized as a government of the state by experts, I have showed that, for the Lévy-Bruhl family, the necessity to prepare for unpredictable events was a way to criticize the state while reforming it.

When social anthropology in France emerged in the late nineteenth century in the context of the Dreyfus Affair, it offered several ways of integrating the irrational within rationality, or accidents within society. Gabriel Tarde and Henri Bergson described the variations of public opinion through the beliefs and desires of inventors and their imitators. Émile Durkheim and Marcel Mauss brought to light the collective representations carved out of the space of sacrifice and the tinkering practices of magicians on its margins. Lucien Lévy-Bruhl chose another option: he analyzed the moral sentiments individuals feel when they prepare for catastrophes to come. This came from his reflection on the false accusations raised against Dreyfus and on Jaurès's invocation of the ideals of truth and justice to counter them. At first, Dreyfus, Lévy-Bruhl, and Jaurès opposed the "civilized mentality" of the French Enlightenment to the "primitive mentality" of the Catholic army. But as the warning signs multiplied of what the Dreyfus Affair prefigured—the rise of colonial violence in the world and anti-Semitism in Europe— "primitive mentality" and its forms of mystical participation appeared as the only intellectual resources available to prepare society for these threats. Where Tarde's and Durkheim's solutions to the problem of rationality opposed individual freedom and social constraint, Lévy-Bruhl made them compatible by describing the participation of individuals in living flows of contagion.

Henri Lévy-Bruhl's work on the sociology of law, taking over from his father's work on the ethnology of "primitive mentality," may then be understood as a contribution to this reflection on the relationship between contingency and society. Henri Lévy-Bruhl, inscribed in the Durkheimian school of the interwar period, studied the transition from the archaic law of ordination to the commercial law of insurance. He showed that a new form of violence, that of confession, infused modern law when the procedures of Roman law were abandoned in favor of the administration of proof and when a new form of criminality, fraud, was introduced to this new administrative rationality. Roman law appeared to him as a "monument" allowing sociologists to compare various forms of the law, because in it the archaic and the modern touch each other without violence. In some statements, this position of Henri Lévy-Bruhl marked a regression in relation to his father's relativism by returning to an evolutionary reading of the history of law and to paternalistic positions on the colonial system. However, it was resolutely in line with

Henri Lévy-Bruhl's socialist commitment in the aftermath of the Second World War and led him to assume the role of the whistleblower that his father cautiously took on at the very end of his life.

The labor and public health statistics mobilized by Raymond and Daniel Lévy-Bruhl in the second half of the twentieth century made it possible to "expect the unexpected" by introducing hazardous events into social regularities. Through random surveys and field epidemiology imported from the US, these two servants of the French state corrected the margins of error of established models by techniques of simulation. They thus continued the reflections that Jean Lévy-Bruhl, the chemist who taught soldiers how to simulate gas attacks, and Marcel Lévy-Bruhl, the microbiologist who thought about the emergence of cross-species pathogens, made in the interwar period, shedding new light on Lucien Lévy-Bruhl's sentence: "Primitive mentality ignores chance." If insurance techniques have allowed the French state to control hazards within the framework of what was called the *état-providence* ("welfare state") through techniques of prevention, the new threats resulting from the globalization of trade led modern societies to invent techniques of preparedness in order to anticipate events whose probability could not be calculated based on the observation of nonmodern societies. By imagining the effects of a natural disaster, a chemical pollution, a new epidemic, or an economic shock as if they had already occurred through sentinels and simulations, modern societies prepare for unpredictable events in ways that can be compared to the techniques of anticipation in societies that Lévy-Bruhl called "primitive," thus opening spaces of collaboration and mutual learning between different societies around the meaning of what is "modernity."

In contemporary global health, the notion of the sentinel refers to human or nonhuman living beings placed at the forefront of the fight against a pathogenic enemy for which they transmit early warning signals, such as unvaccinated chickens in poultry farms to warn of outbreaks of avian influenza. But in French Dreyfusard circles at the end of the nineteenth century, this term designated the victim of a military and colonial system who testified to the violence imposed on his body. Jaurès considered Dreyfus a sentinel for the social rights of the miners and workers he was defending and promoted exercises of simulation in his last book, *L'armée nouvelle*. Lucien Lévy-Bruhl had to experience the First World War and travels in Asia and South America in the ensuing years to understand the politics of vigilance at stake in the Dreyfus Affair, through comparison with other sentinel figures such as Rizal in the Philippines, Rondon in Brazil, Nguyễn in Vietnam, and Baudoux in New Caledonia. The warning signals sent by these sentinels were not heard immediately but in a deferred way, because they were first perceived in a schema of progress from the "primitive" to the "civilized." If these sentinels were designated through the sacrifice of a randomly designated victim, they needed to be equipped to think about hazard or randomness. Far from accepting to be the arbitrary victim of the construction of the collective, the sentinel is a sample equipped to be more sensitive to the tendencies affecting the collective. This is why Raymond Lévy-Bruhl built surveys accounting for economic transformations and Daniel Lévy-Bruhl adapted epidemiological models to virus mutations. While preparedness appeared as a strange conflation between health, economics, and military strategies at the end of the Cold War, it may be understood, if we return to the experience of Dreyfus, Lévy-Bruhl, and Jaurès a century before, as a way to inscribe military sentinels in moral sentiments of truth and justice.

In the genealogy I have traced in this book, the sentinel appears as a vanguard, in the sense that it is at the forefront of a battle to protect humans against unknown threats. If we understand the sentinel as a vanguard, we can mark its difference from the elite in the meritocratic conception of French society. While the elite draws on reflexive consciousness to perceive and represent new norms and forms of truth and justice during times of crisis, which gives it legitimacy to criticize past norms and forms and orient them toward a more enlightened social life, the sentinel perceives and feels in its body the signs of a new norm and form of truth and justice as it casts light on its experience of social injustice, which produces a more cautious and less confident subjectivity on the path to *émancipation*. This is the result of Lucien Lévy-Bruhl's reading of Auguste Comte at the time of the Dreyfus Affair, which describes humanity as a collective subject torn between two "mentalities" on its path to progress. This is also my interpretation of the photograph of the young boy that Viviane Lévy-Bruhl showed me and that I wanted to reproduce on the cover of this book. The sentinel turns to the future by looking back at disasters, in a public space where cocks fight, swallows warble, and chickens are sacrificed. We may understand, then, why Lévy-Bruhl was so fascinated by Amazonian societies where it is said that "humans are birds": what is at stake here is a cognitive and political attitude of vigilance, paying attention to the invisible entities that constitute social life in a troubled environment.

References

Works by Lucien Lévy-Bruhl

Lévy-Bruhl, Lucien. 1881. "Henri Heine et la politique contemporaine." *Nouvelle revue* 11: 340–85.

Lévy-Bruhl, Lucien. 1883. "La morale de Darwin." *Revue politique et littéraire* 31 (6): 174–75.

Lévy-Bruhl, Lucien. 1884a. *L'idée de responsabilité*. Paris: Hachette.

Lévy-Bruhl, Lucien. 1884b. *Quid de Deo Seneca senserit: thesim proponebat Facultati litterarum parisiensi*. Paris: Hachette.

Lévy-Bruhl, Lucien. 1886. "L'évolution et la vie." *Revue politique et littéraire* 38 (3): 84–88.

Lévy-Bruhl, Lucien. 1890a. "La responsabilité des criminels." *Revue politique et littéraire* 56 (21): 643–48.

Lévy-Bruhl, Lucien. 1890b. Review of *La philosophie pénale* by Gabriel Tarde. *Revue philosophique de la France et de l'étranger* 30: 654–66.

Lévy-Bruhl, Lucien. 1890c. Review of *Essai sur les données immédiates de la conscience* by Henri Bergson. *Revue philosophique de la France et de l'étranger* 29: 532–33.

Lévy-Bruhl, Lucien. 1890d. *L'Allemagne depuis Leibniz: Essai sur le développement de la conscience nationale en Allemagne, 1700–1848*. Paris: Hachette.

Lévy-Bruhl, Lucien. 1890e. "Les premiers romantique allemands." *Revue des deux mondes* (September): 120–47.

Lévy-Bruhl, Lucien. 1892a. "Le roman contemporain et le naturalisme en Allemagne." *Revue des deux mondes* 110 (2): 352–73.

Lévy-Bruhl, Lucien. 1892b. Review of *L'Année philosophique* by François Pillon. *Revue philosophique de la France et de l'étranger* 33: 72–81.

Lévy-Bruhl, Lucien. 1892c. "Les origines du socialisme allemand." *Revue politique et littéraire* 49 (18): 553–58.

Lévy-Bruhl, Lucien. 1894. *La philosophie de Jacobi*. Paris: Alcan.

Lévy-Bruhl, Lucien. 1895a. "La crise de la métaphysique en Allemagne." *Revue des deux mondes* 129: 341–67.

Lévy-Bruhl, Lucien. 1895b. "Questions de sociologie." *Revue politique et littéraire* 3 (25): 776–82.

Lévy-Bruhl, Lucien. 1898. "Le centenaire d'Auguste Comte." *Revue des deux mondes* 145: 385–405.

Lévy-Bruhl, Lucien. 1899a. "Introduction." In *Lettres inédites de John Stuart Mill à Auguste Comte*, by Lucien Lévy-Bruhl. Paris: Alcan.

Lévy-Bruhl, Lucien. 1899b. *History of Modern Philosophy in France*. Chicago: Open Court-Kegan Paul.

Lévy-Bruhl, Lucien. 1900. *La philosophie d'Auguste Comte*. Paris: Alcan.

Lévy-Bruhl, Lucien. 1903. *La morale et la science des mœurs*. Paris: Alcan. Translated by Elizabeth Lee as *Ethics and Moral Science* (London: Archibald Constable, 1905).

Lévy-Bruhl, Lucien. 1906. "Émile Boutmy." *Revue de Paris* 13 (1): 795–805.

Lévy-Bruhl, Lucien. 1909. "L'orientation de la pensée philosophique de David Hume." *Revue de metaphysique et de morale* 17 (5): 595–619.

Lévy-Bruhl, Lucien. 1910. *Les fonctions mentales dans les sociétés inférieures*. Paris: Alcan. Translated by Lilian A. Clare as *How Natives Think* (New York: A.A. Knopf, 1926).

Lévy-Bruhl, Lucien. 1911. Preface to Antoine-Augustin Cournot, *Traité de l'enchaînement des idées fondamentales dans les sciences et dans l'histoire*. Paris: Hachette.

Lévy-Bruhl, Lucien. 1915. "Les causes économiques et politiques de la guerre en Allemagne." *Scientia* 17: 35–54.

Lévy-Bruhl, Lucien. 1916a. "L'effort industriel." In *L'effort de la France*, 58–70. Paris-Nancy: Librairie militaire Berger-Levrault.

Lévy-Bruhl, Lucien. 1916b. *Quelques pages sur Jean Jaurès*. Paris: Librairie de l'Humanité.

Lévy-Bruhl, Lucien. 1917a. "Réflexion sur les leçons de la guerre: Force et finesse." Institute for Contemporary Publishing Archives (IMEC), Lucien Lévy-Bruhl (1857–1939) papers (hereafter Lévy-Bruhl papers).

Lévy-Bruhl, Lucien. 1917b. "Les aspects nouveaux de la guerre." *Scientia* 23 (44): 133–41.

Lévy-Bruhl, Lucien [Deuzelles, pseud.]. 1917c. "Les buts de guerre de l'Amérique." *L'Humanité* 4737 (April 6): 1.

Lévy-Bruhl, Lucien [Deuzelles, pseud.]. 1917d. "Le message du président Wilson à la Russie." *L'Humanité* 4804 (June 12): 1.

Lévy-Bruhl, Lucien [Deuzelles, pseud.]. 1917e. "Le message Wilson." *L'Humanité* 4981 (December 6): 1.

Lévy-Bruhl, Lucien. 1918a. "Note sur la guerre." IMEC, Lévy-Bruhl papers.

Lévy-Bruhl, Lucien [Deuzelles, pseud.]. 1918b. "M. Wilson et la Russie." *L'Humanité* 5017 (January 11): 1.

Lévy-Bruhl, Lucien. 1919a. "Note sur les réparations de guerre." IMEC, Lévy-Bruhl papers.

Lévy-Bruhl, Lucien. 1919b. "Note sur la mission aux Philippines." IMEC, Lévy-Bruhl papers.

Lévy-Bruhl, Lucien [anon.]. 1920. "L'ébranlement du monde jaune." *Revue de Paris* 27 (5): 871–94.

Lévy-Bruhl, Lucien. 1922. *La mentalité primitive*. Paris: Alcan.

Lévy-Bruhl, Lucien. 1923a. "La mentalité primitive." *Bulletin de la Société Française de Philosophi* 32 (2): 17–48.

Lévy-Bruhl, Lucien. 1923b. "La religion de Renan." *Journal de psychologie normale et pathologique* 20: 335–44.

Lévy-Bruhl, Lucien. 1924a. "L'idéal républicain." *Revue de Paris* 31 (1): 805–22.

Lévy-Bruhl, Lucien. 1924b. "Primitive Mentality and Gambling." *The Criterion* 188–200. Translated as "Mentalité primitive et jeu de hasard" in *La Revue de Paris* (March 1926): 317–27. Edited and republished as "Primitive Mentality and Games of Chance," in *HAU: Journal of Ethnographic Theory* 10 (2) (2020): 420–24.

Lévy-Bruhl, Lucien. 1925. "L'Institut d'Ethnologie de l'Université de Paris." *Revue d'Ethnologie et des Traditions Populaires* 6 (23): 233–36.

Lévy-Bruhl, Lucien. 1926. "Research as It Is Today." *Johns Hopkins Alumni Magazine* 15 (1): 25–34.

Lévy-Bruhl, Lucien. 1927. *L'âme primitive*. Paris: Alcan.

Lévy-Bruhl, Lucien. 1928a. "Henri Bergson à l'École normale." *Les Nouvelles littéraires* 322: 1–2.

Lévy-Bruhl, Lucien. 1928b. "Foreword." In *Légendes canaques*, by Georges Baudoux. Paris: Rieder.

Lévy-Bruhl, Lucien. 1929a. "Une heure avec Lévy-Bruhl." In *Une heure avec …*, edited by Frédéric Lefèvre, 75–86. Paris: Gallimard.

Lévy-Bruhl, Lucien. 1929b. "L'âme primitive." *Bulletin de la société française de philosophie* 29: 105–39.

Lévy-Bruhl, Lucien. 1930. Preface to *Les Carnets de Schwartzkoppen: La Vérité sur Dreyfus*. Edited by Bernhardt Schwertfeger. Translated by Alexandre Koyré. Paris: Rieder.

Lévy-Bruhl, Lucien. 1931. *Le surnaturel et la nature dans la mentalité primitive*. Paris: Alcan. Translated by Lilian A. Clare as *Primitives and the Supernatural* (New York: Dutton, 1935).

Lévy-Bruhl, Lucien. 1933. "Quelques aspects de la mentalité primitive." *Nouvelle Revue Française* 240: 321–52.

Lévy-Bruhl, Lucien. 1934. "Vues sur la mythologie primitive." *Nouvelle Revue Française* 250: 50–75.

Lévy-Bruhl, Lucien. 1935. *La mythologie primitive: Le monde mythique des Australiens et des Papous*. Paris: Alcan.

Lévy-Bruhl, Lucien. 1936. "L'esprit européen." *Les Nouvelles littéraires* 692: 1–5.

Lévy-Bruhl, Lucien. 1938. *L'expérience mystique et les symboles chez les primitifs*. Paris: Alcan.

Lévy-Bruhl, Lucien. 1949. *Carnets de Lucien Lévy-Bruhl*. Foreword by Maurice Leenhardt. Paris: Presses universitaires de France.

Lévy-Bruhl, Lucien. 1957. "Une lettre de Lucien Lévy-Bruhl au professeur Evans Pritchard." *Revue philosophique de la France et de l'étranger* 147: 407–13.

Works by Henri Lévy-Bruhl

Lévy-Bruhl, Henri, and André Prudhomme. 1909. "L'Organisation économique de la commune." *Cahiers du socialiste* 7.

Lévy-Bruhl, Henri. 1922. "La libération d'André Marty." *L'Humanité*, December 1: 4.

Lévy-Bruhl, Henri. 1933. *Histoire de la lettre de change en France aux XVIIe et XVIIIe siècles*. Paris: Sirey.

Lévy-Bruhl, Henri. 1938. *Histoire juridique des sociétés de commerce*. Paris: Domat-Montchrestien.

Lévy-Bruhl, Henri. 1945. "Histoire et bergsonisme." *Revue de synthèse* 40: 140–51.

Lévy-Bruhl, Henri. 1946. "Le droit des peuples à disposer d'eux-mêmes: formule dépassée." *Revue socialiste* (October): 450–70.

Lévy-Bruhl, Henri, and André Davidovitch. 1957–58. "La statistique et le droit." *L'Année sociologique* 9: 353–60.

Lévy-Bruhl, Henri. 1961. *Sociologie du droit*. Paris: Presses universitaires de France.

Lévy-Bruhl, Henri. 1964. *La preuve judiciaire: Études de sociologie juridique*. Paris: Marcel Rivière.

Lévy-Bruhl, Henri. 1968. "Ethnologie juridique." In *Ethnologie générale, Encyclopédie de la Pléiade*, edited by Jean Poirier, 1118–83. Paris: Gallimard.

Works by Marcel Lévy-Bruhl

Forgeot, P., P. Halbron, and Marcel Lévy-Bruhl. 1940. "Pyobacillose généralisée mortelle chez un berger." *Annales de l'Institut Pasteur* 65 (11): 326–35.

Launoy, L., and Marcel Lévy-Bruhl. 1915. "Sur la résistance des poules à l'infection par le 'Spirochæta Gallinarum' après Thyroïdectomie ou splénectomie." *Annales de l'Institut Pasteur* 29 (5): 213–20.

Lévy-Bruhl, Marcel. 1938. "Les pasteurelloses humaines." *Annales de médecine* 44 (5): 406–37.

Lévy-Bruhl, Marcel, and Jeanne Courtois. 1940. "Recherches immunologiques sur les bacilles muqueux." *Annales de l'Institut Pasteur* 64 (4): 316–39.

Works by Raymond Lévy-Bruhl

Azéma, Jean-Pierre, Raymond Lévy-Bruhl, and Béatrice Touchelay. 1998. *Mission d'analyse historique sur le système statistique français de 1940 à 1945*. Paris: Institut national de la statistique et des études économiques.

Lévy-Bruhl, Raymond. 1951. "Les sondages d'opinion et l'échec des prévisions électorales de Gallup." *Journal de la société statistique de Paris* 92: 63–70.

Works by Daniel Lévy-Bruhl

Bonmarin, Isabelle, and Daniel Lévy-Bruhl. 2007. "Contribution of Simulation Models to Public Health Decisions: The Influenza Pandemic." *Médecine et Maladies Infectieuses* 37 (S3): S204–9. https://doi.org/10.1016/j.medmal.2007.02.004.

Doyle, Aoife, Isabelle Bonmarin, Daniel Lévy-Bruhl, Yann Le Strat, and Jean-Claude Desenclos. 2006. "Influenza Pandemic Preparedness in France: Modelling the Impact of Interventions." *Journal of Epidemiological Community Health* 60 (5): 399–404. https://doi.org/10.1136/jech.2005.034082.

Guerrisi, Caroline, Clément Turbelin, Cécile Souty, Chiara Poletto, Thierry Blanchon, Thomas Hanslik, Isabelle Bonmarin, Daniel Lévy-Bruhl, and Vittoria Colizza. 2018. "The Potential Value of Crowdsourced Surveillance Systems in Supplementing Sentinel Influenza Networks: The Case of France." *Euro Surveillance* 23 (25). https://doi.org/10.2807/1560-7917.ES.2018.23.25.1700337.

Lévy-Bruhl, Daniel. 2010. "Apport de la modélisation mathématique à la décision vaccinale: Illustrations avec les vaccinations contre la varicelle, le rotavirus et le papillomavirus." *Bulletin de l'Académie Nationale de Médecine* 194 (8): 1545–56. https://doi.org/10.1016/S0001-4079(19)32184-3.

Lévy-Bruhl, Daniel. 2011. "Infections à caractère vaccinal." In *Surveillance épidémiologique: Principes, méthodes et applications en santé publique*, edited by Pascal Astagneau and Thierry Ancelle, 131–38. Paris: Lavoisier.

Lévy-Bruhl, Daniel, Jon Cook, Blandine Legonou, Yannick Jaffré, Philippe D. Amévigbe, Gilbert Sanou, and Nicole Guérin. 1993. "Approches méthodologiques dans l'étude de l'acceptabilité de la vaccination: exemple de trois enquêtes menées en Afrique de l'Ouest." *Sciences sociales et santé* 11 (2): 9–25.

Lévy-Bruhl, Daniel, C. Six, and Isabelle Parent. 2004. "Rubella Control in France." *Euro Surveillance* 9 (4): 15–16.

Lévy-Bruhl, Daniel, Agnes Soucat, Raimi Osseni, Jean-Michel Ndiaye, Boubacar Dieng, Xavier de Bethune, Alpha T. Diallo, Mamadou Conde, Mohamed Cisse, Yarou Moussa, Kandjoura Drame, and Rudolf Knippenberg. 1997. "The Bamako Initiative in Benin and Guinea: Improving the Effectiveness of Primary Health Care." *International Journal of Health Planning Management* 12 (Suppl. 1): S49–79. https://doi.org/10.1002/(SICI)1099-1751(199706)12:1+<S49::AID-HPM466>3.0.CO;2-P.

General references

Alam, Thomas. 2010. "Les mises en forme savante d'un mythe d'action publique: la sécurité sanitaire." *Genèses* 78 (1): 48–66. https://doi.org/10.3917/gen.078.0048.

Albert, Bruce. 2003. "Anthropologie et recherche biomédicale: le cas yanomami (Venezuela et Brésil)." *Autrepart* 28 (4): 125–46. https://doi.org/10.3917/autr.028.0125.

Albert, Pierre. 2004. "Les sociétés du journal *L'Humanité* de 1904 à 1920." In *L'Humanité de Jaurès à nos jours*, edited by Christian Delport, Claude Pennetier, and Jean-François Sirinelli, 21–33. Paris: Nouveau Monde éditions.

Anderson, Benedict. 2007. *Under Three Flags: Anarchism and the Anti-Colonial Imagination*. London: Verso.

Anderson, Warwick. 2006. *Colonial Pathologies: American Tropical Medicine, Race, and Hygiene in the Philippines*. Durham, NC: Duke University Press.

Arendt, Hannah. 1968. *Antisemitism: Part One of The Origins of Totalitarianism*. New York: Harcourt Brace Jovanovich.

Argon, Charles. 2015. "The Problem of China: Orientalism, 'Young China,' and Russell's Western Audience." *Russell: Journal of the Bertrand Russell Studies* 35 (2): 154–76. https://doi.org/10.15173/russell.v35i2.2756.

Aron, Raymond. 1961. *Introduction to the Philosophy of History: An Essay on the Limits of Historical Objectivity*. Boston, MA: Beacon Press.

Audren, Frédéric, and Jean-Louis Halpérin. 2013. *La culture juridique française: Entre mythes et réalités, XIXe–XXe siècles.* Paris: CNRS Editions.

Azéma, Jean-Pierre, and Olivier Wieviorka. 1997. *Vichy, 1940–1944.* Paris: Perrin.

Azouvi, François. 2007. *La gloire de Bergson: Essai sur le magistère philosophique.* Paris: Gallimard.

Baker, Lee. 1998. *From Savage to Negro. Anthropology and the Construction of Race, 1896–1954.* Berkeley: University of California Press.

Baruch, Marc-Olivier. 1997. *Servir l'état français.* Paris: Odile Jacob.

Becker, Annette. 2003. *Maurice Halbwachs, un intellectuel en guerres mondiales 1914–1945.* Paris: Agnès Viénot.

Benamouzig, Daniel, and Julien Besançon. 2005. "Administrer un monde incertain: Le cas des agences sanitaires." *Sociologie du travail* 47 (3): 301–22. https://doi.org/10.4000/sdt.26600.

Benda, Julien. 1968. *La jeunesse d'un clerc.* Paris: Gallimard.

Bensa, Alban. 2015. *Les Sanglots de l'aigle pêcheur: Nouvelle-Calédonie: la Guerre kanak de 1917.* Toulouse: Anacharsis.

Bensaude-Vincent, Bernadette. 1987. *Langevin: Science et vigilance.* Paris: Belin.

Bergson, Henri. 1888. *Essai sur les données immédiates de la conscience.* Paris: Alcan.

———. 1896. *Matière et mémoire: Essai sur la relation du corps à l'esprit.* Paris: Alcan.

———. (1907) 2013. *L'évolution créatrice.* Edition by Arnaud François. Paris: Presses universitaires de France.

———. 1932. *Les deux sources de la morale et de la religion.* Paris: Alcan. Translated by Ashley Audra and Cloudesley Brereton as *The Two Sources of Morality and Religion* (London: MacMillan, 1935).

Birnbaum, Pierre. 1992. *Les fous de la République: Histoire politique des Juifs d'État de Gambetta à Vichy.* Paris: Fayard.

Blais, Marie-Claire. 2000. *Au principe de la République: Le cas Renouvier.* Paris: Gallimard.

Blanckaert, Claude. 1994. "Des sauvages en pays civilisé: L'anthropologie des criminels." In *Histoire de la criminologie française,* edited by Laurent Mucchielli, 55–88. Paris: L'Harmattan.

Blondel, Charles. 1914. *La conscience morbide: Essai de psycho-pathologie générale.* Paris: Alcan.

Blondiaux, Loïc. 1998. *La fabrique de l'opinion: Une histoire sociale des sondages*. Paris: Seuil.

Blum, Léon. 1935. *Souvenirs sur l'affaire*. Paris: Gallimard.

———. 1939. "Lucien Lévy-Bruhl." *Le Populaire*, March 14, 1939, 1.

Boas, Franz. (1911) 1938. *The Mind of Primitive Man*. New York: MacMillan.

Bonah, Christian. 2007. *Histoire de l'expérimentation humaine en France: Discours et pratiques, 1900–1940*. Paris: Les Belles Lettres.

Bonaparte, Marie, and Sigmund Freud. 2022. *Correspondance intégrale: 1925–1939*. Translated from German by Olivier Mannoni, edited by Rémy Amouroux. Paris: Flammarion.

Bonneuil, Christophe, and Patrick Petitjean. 1996. "Les chemins de la création de l'ORSTOM, du Front populaire à la Libération en passant par Vichy, 1936–1945: Recherche scientifique et politique coloniale." In *Les sciences hors d'Occident au 20è siècle*, vol. 2: *Les sciences coloniales: figures et institutions*, edited by Patrick Petitjean, 113–61. Paris: Office de la recherche scientifique et technique outre-mer.

Borel, Émile. 1914. *Le hasard*. Paris: Alcan.

Bosserman, Philippe. 1981. "Georges Gurvitch et les durkheimiens en France, avant et après la seconde guerre mondiale." *Cahiers internationaux de Sociologie* 70: 35–53. https://doi.org/10.3917/cis.110.0097.

Bouchet, Thomas. 2010. *Noms d'oiseaux: L'insulte en politique*. Paris: Stock.

Bouché-Leclercq, Auguste. 1879–82. *Histoire de la divination*. 4 vol. Paris: Ernest Leroux.

Bourdelais, Patrice. 2001. *Les Hygiénistes: Enjeux, modèles et pratiques (18e–20e siècles)*. Paris: Belin.

Bourgeois, Bernard. 1989. "Lévy-Bruhl et Hegel." *Revue philosophique de la France et de l'étranger* 179 (4): 449–51.

Bourgin, Hubert. 1938. *De Jaurès à Léon Blum: L'École normale et la Politique*. Paris: Arthème Fayard.

Boutroux, Émile. 1902. "Comte et la métaphysique." *Bulletin de la Société Française de philosophie*.

Braudel, Fernand, and Ernest Labrousse. 1979. *Histoire économique et sociale de la France*. Paris: Presses universitaires de France.

Bréhier, Émile. 1907. *La théorie des incorporels dans l'ancien stoïcisme*. Paris: Alphonse Picard & Fils.

Brian, Eric. 1994. *La mesure de l'État: Administrateurs et géomètres au XVIIIe siècle*. Paris: Albin Michel.

Broszat, Michael. 1981. *The Hitler State: The Foundation and Development of the Internal Structure of the Third Reich*. London: Routledge.

Burns, Michael. 1991. *Dreyfus: A Family Affair (1789–1945)*. New York: Harper Collins.

Burrell George, and Seibert Frank. 1914. "Experiments with Small Animals and Carbon Monoxide." *Journal of Industrial and Engineering Chemistry* 6 (3): 241–44. https://doi.org/10.1021/ie50063a027.

Buton, François, and Frédéric Pierru. 2012. "Instituer la police des risques sanitaires: Mise en circulation de l'épidémiologie appliquée et agencification de l'État sanitaire." *Gouvernement et action publique* 4 (4): 67–90. https://doi.org/10.3917/gap.124.0067.

Candar, Gilles. 2008. "Jaurès et le parti, retour sur un itinéraire." *Cahiers Jaurès* 187–88: 15–27. https://doi.org/10.3917/cj.187.0015.

Candar, Gilles, and Vincent Duclert. 2014. *Jean Jaurès*. Paris: Fayard.

Candide. 1939. "Lucien Lévy-Bruhl est mort." *Candide*, March 29, 1939: 7.

Cassirer, Ernst. 1946. *The Myth of the State*. New Haven, CT: Yale University Press.

Charpentier, Antoine. 1939. "Lucien Lévy-Bruhl." *La Griffe*, March 4, 1939.

Charvolin, Florian, and Christophe Bonneuil. 2007. "Entre écologie et écologisme: la protection de la nature au Muséum dans les années 1950." *Responsabilités et Environnement* 46: 46–53.

Chateauraynaud, Francis, and Didier Torny. 1999. *Les sombres précurseurs: Une sociologie pragmatique de l'alerte et du risque*. Paris: École des hautes études en sciences sociales.

Chaubet, François. 2006. *La politique culturelle française et la diplomatie de la langue: L'Alliance Française (1883–1940)*. Paris: L'Harmattan.

Chaumont, Jean-Philippe, and Jean-Claude Kuperminc. 2007. *Zadoc Kahn: Un grand rabbin entre culture juive, affaire Dreyfus et laïcité*. Paris: Editions de l'Éclat.

Chavannes, Edouard. 1895–1905. *Shiji: Les Mémoires historiques de Se-ma Ts'ien*. 6 vols. Paris: Ernest Leroux.

Chestov, Léon, and B. de Schloczer. 1933. "Martin Buber: Un mystique juif de langue allemande." *Revue philosophique de la France et de l'étranger* 116: 430–42.

Chestov, Léon. 1938. "Le mythe et la vérité: À propos du livre de L. Lévy-Bruhl, *La mythologie primitive.*" *Philosophia* 3 (1): 60–71.

Chevreau, Emmanuelle, Frédéric Audren, and Raymond Verdier, eds. 2018. *Henri Lévy-Bruhl: Juriste sociologue.* Paris: Mare & Martin.

Chimisso, Cristina. 2001. "Hélène Metzger: The History of Science between the Study of Mentalities and Total History." *Studies in History and Philosophy of Science* 32: 203–41. https://doi.org/10.1016/S0039-3681(01)00006-1.

Clark, Christopher. 2013. *The Sleepwalkers: How Europe Went to War in 1914.* New York: Harper Collins.

Clark, Terrence. 1973. *Prophets and Patrons: The French University and the Emergence of the Social Sciences.* Cambridge, MA: Harvard University Press.

Clifford, James. 1982. *Person and Myth: Maurice Leenhardt in the Melanesian World.* Berkeley: University of California Press.

———. 1983. "On Ethnographic Authority." *Representations* 2: 118–46. https://doi.org/10.2307/2928386.

Collier, Stephen, and Andrew Lakoff. 2022. *The Government of Emergency: Vital Systems, Expertise, and the Politics of Security.* Princeton, NJ: Princeton University Press.

Collier, Stephen, Andrew Lakoff, and Paul Rabinow. 2004. "Biosecurity: Towards an Anthropology of the Contemporary." *Anthropology Today* 20 (5): 3–7. https://doi.org/10.1111/j.0268-540X.2004.00292.x.

Conklin, Alice. 1997. *A Mission to Civilize: The Republican Idea of Empire in France and West Africa, 1895–1930.* Stanford, CA: Stanford University Press.

Conybeare, Frederick. 1899. *The Dreyfus Case.* London: George Allen.

Cournot, Antoine-Augustin. 1843. *Exposition de la théorie des chances et des probabilités.* Paris: Hachette.

———. 1911. *Traité de l'enchaînement des idées fondamentales dans les sciences et dans l'histoire.* New edition. Paris: Hachette.

Crosby, Alfred. 1989. *America's Forgotten Pandemic: The Influenza of 1918.* Cambridge: Cambridge University Press.

Daston, Lorraine. 1988. *Classical Probability in the Enlightenment.* Princeton, NJ: Princeton University Press.

Debaene, Vincent. 2014. *Far Afield: French Anthropology between Science and Literature.* Chicago: University of Chicago Press.

Debré, Patrice. 2018. *Robert Debré: Une vocation française*. Paris: Odile Jacob.

De Groot, Jan Jakob Maria. 1892. *The Religious System of China*. Leyden: Brill.

Derrida, Jacques. 1976. *Of Grammatology*. Baltimore, MD: The Johns Hopkins University Press.

Desrosières, Alain. 1993 *The Politics of Large Numbers: A History of Statistical Reasoning*. Cambridge, MA: Harvard University Press.

Desrosières, Alain, and Béatrice Touchelay. 2008. "Raymond Lévy-Bruhl (1922–2008): Un statisticien innovateur et un serviteur de l'État." *Courrier des statistiques* 124: 49–53.

Dewey, John. 1910. *How We Think*. Boston, MA: D. C. Heath.

———. 1925. *Experience and Nature*. Chicago: Open Court.

Diacon, Todd. 2004. *Stringing together a Nation: Cândido Mariano da Silva Rondon and the Construction of a Modern Brazil, 1906–1930*. Durham, NC: Duke University Press.

Didier, Emmanuel. 2020. *America by the Numbers: Quantification, Democracy, and the Birth of National Statistics*. Boston, MA: MIT Press.

Digeon, Claude. 1959. *La crise allemande de la pensée française (1870–1914)*. Paris: Presses universitaires de France.

Dorst, Jean. 1965. *Avant que nature meure*. Neuchatel: Delachaux et Niestlé. Translated by Constance D. Sherman as *Before Nature Dies* (Boston, MA: Houghton, 1969).

Douglas, Mary, and Aaron Wildavsky. 1982. *Risk and Culture: An Essay on the Selection of Technological and Environmental Dangers*. Berkeley: University of California Press.

Dreyfus, Alfred. 1898. *Lettres d'un innocent*. Edited by P.-V. Stock. Paris: Ed. de l'Aurore.

Dreyfus, Alfred. 2017. *Lettres à la marquise*. Paris: Grasset.

Drucker, Jacques. 1997. "Des CDC d'Atlanta à l'Institut de veille sanitaire en passant par le Réseau national de santé publique: L'essor de l'épidémiologie d'intervention en France." *Revue française des affaires sociales* 3–4: 63–70.

Duclaux, Émile. 1899. *Propos d'un solitaire: L'Affaire Dreyfus*. Paris: Stock.

Duclert, Vincent. 1993. "Émile Duclaux, le savant et l'intellectuel." *Mil neuf cent: Revue d'histoire intellectuelle* 11: 21–26.

———. 2006. *Alfred Dreyfus: L'honneur d'un patriote*. Paris: Fayard.

Dumont, Louis. 2006. *An Introduction to Two Theories of Social Anthropology: Descent Groups and Marriage Alliance.* New York: Berghahn.

Durkheim, Émile. 1897. *Le suicide: Étude de sociologie.* Paris: Alcan.

———. 1912. *Les formes élémentaires de la vie religieuse: le système totémique en Australie.* Paris: Alcan.

———. 1933. *The Division of Labour in Society.* Translated by George Simpson. New York: MacMillan.

———. 1982. *The Rules of Sociological Method.* Edited by Steven Lukes. Translated by William Halls. New York: The Free Press. Originally published as *Les Règles de la méthode sociologique* (Paris: Alcan, 1895).

———. 1992. *Le socialisme.* Paris: Presses universitaires de France.

———. 2002. *L'individualisme et les intellectuels.* Paris: Mille et une nuits.

Ellis, William. 1838. *A Treatise on the Nature, Symptoms, Causes, and Treatment of Insanity.* London: S. Holdsworth. Translated by Th. Archambault as *Traité de l'aliénation mentale, ou De la nature, des causes, des symptômes et du traitement de la folie.* (Paris: Rouvier, 1840).

Esquirol, Jean-Étienne. 1805. "Des passions considérées comme causes, symptômes et moyens curatifs de la maladie mentale." PhD diss., Paris.

Etheridge, Elizabeth. 1992. *Sentinel for Health: A History of the Centers for Disease Control.* Berkeley: University of California Press.

Evans-Pritchard, Edward. 1937. *Witchcraft, Oracles and Magic Among the Azande.* Oxford: Oxford University Press.

———. 1940. *The Nuer: A Description of the Modes of Livelihood and Political Institutions of a Nilotic People.* Oxford: Oxford University Press.

———. 1965. *Theories of Primitive Religion.* Oxford: Oxford University Press.

Ewald, François. 2020. *The Birth of Solidarity: The History of the French Welfare State.* Durham, NC: Duke University Press.

Fabiani, Jean-Louis. 1988. *Les philosophes de la République.* Paris: Minuit.

Fabre, Daniel. 2012. "D'Isaac Strauss à Claude Lévi-Strauss: Le judaïsme comme culture." In *Claude Lévi-Strauss, un parcours dans le siècle*, edited by Philippe Descola, 267–93. Paris: Odile Jacob.

Farmer, Paul. 1999. *Infections and Inequalities: The Modern Plagues.* Berkeley: University of California Press.

Fearnley, Lyle. 2010. "Epidemic Intelligence: Langmuir and the Birth of Disease Surveillance." *Behemoth* 3: 37–56.

Fondane, Benjamin. 1938. "Léon Chestov et la lutte contre les évidences." *Revue philosophique de la France et de l'étranger* 126 (7–8): 113–50.

———. 1940. "Lévy-Bruhl et la métaphysique de la connaissance." *Revue philosophique de la France et de l'étranger* 129 (5/6): 289–316; 130 (7/8): 29–54.

———. 1982. *Rencontres avec Léon Chestov*. Paris: Plasma.

Foucault, Michel. 1994. "L'évolution de la notion d'individu dangereux dans la psychiatrie légale du 19e siècle." In *Dits et écrits III*, 443–64. Paris: Gallimard.

———. 2009. *History of Madness*. Unabridged edition translated by Jean Khalfa. New York: Routledge.

———. 2016. *Abnormal: Lectures at the Collège de France, 1974–1975*. Edited by Valerio Marchetti and Antonella Salomoni. Translated by Graham Burchel. London: Verso.

Fournier, Marcel. 1994. *Marcel Mauss*. Paris: Fayard.

———. 2007. *Émile Durkheim*. Paris: Fayard.

Fressoz, Jean-Baptiste. 2012. *L'apocalypse joyeuse: Une histoire du risque technologique*. Paris: Seuil.

Freud, Sigmund, and William Bullit. 1966. *Woodrow Wilson: A Psychological Study*. London: Transaction Publishers.

Freudenthal, Gad, ed. 1990. *Études sur Hélène Metzger/Studies on Hélène Metzger*. Leiden: Brill.

Friedmann, Georges. 1946. *Problèmes humains du machinisme industriel*. Paris: Gallimard.

Fruteau de Laclos, Frédéric. 2007. "Œuvre, fonction et société dans la psychologie historique d'Ignace Meyerson." *Revue d'Histoire des Sciences Humaines* 2 (17): 119–36.

Fustel de Coulanges, Numa. 1984. *La cité antique: Étude sur le culte, le droit, les institutions de la Grèce et de Rome*. Paris: Flammarion.

Geertz, Clifford. 1973. "Deep Play: Notes on the Balinese Cockfight." In *The Interpretation of Cultures*, 412–453. New York: Basic Books.

Gide, André. 1927. *Voyage au Congo*. Paris: Gallimard.

Glotz, Gustave. 1904. *L'ordalie dans la Grèce primitive: Étude de droit et de mythologie, en ouvrant à une approche comparative*. Paris: Albert Fontemoing.

Goldman, Marcio. 1994. *Razão e diferença: afetividade, racionalidade e relativismo no pensamento de Lévy-Bruhl.* Rio de Janeiro: Universidade Federal do Rio de Janeiro.

Goody, Jack. 1977. *The Domestication of the Savage Mind.* Cambridge: Cambridge University Press.

Gottlieb, Nathan. 1939. "Lucien Lévy-Bruhl." *L'Univers israelite*, March 24, 1939: 1–2.

Gregg, Michael. 1996. *Field Epidemiology.* New York: Oxford University Press.

Greilsamer, Laurent. 2018. *La tragédie du capitaine Dreyfus.* Paris: Tallandier.

Guiart, Jean. 1962. *Les religions de l'Océanie.* Paris: Presses universitaires de France.

Gurvitch, Georges. 1955. "Le concept de structure sociale." *Cahiers Internationaux de Sociologie* 19: 3–44.

Hacking, Ian. 1975. *The Emergence of Probability: A Philosophical Study of Early Ideas about Probability, Induction and Statistical Inference.* Cambridge: Cambridge University Press.

———. 1990. *The Taming of Chance.* Cambridge: Cambridge University Press.

Halbwachs, Maurice. 2012. *Écrits d'Amérique.* Paris: L'École des hautes études en sciences sociales.

Halpérin, Jean-Louis. 2009. "Le dossier Henri Lévy-Bruhl, une contribution à l'histoire des professeurs de droit pendant la seconde guerre mondiale." *Revue d'histoire des facultés de droit et de la culture juridique* 29–30: 189–96.

Hamayon, Roberte. 2016. *Why We Play: An Anthropological Study.* Chicago: Hau Books.

Hamelin, Octave. 1902. "Sur la logique des stoïciens." *Année philosophique* 12: 13–52.

Harper, Tim. 2020. *Underground Asia: Global Revolutionaries and the Assault on Empire.* London: Penguin.

Harris, Ruth. 2010. *Dreyfus: Politics, Emotion, and the Scandal of the Century.* New York: Henry Holt.

Heilbron, Johan. 1991. "Pionniers par défaut? Les débuts de la recherche au Centre d'études sociologiques (1946–1960)." *Revue Française de Sociologie* 32: 365–79.

Heim, Roger. (1952) 2020. *Destruction et protection de la nature.* With a foreword by Bernadette Lizet. Paris: CNRS Editions.

Heine, Henri. (1851) 1997. *Romancero.* Translated by Isabelle Kalinowski. Paris: Cerf.

Héran, François. 1987. "L'institution démotivée: De Fustel de Coulanges à Durkheim et au-delà." *Revue Française de Sociologie* 27: 67–97.

———. 1987b. "Le hasard et la prérogative." *Ethnologie française* 17 (2–3): 158–66.

———. 2009. *Figures de la parenté: Une histoire critique de la raison structurale.* Paris: Presses universitaires de France.

Hertz, Robert. 2002. *Un ethnologue dans les tranchées, août 1914–avril 1915: Lettres de Robert Hertz à sa femme Alice.* Paris: CNRS Editions.

Hirsch, Thomas. 2016. *Le temps des sociétés: d'Émile Durkheim à Marc Bloch.* Paris: L'École des hautes études en sciences sociales.

Holbraad, Martin. 2012. *Truth in Motion: The Recursive Anthropology of Cuban Divination.* Chicago: University of Chicago Press.

Hubert, Henri, and Marcel Mauss. 1902–3. "Esquisse d'une théorie générale de la magie." *L'Année sociologique* T7: 1–146.

Husserl, Edmund. 1998. "Lettre à Lévy-Bruhl du 11 mars 1935." *Gradhiva* 4: 64–68.

Hyman, Paula E. 1998. *The Jews of Modern France.* Berkeley: University of California Press.

Informations (*Informations industrielles et commerciales*). 1955. "Raymond Lévy-Bruhl à l'INSEE." April 8, 1955.

Israël, Liora. 2001. "Action collective et identités professionnelles en temps de guerre: La résistance dans les milieux judiciaires." *Genèses* 45: 45–68. https://doi.org/10.3917/gen.045.0045.

Itzen, Peter, Birgit Metzger, and Anne Rasmussen, eds. 2022. *Accidents and the State: Understanding Risk in the 20th Century.* New York: Columbia University Press.

Jaurès, Jean. 1900. "Préface." In *Les hommes de révolution: Aguinaldo et les Philippins,* by Henri Turot. Paris: Cerf.

———. 1915. *L'armée nouvelle.* Paris: L'Humanité.

———. 1998. *Les preuves: Affaire Dreyfus.* Paris: La Découverte.

———. 2009. *Œuvres 1: Les années de jeunesse.* Paris: Fayard.

———. 2014. *Discours et conférences.* Paris: Flammarion.

Jeanpierre, Laurent. 2004. "Une opposition structurante pour l'anthropologie structurale: Lévi-Strauss contre Gurvitch, la guerre de deux exilés français aux États-Unis." *Revue d'Histoire des Sciences Humaines* 11 (2): 13–44. https://doi.org/10.3917/rhsh.011.0013.

Jourmas, Georges. 2011. *Alfred Dreyfus, officier en 14–18*. Orléans: Corsaire Editions.

Kalifa, Dominique. 2009. *Biribi: Les bagnes coloniaux de l'armée française*. Paris: Perrin.

Karsenti, Bruno. 1997. *L'homme total: Sociologie, anthropologie et philosophie chez Marcel Mauss*. Paris: PUF.

———. 2006. *Politique de l'esprit: Auguste Comte et la naissance de la science sociale*. Paris: Hermann.

———. 2013. *D'une philosophie à l'autre: Les sciences sociales et la politique des modernes*. Paris: Gallimard.

———. 2017. *La question juive des modernes: Philosophie de l'émancipation*. Paris: Presses universitaires de France.

Kaspi, André, ed. 2010. *Histoire de l'Alliance Israelite Universelle de 1860 à nos jours*. Paris: Armand Colin.

Keck, Frédéric. 2008. *Lévy-Bruhl, entre philosophie et anthropologie: Contradiction et participation*. Paris: CNRS Editions.

———. 2020. *Avian Reservoirs: Virus Hunters and Birdwatchers in Chinese Sentinel Posts*. Durham, NC: Duke University Press.

Kelty, Chris. 2020. *The Participant: A Century of Participation in Four Stories*. Chicago: University of Chicago Press.

Kuper, Adam. 1973. *Anthropologists and Anthropology: The British School 1922–1972*. New York: Pica Press.

Laurière, Christine. 2008. *Paul Rivet: le savant et le politique*. Paris: Muséum national d'histoire naturelle.

Lécuyer, Bernard. 1987. "Probability in Vital and Social Statistics. Quételet, Farr and the Bertillons." In *The Probability Revolution*, edited by Lorenz Kruger, Gerd Gigerenzer, and Mary Morgan, 317–35. Cambridge, MA: MIT Press.

Leenhardt, Maurice. 1949. "Les carnets de Lucien Lévy-Bruhl." In Lucien Lévy-Bruhl, *Carnets*, I–XX. Paris: Les Presses universitaires de France.

Leiris, Michel. 1995. *Miroir de l'Afrique*. Paris: Gallimard.

Lepick, Olivier. 1998. *La Grande Guerre chimique, 1914–1918*. Paris: Presses universitaires de France.

Lévi, Bernard. 2007. "Autour de l'éclipse de soleil du 17 avril 1912, à la villa 'La Marguerite' au Vésinet." *Revue du cercle de généalogie juive* 92: 4–16.

Levinas, Emmanuel. 1957. "Lévy-Bruhl et la philosophie contemporaine." *Revue philosophique de la France et de l'étranger* 147: 556–69.

———. (1963) 1998. *De l'existence à l'existant*. Paris: Vrin.

———. 2001. *En découvrant l'existence avec Husserl et Heidegger*. Paris: Vrin.

Lévi-Strauss, Claude. 1945. "French Sociology." In *Twentieth Century Sociology*, edited by Georges Gurvitch and William Moore, 503–37. New York: The Philosophical Library.

———. 1949. *Les structures élémentaires de la parenté*. Paris: Presses universitaires de France.

———. 1950. "Introduction à l'œuvre de Marcel Mauss." In *Sociologie et Anthropologie*, by Marcel Mauss. Paris: Presses universitaires de France.

———. 1955. "Diogène couché." *Les Temps modernes* 110: 1186–220.

———. 1958. *Anthropologie structurale*. Paris: Plon.

———. 1988. *De près et de loin, Entretiens avec Didier Eribon*. Paris: Odile Jacob.

———. 2008. *Œuvres*. Paris: Gallimard.

Littré, Émile. 1957. *Dictionnaire de la langue française*, vol. 5. Paris: Gallimard-Hachette.

Lombroso, Cesare. 1876. *L'uomo delinquente*. Turin: Fratelli Bocca.

Loyer, Emmanuelle 2015. *Lévi-Strauss*. Paris: Gallimard.

Lyautey, Hubert. 1900. *Du rôle colonial de l'armée*. Paris: Armand Colin.

Malinowski, Bronislaw. 1922. *Argonauts of the Western Pacific: An Account of Native Enterprise and Adventure in the Archipelagoes of Melanesian New Guinea*. London: Routledge and Kegan Paul.

Mallard, Grégoire. 2019. *Gift Exchange: The Transnational History of a Political Idea*. Cambridge: Cambridge University Press.

Marcel, Jean-Christophe. 1999. "Maurice Halbwachs à Chicago ou les ambiguïtés d'un rationalisme durkheimien." *Revue d'Histoire des Sciences Humaines* 1: 47–68. https://doi.org/10.3917/rhsh.001.0047.

———. 2001. "Georges Gurvitch: les raisons d'un succès." *Cahiers Internationaux de Sociologie* 110: 97–119. https://doi.org/10.3917/cis.110.0097.

Mariot, Nicolas. 2013. *Histoire d'un sacrifice: Robert, Alice et la guerre*. Paris: Seuil.

Marrou, Henri-Irénée (Davenson). 1941. "Bergson et l'histoire." In *Essais et témoignages inédits*, edited by Henri Bergson, 32–45. Neuchâtel: La Baconnière.

Marrus, Michael. 1980. *The Politics of Assimilation: The French Jewish Community at the Time of the Dreyfus Affair*. New York: Oxford University Press.

Martin, Thierry. 1996. *Probabilités et critique philosophique selon Cournot*. Paris: Vrin.

Masson-Oursel, Paul. 1938. *La philosophie en Orient*. Paris: Alcan.

Mauss, Marcel. 1939. "Lucien Lévy-Bruhl." *Le Populaire*, March 16, 1939, 4.

Mauss, Marcel, and Henri Hubert. 1897–98. "Essai sur la nature et la fonction du sacrifice." *L'Année sociologique* T2: 29–138.

McWilliam, Neil, Catherine Méneux, and Julie Ramos, eds. 2014. *L'Art social en France: de la Révolution à la Grande Guerre*. Rennes: Presses universitaires de Rennes.

Merleau-Ponty, Maurice. 1975. *La phénoménologie et les sciences de l'homme*. Paris: Centre de Documentation Universitaire.

Merllié, Dominique. 1989. "Présentation: Le cas Lévy-Bruhl." *Revue philosophique de la France et de l'étranger* 179 (4): 419–48.

———. 1992. "Les rapports entre la *Revue de métaphysique* et la *Revue philosophique*: Xavier Léon, Théodule Ribot, Lucien Lévy-Bruhl." *Revue de Métaphysique et de Morale* 98 (1/2): 59–108.

Metzger, Hélène. 1930. "La philosophie de Lucien Lévy-Bruhl et l'histoire des sciences." *Archeion* 12: 15–24.

Meyerson, Émile. 2008. *Essais*. Paris: Corpus.

———. 2009. *Lettres françaises*. Edited by Bernadette Bensaude-Vincent and Eva Telkes-Klein. Paris: CNRS Editions.

Meyerson, Ignace. 1925. "La mentalité primitive: A propos de l'ouvrage de L. Lévy-Bruhl." *Année psychologique* 23: 214–22.

Michel, Florian. 2018. *Étienne Gilson: Une biographie intellectuelle et politique*. Paris: Vrin.

Mill, John Stuart. 1865. *Auguste Comte and Positivism*. London: Trübner.

Milner, Jean-Claude. 2006. *Le Juif de savoir*. Paris: Grasset.

Moissinat, Christine. 2015. *Émile Duclaux: de Pasteur à Dreyfus*. Paris: Hermann.

Mucchielli, Laurent. 1998. *La découverte du social: Naissance de la sociologie en France*. Paris: La Découverte.

Murard, Lion, and Patrick Zylberman. 1996. *L'Hygiène dans la République: la santé publique en France ou l'utopie contrariée (1870–1918)*. Paris: Fayard.

Nguyen, Phuong Ngoc. 2012. *À l'origine de l'anthropologie au Vietnam: Recherche sur les auteurs de la première moitié du XXe siècle*. Aix-en-Provence: Presses universitaires de Provence.

Nguyen, Van Hyuen. 1944. *La Civilisation annamite*. Hanoi: IPP du Tonkin.

Nicolle, Charles. 1930. *Naissance, vie et mort des maladies infectieuses*. Paris: Alcan.

Nisio, Francesco S. 2019. *Lucien Lévy-Bruhl: Filosofia, Scienze sociali, giustizia*. Milano: Giuffré Francis Lefebvre.

Nizan, Paul. 1937. "Les primitifs et nous." *L'Humanité* 25 (March): 8.

———. 1971. *The Watchdogs: Philosophers and the Established Order*. New York, Monthly Review Press.

O'Reilly, Patrick. 1950. "Georges Baudoux, prospecteur et écrivain calédonien." *Journal de la Société des Océanistes* 6: 185–206.

Ostrogorski, Moisei. 1993. *La démocratie et les partis politiques*. Paris: Fayard.

Palmer, David. 2019. "Marcel Granet and Chinese Religion in the History of Social Theory." *Review of Religion and Chinese Society* 6 (2): 160–87.

Paulhan, Jean. 1945. "La mentalité primitive et l'illusion des explorateurs." In *Oeuvres complètes*, vol. 2, *Langage 1: La marque des lettres, le poids du sanctuaire*, 143–53. Paris: Gallimard.

Paulme, Denise, and Deborah Lifchitz. 2015. *Lettres de Sanga*. Paris: CNRS Editions.

Pelis, Kim. 2007. *Charles Nicolle, Pasteur's Imperial Missionary: Typhus and Tunisia*. Rochester, NY: University of Rochester Press.

Perthuis, Bertrand de. 2003. "Les animalisations de Jaurès." *Ridiculosa* 10.

Pinault, Michel. 2017. *Émile Borel: Une carrière intellectuelle sous la Troisième République*. Paris: L'Harmattan.

Pinel, Philipp. 1798. *Traité medico-philosophique sur l'aliénation mentale, ou la manie*. Paris : Richard, Caille et Ravier Libraires.

Poulat, Émile. 1962. *Histoire, dogme et critique dans la crise moderniste*. Paris: Albin Michel.

Prochasson, Christophe. 1993. *Les intellectuels, le socialisme et la guerre 1900–1938*. Paris: Seuil.

Prochasson, Christophe, and Anne Rasmussen. 1996. *Au nom de la patrie: Les intellectuels et la Première Guerre mondiale (1910–1919)*. Paris: La Découverte.

Proust, Marcel. 1988. *À la recherche du temps perdu*. Paris: Gallimard.

Rabinow, Paul. 1989. *French Modern: Norms and Forms of the Social Environment*. Chicago: University of Chicago Press.

———. 1999. *French DNA: Trouble in the Purgatory*. Chicago: University of Chicago Press.

Redfield, Peter. 2000. *Space in the Tropics: From Convicts to Rockets in French Guiana*. Berkeley: University of California Press.

Reinach, Salomon. 1880. *Manuel de philologie classique*. Paris: Hachette.

Renouvier, Charles. 1874. "L'origine du sentiment moral." *Critique philosophique* 1: 321–45.

———. 1879. "L'homme primitif selon M. Spencer." *Critique philosophique* 1: 91–103.

Riché, Pierre. 2003. *Henri Irénée Marrou, historien engagé*. Paris: Cerf.

Rizal, José. 1887. *Noli Me Tángere*. Berlin: Berliner Buchdruckerei-Aktiengesellschaft.

———. 1891. *El filibusterismo*. Ghent: F. Meyer van Loo Press. Translated by Charles Derbyshire as *The Reign of Greed* (Manila: Philippine Education Company, 1912). Translated by Jovita Ventura Castro as *Révolution aux Philippines* (Paris: Gallimard, 1984).

Rusche, Georg, and Otto Kirchheimer. 1939. *Punishment and Social Structure*. New York: Columbia University Press.

Sahlins, Marshall. 1995. *How "Natives" Think: About Captain Cook, for Example*. Chicago: University of Chicago Press.

Saleilles, Raymond. 1898. *L'individualisation de la peine: Étude de criminalité sociale*. Paris: Alcan.

Sartre, Jean-Paul. 1946. *Réflexions sur la question juive*. Paris: Gallimard. Translated by George J. Becker as *Anti-Semite and Jew*. London: Morihien, 1948.

Schaper, Bertus Willem. 1960. *Albert Thomas: Trente ans de réformisme social*. Paris: Presses universitaires de France.

Schnerr, Jonathan. 1982. *Ben Tillett: Portrait of a Labour Leader*. London: Croom Helm.

Sellers, Peter. 1997. *Hazards of the Job: From Industrial Disease to Environmental Health Science*. Chapel Hill: University of North Carolina Press.

Sibeud, Emmanuelle. 2002. *Une science impériale pour l'Afrique? La construction des savoirs africanistes en France, 1878–1930.* Paris: École des hautes études en sciences sociales.

Simon-Nahum, Perrine. 2018. *Les Juifs et la modernité: L'héritage du judaïsme dans les sciences de l'homme en France au XIXème siècle.* Paris: Albin Michel.

Singaravélou, Pierre. 2011. *Professer l'Empire: Les "Sciences coloniales" en France sous la IIIᵉ République.* Paris: Publications de la Sorbonne.

Soula, Mathieu. 2015. "Au-delà de l'histoire du droit: Retour sur la trajectoire d'un entrepreneur scientifique, Henri Lévy-Bruhl (1884–1964)." *ClioThemis: Revue électronique d'histoire du droit.* https://www.cliothemis.com/Au-dela-de-l-histoire-du-droit.

Soulez, Philippe, and Frédéric Worms. 1997. *Bergson.* Paris: Flammarion.

Stocking, George. 1974. *The Shaping of American Anthropology 1883–1911: A Franz Boas Reader.* New York: Basic Books.

Stoczkowski, Wiktor. 2008. *Anthropologies rédemptrices: Le monde selon Lévi-Strauss.* Paris: Hermann.

Tabuteau, Didier. 2002. *La sécurité sanitaire.* Paris: Berger-Levrault.

Tesnières, Valérie. 2001. *Le Quadrige: Un siècle d'éditions universitaires.* Paris: Presses universitaires de France.

Thomas, Gaëtan. 2018. "La routine vaccinale: Essai sur un programme français de rationalisation par les nombres 1949–1999." PhD diss., École des Hautes Études en Sciences Sociales.

Topalov, Christian. 2006. "Maurice Halbwachs: L'expérience de Chicago (automne 1930)." *Annales: Histoire, Sciences Sociales* 3: 555–81.

Vatin, François. 1998. *Économie naturelle et économie politique chez Antoine-Augustin Cournot.* Paris: Presses universitaires de France.

Vidal-Naquet, Pierre. 1981. *Les Juifs, la mémoire et le présent.* Paris: Maspéro.

———. 1989. *L'affaire Audin (1957–1978).* Paris: Minuit.

Wang, Jessica. 2007. *John Dewey in China: To Teach and to Learn.* Albany: State University of New York Press.

Webster, Robert. 2018. *Flu Hunter: Unlocking the Secrets of a Virus.* Dunedin: Otago University Press.

Wolff, E. 2011. *Political Responsibility for a Globalised World: After Levinas' Humanism.* Bielefeld: Transcript.

Worcester, Dean. 1914. *The Philippines Past and Present.* New York: MacMillan.

Zambelli, Paola. 1995. "Alexandre Koyré versus Lucien Lévy-Bruhl: From Collective Representations to Paradigms of Scientific Thought." *Science in Context* 8 (3): 531–55. https://doi.org/10.1017/S0269889700002155.

Zamora, Mario, ed. 1967. *Studies in Philippine Anthropology: In Honor of H. Otley Beyer*. Quezon City: Phoenix Press.

Zimmer, Alexis. 2016. *Brouillards toxiques: Vallée de la Meuse 1930, Contre-enquête*. Bruxelles: Zones sensibles.

Zola, Émile. 2010. *L'Affaire Dreyfus*. Edited by Henri Mitterrand. Paris: Librairie Générale Française.

Index of Names

Index of Notions

accident, xii, 3, 23–25, 27, 30, 68, 72, 75–77, 93, 94, 108, 114, 119, 175, 185, 211–13

anarchism; anarchist, 23, 33, 54, 100

ancient, 11, 14, 25, 26, 47, 49, 51, 81, 86, 134, 159

animal, 49, 59, 88–90, 119, 199, 205, 207

anti-Semitism; anti-Semitic, xi, xii, 6, 31–36, 42, 59, 64, 65, 67, 69, 120, 131, 139, 140, 158, 159, 165, 182, 208, 212, 213

art; artist, 16, 54, 55, 84, 98, 138, 163, 197, 206

attention, xii, 3, 4, 49, 55, 109, 139, 141, 160, 172, 208, 215

avant-garde; vanguard, 39, 43, 103, 215

belief, 25, 26, 32, 46, 48, 56, 79, 83, 84, 86, 92, 101, 108, 114, 128, 189, 213

biology; biological, 39, 59, 78, 79, 82, 88

body, 15, 40, 42, 51, 76, 78, 82, 92, 97, 119, 158, 211, 214, 215

calculation, xii, 3, 68, 72, 76, 78, 81, 83, 86, 175, 176, 200

catastrophe, xi, xii, 2, 4, 161, 202, 212, 213

causality, 75, 77, 79, 89, 109, 165, 212

chance, xii, 6, 75–79, 81–84, 86, 87, 109, 136, 174–76, 178, 211, 214

chemistry, 5, 39, 51, 91, 132, 159, 206

civilization; civilized; civilizing, xii, xiv, 1, 2, 35, 37, 40–43, 47, 50, 55, 80, 89, 90, 93, 97, 102, 104, 106, 108–11, 113, 114, 116, 119, 123, 128, 141, 158, 163, 178, 189, 207, 208, 213, 215

class struggle (workers/employers), 17, 20, 21, 67

collective representation, xiv, xv, 7, 53, 55, 56, 76, 80, 94, 141, 163, 211, 213

numeration; numbers; numbering,
8, 32, 45, 46, 55, 76, 78, 79, 82,
93, 101, 109, 126, 133, 136,
172, 176, 177, 180, 187, 192

objective, 26, 31, 46, 51, 57, 68, 69,
79, 128, 174, 180, 196, 203
opinion, 35, 47, 102, 125, 175,
184, 201, 213
oracles, 109
ordeal, 85, 86, 93, 94, 190
organic; organism; organization,
xiii, 2, 4, 5, 19, 27, 28, 33, 42,
46, 47, 52, 57, 63, 78, 87, 88,
94, 118, 122, 133, 188, 198

pandemic, 1, 90, 201–205, 212
participation, xii, xiv, 2, 3, 4, 6,
18, 55–60, 63–65, 75, 87, 94,
108, 116, 128, 129, 138, 139,
141, 162, 163, 168, 175, 176,
211–13
phenomenology, xii–xiv, 134, 139,
163, 169
philosophy, 6, 13–15, 18, 20, 23,
25–27, 30, 34, 37–39, 41, 42,
49, 50, 56, 58, 64, 77–79, 81,
85, 99, 118, 122–32, 134–39,
141, 160, 165, 167, 168, 197
piety, 26, 32, 50, 163
positivism; positivist, 2, 20, 26–28,
37, 38, 43, 78, 105, 166
pragmatism; pragmatist, 126, 131,
134, 176
precaution; precautionary, 4, 7, 15,
204
predictable; unpredictable;
unpredictability, 2, 4, 63,
71–73, 75, 77, 79, 80, 90, 114,
201, 205, 213, 214

preparedness; prepare;
preparation, xii, xv, 2, 4, 6–8,
34, 65–68, 71, 73, 83, 90,
91, 112, 125, 130, 162, 165,
176, 181, 201, 202, 205, 207,
212–15
prevention, xii, xv, 7, 8, 27, 112,
176, 200, 212, 214
primitive man; primitive
humanity; primitive state;
primitive mentality; primitive
society; primitive solidarity;
primitive law, xi, xii, xiv, 1–5,
7, 8, 25–27, 35, 37, 41–43,
47–49, 53, 55, 60, 63, 72,
75–77, 80, 82–86, 89, 90–94,
98, 100–103, 108–10, 112–
17, 119, 121–23, 125–29,
134–39, 141, 158, 162, 163,
165, 167, 168, 175, 176,
178, 185–90, 202, 207, 211,
213–15
probability, 8, 68, 78, 79, 81, 176,
214
progress, xviii, 16, 37, 43, 53, 69,
79, 119, 174, 175, 190, 209,
215
protection, 86, 89, 113, 134,
205–207
psychology, xiv, 18, 20, 24, 25, 38,
64, 71, 80, 82, 127, 129, 135,
136
public health; public hygiene, xii,
xvii, 5, 85, 87, 92, 93, 99, 101,
103, 195–98, 200–204, 214
punishment, xiii, 27, 29, 30, 203

race; racism; racist, xiv, 36, 59, 71,
76, 104, 111, 113, 126–28, 132,
134, 138–41, 180, 211

solidarity, xiv, 25, 27, 32, 33,
35–37, 39, 46, 47, 52, 57, 59,
88, 89, 130, 162, 205, 211
sophistry, 34, 38
spirit; spiritualism; spiritualist, 2,
3, 7, 15, 17, 20, 37, 38, 49, 56,
58, 67, 82, 86, 92, 97, 101, 111,
121, 124–26, 138, 158, 163,
186
state, xi, xvi, 1–3, 5–8, 18–20, 23,
34, 43, 52, 53, 55, 57, 58, 67–
69, 84, 85, 105, 107, 133, 161,
172, 174, 178–81, 183, 186,
189, 190, 192, 198, 201–203,
205, 211–14
statistics; statistician; statistical,
xi–xiii, xv, xvi, 5, 8, 18, 24, 28,
34, 46, 53, 64, 68, 76, 77, 79,
81, 84, 85, 93, 169, 171–80,
183, 190, 193, 199–202, 212,
214
structuralism; structure;
superstructure, xii, xiii, 57, 105,
116, 169, 174, 188, 190
subjective, subjectivity 25, 26, 31,
37, 38, 46, 51, 69, 79, 128, 139,
165, 215
supernatural, 56, 123, 186
superstition, 38, 55, 101
symbolic, 4, 188, 209

techniques, xii, xv, 3, 7, 8, 51, 68,
81, 84, 85, 99, 171, 199–201,
205, 212, 214
theology; theological, 37–39, 42,
94, 113, 123, 124

tradition; traditional, xi, xiii, 14,
15, 46, 49–51, 56, 82, 93, 128,
129, 137, 141
truth, xiii, 7, 8, 16, 34–38, 53, 98,
113, 117, 161, 183, 184, 186,
190, 212, 213, 215

uncertainty, 3, 86, 87, 93, 94, 199,
202, 205
unconscious, xiii, 134, 136, 137,
139, 167, 168, 188, 189

vaccine; vaccination, xi, xii, xviii, 6,
52, 93, 103, 195, 196, 198–202,
204, 212, 214
vigilance, 5, 43, 66, 94, 95, 139,
140, 141, 176, 193, 197, 200,
203, 209, 214, 215
violence, xii, 1, 41–43, 73, 95, 106,
108, 117, 186, 188, 189, 191,
213, 214
virus; virulence, 2, 33, 52, 53, 88,
89, 94, 113, 196, 202, 203, 215

warning signal, xii, 4, 8, 43, 161,
206, 213–15
watchdog, 124
whistleblower, 4, 42, 43, 83, 95,
138, 184, 189, 214
witchcraft, 109
writing, xiv, xviii, 6, 20, 31, 34, 35,
39, 45, 47, 52, 69, 76, 84, 100,
109, 111, 114–17, 123, 141,
164, 168, 189, 190, 203